I'M WRITING YOU FROM TEHRAN

I'm Writing You from Tehran

A GRANDDAUGHTER'S SEARCH

FOR HER FAMILY'S PAST AND

THEIR COUNTRY'S FUTURE

Delphine Minoui

Translated from the French by
Emma Ramadan

Farrar, Straus and Giroux | New York

Farrar, Straus and Giroux
175 Varick Street, New York 10014

Copyright © 2015 by Éditions du Seuil
Translation copyright © 2019 by Emma Ramadan
All rights reserved
Printed in the United States of America
Originally published in French in 2015 by Éditions du Seuil,
France, as *Je vous écris de Téhéran*
English translation published in the United States
by Farrar, Straus and Giroux
First American edition, 2019

Library of Congress Cataloging-in-Publication Data
Names: Minoui, Delphine, author. | Ramadan, Emma, translator.
Title: I'm writing you from Tehran : a granddaughter's search for her
family's past and their country's future / Delphine Minoui ;
translated from the French by Emma Ramadan.
Other titles: Je vous écris de Téhéran. English | I am writing you
from Tehran
Description: First American edition. | New York : Farrar, Straus
and Giroux, 2019.
Identifiers: LCCN 2018035766 | ISBN 9780374175221 (hardcover)
Subjects: LCSH: Iran—Social conditions—1997– | Iran—Politics
and government—1997– | Minoui, Delphine. | Minoui, Delphine—
Family. | Minoui family.
Classification: LCC HN670.2.A8 M56 2019 | DDC 306.0955—dc23
LC record available at https://lccn.loc.gov/2018035766

Designed by Richard Oriolo

Our books may be purchased in bulk for promotional, educational, or
business use. Please contact your local bookseller or the Macmillan
Corporate and Premium Sales Department at 1-800-221-7945, extension
5442, or by e-mail at MacmillanSpecialMarkets@macmillan.com.

www.fsgbooks.com
www.twitter.com/fsgbooks • www.facebook.com/fsgbooks

1 3 5 7 9 10 8 6 4 2

For my daughter, Samarra

I'M WRITING YOU FROM TEHRAN

THE TAXI ROLLS along gray lines. That's all we can make out in the darkness: gray lines, as far as the eye can see, marking out the road to the airport. Outside, beyond the window, the night devours the last forbidden words I heard. How many will still dare to shout "*Allahu Akbar*" ("God is great") and "Death to the dictator" from the rooftops of Tehran?

This is no article—it is a stillborn idea, just a thought. A thought that stretches out as the taxi speeds along those never-ending gray lines. This time, though, is no false start, no trial run. I am leaving for good.

The minutes pass, seeming like hours. The drive to the airport feels so long when you're heading toward the unknown. I move forward, I rewind. I think of the disappeared, of friends who no longer answer my calls. Of the bloodstains on the pavement. Of assassinated dreams. Of threats scratched on paper. Of stories I can no longer tell. And this fear I can't shake. This fear is inescapable. It cannot be tamed. It's like swimming against the current: we are pushed back, we fight to recover, again and again, until we drown.

Suddenly, the gray lines vanish within a blinding beam of light. I lift my head. We have arrived at the airport. Whatever you do, don't look back. Get out of the taxi as if nothing has happened. Take your suitcase, the only one you were able to salvage. Pass through the X-rays. Endure the gloved prodding of the veiled policewoman. At Security, present your passport—the Iranian one, not the French one. Conceal the ball of anxiety in a fold of your headscarf. Walk carefully toward the gate. Board the plane without running. No running; be careful. Find your place and sit down. Pray for the imminent closing of the doors; pray that they close before the security agents storm in.

The plane takes off. Finally! From the sky, the mausoleum of Imam Khomeini is nothing but a dot in the night before it's engulfed by clouds. What does a person think about once she is free? Of those pages of gray lines, ones she can newly fill in however she pleases. She tells herself that the nightmare is over. That she will learn to breathe again. In reality, the hardest part has only just begun. The hardest part is abandoning Iran to its own blank page.

LETTER TO BABAI, MY GRANDFATHER; PARIS, SUMMER 2014

I LEFT YOUR country without looking back. How could I say good-bye to a rediscovered part of myself? It was the beginning of summer 2009, Tehran was mourning its martyrs, and the prison cells were overflowing. Over the course of a sham election, we had passed from the green of hope to the red of blood. The dream of change had shattered against the wall of repression. I was reluctantly putting the finishing touches on a long report whose secret you still guarded. Back in Paris, I could not write a single line. Words waged war on my page. Emotions battled facts. A journalist by trade, I had returned to being a simple citizen. I had lost the necessary distance for telling this story. So I surrendered my pen. For a long time, a very long time—and then I remembered the lines from Hafez you had bequeathed to me.

> *He who binds himself to darkness fears the wave.*
> *The whirlpool frightens him.*
> *And if he wants to share our journey,*
> *He has to venture well beyond the comforting sand of the shore.*

You had offered these to me in Paris, one November morning in 1997. I didn't know it yet, but this poem would become my profession of faith. You had just arrived from Iran for heart surgery that day. A routine operation, the doctors had said. I was twenty-three years old. You were at least three times older, and I believed you were immortal. No doubt because of the distance, which had always kept us apart. During your rare trips to France, you had a way of always expressing yourself through poems that you neglected to translate. You, who had represented Iran in UNESCO at the end of the '50s, you knew Hafez like the back of your hand. You claimed that the illustrious fourteenth-century poet had an answer for everything, that his writings were more valuable than any crystal ball, that all one had to do was dip into them at random in order to glimpse the near future. There was something magical about listening to you recite what was, to my ear, gibberish. That day, in your hospital bed, you had taken the time to explain. You expressed an unexpected desire to initiate me into your native tongue. An astonishing whim. Like a fundamental need. No one at home had ever bothered to teach me about my origins. From right to left, your pen began to dance, dressing the consonants in tiny colorful accents. On each line, a short French translation followed on the heels of your calligraphy. This poem, my first lesson in Persian. One of your last breaths.

Your sudden disappearance from the world knocked me flat. I knew so little about you. And even less about your country. As a child, I would send you letters, my way of challenging the unknown. I would always embellish them with colorful drawings of unchanging characters. Papa. Maman. My sister, Nasrine, and me. A little sample of your family spread across the planet by way of miniature chronicles written in French. They were my first dispatches. They say that writing is liberating. At the time, I thought of it as a game of hide-and-seek with your shadow. Or else an intriguing puzzle, for whose missing pieces I obstinately kept searching.

So many years have passed since your death. What an unsettling feeling, to reach once again for my pen, knowing everything about you. To dedicate this long letter to you when you are no longer with us. As a little girl, when I would write to you from Paris with my chubby hands, I'd imagine you leafing through my missives, sitting on your pretty Tehran patio where I had spent the summer when I was four. The Iran of my childhood memory was that and nothing else: a patio adorned with forsythias, rosewater ice cream, an inflatable pool to wade around in, and Persian laments reverberating in the background. Papa had sent the three of us there for vacation. It was August 1978. In the middle of the garden, Maman was bronzing her fair skin, her face framed by a homemade aluminum reflector to capture the reflection of the UV rays, to the great distress of Grandmother, who said she looked like a toaster. In the East, whiteness is sacred. At the foot of a persimmon tree, cousins were playing backgammon as they sipped pomegranate juice. The crackling of the radio was accompanying their laughter when, suddenly, a terrible piece of news rattled that little corner of Paradise. I remember a crash of voices, and that indecipherable language abruptly losing its musicality. Then my panicked mother, glued to the telephone, murmuring in French to Papa, who was still in Paris, "Things are heating up in Iran . . . The Cinema Rex in Abadan was torched . . . Hundreds of people are dead . . . No one knows who's behind it . . . The protests against the shah have multiplied." These events, which seemed to me like fables for adults, announced the seeds of the revolution against the sitting monarchy. But, at the time, I saw them only as the unjust trigger of our hasty return to France. Two months later, a new face invaded our little French TV screen. An old bearded man who looked like a sorcerer, a "Gargamel" in a black turban, shriveled under his apple tree at a château called "Neauphle": Ayatollah Khomeini, whose enemy was, to my ears, not the *shah* but the *chat* (cat) of Iran, a greedy and cruel king hidden away in his golden palace. Rumor had it that the sorcerer wanted the shah's hide and his position, and that, since his exile to France, he had dreamed of dethroning him. Nose glued to the television of our apartment in Paris, Papa said nothing. He watched, powerless, as that grand pooh-bah cast a spell over his distant country. Over there, many people, religious and secular, were drunk on his evil potion: "Revolution, liberty, Islamic Republic!" his supporters cried at the top of their lungs. You know the rest: January 6, 1979, the monarch ended up making a run for it. Three weeks later, the sorcerer was back in Tehran.

At our home in Paris, Iran became a taboo subject. There would be no more questions about your pomegranate-scented country. From then on, the description of Iran in the French newspapers could be summed up in three words: *Islam, chador,* and *terrorism.* It made Papa sick. One night when he came back from work, he collapsed on the sofa. "I was stopped by the police! They called me a 'towelhead'!" Papa, whom you had enrolled in French boarding school from the age of eleven, until you returned to Tehran once your mission for UNESCO was finished, couldn't stand the image of his homeland being thrown in his face. From that day on, he called himself "Henri." Except for the *H* of "Homayoun," this pseudonym had nothing in common with his given name. Powerless to change his country, he changed himself.

I concluded that I was French. One hundred percent. Nothing in our home led me to think otherwise. We spoke French. We ate French. We dreamed in French. When, during each first day back to school, the teacher asked the country of my origin, I would respond, "France!" without hesitating. Out of imitation, probably. Out of fear, also, of hurting Papa if I were to reveal what seemed to be a state secret. A giant concern, however, nagged at me. Your trips to France, which had become more and more spaced out, came to a halt entirely in 1980. In your country, a deadly conflict had just broken out with neighboring Iraq, which was backed by the majority of Western powers. At night, I had nightmares thinking of the bombs falling on Tehran. For me, war had existed in grown-ups' movies. Suddenly, it took on a dimension much closer to home. Was your life in danger? What was the day-to-day like for you and Grandmother? Why didn't you take refuge in Paris? I would have lent you my room. My bed, too, and my toys. In my letters, I declared my love for you. I sketched out our daily life, school, weekends in the countryside, Santa Claus and his bag of toys, naïvely praying that my stories might give you the strength to hold on. But did they make it through to you, these unanswered missives?

Once the war was over, eight years later, I learned with relief that you were in good health. A precious solace. With age, I also started to become aware of my origins. But the star of your country did not cease fading. In 1992, the international bestseller *Not Without My Daughter*, by Betty Mahmoody, dealt a blow to its image. Who could have imagined? This sensationalist memoir of an American woman married to a violent Iranian man, sequestered in Tehran with her daughter, also ended up poisoning my daily life. From the doctor's waiting room to the neighborhood butcher, everyone brought it up with a little condescending phrase about the "poor Iranian women." "And you?" they asked me. "You're not afraid that the same thing will happen to you?" In high school, I fled the inquisitive stares. One day, the father of a friend asked me, "Is it because your father is Iranian that you don't wear miniskirts?" What business was it of his? Short dresses had never been my cup of tea.

Comments from various people stirred up my curiosity. What, then, did this Islamic Republic that the entire planet denigrated look like? Did we have to throw all Iranians in the same basket? At journalism school, which I had begun in 1995, my professors encouraged me to go beyond the clichés. One of the golden rules of our profession. See, feel, get as close as possible, before judging. Two years later, I made the "Iranian press" the subject of my master's thesis. An ideal pretext to return to your country. And find you again. "*Khosh amadid*—welcome— to the land of your ancestors!" you had flung at me upon my arrival, with that habit of navigating between words from your mother tongue and the French you learned in your youth at the Sorbonne. I had two weeks to do my research. Astonished by my fascination, you laughed at seeing me put on the obligatory veil as one dons a theater costume, at hearing me negotiate the price of a taxi without speaking a word of Persian. I innocently gushed over the tiniest things. At night, we flipped through all the new magazines that were flourishing thanks to the efforts of a certain Mohammad Khatami. This reformist mullah, minister of culture for ten years, had laboriously fought to soften censorship. A man of dialogue, he embodied a new generation of politicians, eager for political openness in an Islamic Republic that had been isolated for too long. A real *roshanfekr*—

an "enlightened thinker," as you would say. By May 23, 1997, when he won the presidential election to widespread surprise, I was already back in Paris, in the middle of writing my thesis. I rushed to call you. On the telephone, your voice was trembling with joy. You were celebrating. You wanted to believe this was a turning point for your country. For the first time since the revolution, Iran was reaching its hand out to the world.

Your sudden death, six months later, coincided with these changes. Your heart, too fragile, stopped beating before the French doctors could operate. The day of your funeral, at Montparnasse Cemetery, I felt injustice crashing down on my shoulders. You had left too soon. And I had come too late to meet you. The irony of history: you, who had always wanted to remain in your country, had, for reasons I was unaware of at the time, ended up dying beyond its borders. Heart on my sleeve, I placed my hand on your coffin. Under this damp ground, the dust of your secrets would be forever buried. The air was heavy that day. Above my head, the sky was moving toward a storm. I thought again of that poem by Hafez. "Venture well beyond the comforting sand of the shore." A poem: this was the only inheritance you left me. With a message between the lines. Like a debt to be honored. On a bright morning, after a few months of hesitation, I jumped onto the Métro and headed toward Opéra. At a travel agency counter, I asked for a ticket to Tehran. "For how long?" the agent asked. "One week," I replied. In the end, I stayed for ten years.

IT ALL STARTED with flowers. Flowers, everywhere flowers. And all those shouts of joy escaping from chadors. I remember that May 23, 1998, as if it were yesterday. The second of Khordad, according to the Iranian calendar. A year had gone by since Khatami was elected. The scent of spring permeated the Iranian capital. On Enghelab (Revolution) Street, Iranians were celebrating the first anniversary of his victory. I had landed in Tehran a few days earlier. I was staying with Grandmother, my last family connection to Iran since your passing. Despite her inordinate protectiveness, I had managed to extricate myself from her house. It was my first outing. To help pay for my journey, I had pitched a documentary project on Iranian youth to Radio France. In the West, Iran had become respectable again, and in Parisian newsrooms, questions were pouring in from all sides. Did Khatami's victory signal the end of repressive theocracy? Was democracy compatible with Islam? What did "Generation K"—all those young people my age born under Khomeini; raised under his successor, Khamenei; and the main electors of the new president—dream of? The stipend for my freelancing only just about covered my plane ticket. But the idea of working for one of the biggest French media companies and being in the land of my ancestors was more than enough compensation for me.

Hijab plastered to my head, I looked all around me. Enghelab

Street was black with people. There were thousands of them, girls and boys mixed together, silently marching on this long strip of pavement that crossed through the capital from east to west, where, twenty years earlier, their parents had over-thrown the shah. I watched them timidly trample on the "Islamic Revolution" they had inherited. I was hungry to decode their tiniest gestures, their rediscovered zest for life. I scrutinized their faces, their way of brandishing red roses as though defying the past. Through them, I imagined the woman I could have been if I had been born in your country. With a slow and de-termined gait, they advanced toward that unprecedented some-thing that seemed crystallized in Khatami's person. Elected a year earlier with more than 70 percent of the vote, he embodied their hopes for change. On his posters, fluttering like totems above their heads, he had a mischievous laugh, a salt-and-pepper beard. Even his elegant Italian slippers contrasted with the aus-terity of his peers. In one of his photos, someone had written in English, "Iran Is in Love Again."

Carried along by the crowd, I cleared a path for myself up to the main entrance of the campus. Approaching the platform, I recognized his black turban, usually worn by the descendants of the Prophet. The president had just arrived. Immediately, a thick murmur ran through the space. *"Dadash Khatami, doostet darim!"* "Brother Khatami, we love you!" In four words, the im-age of the father, so sacred in Iran, was shattered. The monarchs of Persia, then Imam Khomeini in his turn, had always happily abused that image to infantilize the people. Not even with the death of the Supreme Leader in 1989 did Ayatollah Khamenei break with tradition. In the pyramid of power, President Kha-tami exercised limited privileges. But he had refused to give in to the temptations of the throne. They said that during his cam-paign he traveled throughout the country on a modest bus.

Since his victory, he continued to shake hands, dared to mingle with the crowd. A new way of being, a style unto himself. "Iran for all Iranians," ran one of his favorite slogans, which was repeated across college campuses. Once onstage, Khatami scanned the crowd before beginning his speech. At my side, a student gave me a summarized translation. It centered on questions of "civil society," "human rights," and "freedom of expression." With the candor of a child, the student drank in Khatami's words.

Young men suddenly took over a path bordered by trees. They were dressed in black, sporting badly trimmed beards. They were all cupping their hands to scream, "Death to America!" One of the raisons d'être of the Islamic Republic. A refrain that gave rhythm to the Friday prayer and decorated the walls of the former U.S. embassy, mobbed nineteen years earlier. That day, Khatami had purposely omitted it from his speech. A few weeks earlier, he had even granted an interview to CNN in which he expressed his regrets about the notorious hostage crisis of 1979, which resulted in the break in diplomatic relations between the two countries. An unprecedented boldness that the new intruders in black would not tolerate. The student at my side whispered to me that they were with the Basij, the regime's voluntary militia, who pledged themselves to a radical form of Islam. Far from letting himself get flustered, the celebrity president let slip the hint of a smile: "Death is a thing of the past," he shouted, before adding, "It's life we must look toward!" Silence took hold of the crowd. My young neighbor was trembling. Life versus death. So that was Khatami's credo, the secret to his success in the eyes of his supporters. His speech made me shiver. Within it, I heard a singular echo. Life versus death . . . My life versus your death. What message was I supposed to read between the lines?

"Death to America!" the militiamen roared. But this time their slogans were drowned out by applause for the Iranian president. Like taunting the darkness of the past.

It was at that instant, I think, that my gaze met that of a young girl. In her slender hand, she made a red rose dance in the azure sky as she let fly little cries of ecstasy. A *maghnaeh*, the hood worn by female students, framed her pale face. She was proud, it was clear. Proud to belong to an Iran that loved again. To a country that was turning its back on old demons. Tears of emotion escaped from her almond-shaped eyes and drew lines of mascara on her baby cheeks. I handed her a tissue.

"Thank you," she said to me.

"*Esmet chiye?*" I asked her. What's your name?

I knew only a few words of Persian.

"Sepideh," she replied.

"Why are you crying?"

"I'm feeling so much . . . You know, today, I feel like the doors of a great prison have been cracked open."

"Really? It means that much to you?" I asked skeptically.

"You're not from here?" she asked.

"No, well, not really."

"Well then, you can't understand."

⁕

"You can't understand." I felt a pang at hearing those words. It's true that I wasn't really from her country. From your country. At first glance, we looked alike. We were both wearing Adidas sneakers, and blue jeans beneath *mantos*—our obligatory long coats. Maybe we had the same taste in music, the same passion for books and chocolate? And yet, she was right. I had grown up in the comfort of democracy; how could I understand the true extent of the dreams of change that made her tremble? How could I put myself in her place? I was there precisely in order to understand. At least, to try.

SEPIDEH MET ME a few days later, at Shouka, one of the new hip cafés in the capital that didn't exist in your time. When I entered, I immediately recognized her round, porcelain doll face. She had swapped her usual black *maghnaeh* for a light blue shawl that made me, in my thick gray headscarf, look like a nun by comparison. On the glass door, a small sign accompanied by a drawing of a woman in a black veil reminded "Dear Sisters" to "Respect Islamic Traditions"—in other words, to favor an outfit like mine. Thinking I would save Sepideh some trouble, I couldn't help but wink at her and point out the warning. She burst out laughing:

"You've got to get into Tehran's fashion!"

Such self-confidence for a young woman who had never left Iran, who had spent the majority of her life under a heavy weight of restrictions! This was only the beginning of the surprises awaiting me. At the table next to ours, a young man with slicked-back hair was murmuring sweet nothings to his companion, a beauty who had tucked her fake Hermès scarf behind her ears to keep it from falling into her chocolate ice cream. Between spoonfuls, she played around, planting little kisses on her boyfriend's neck. Only recently had unmarried couples started going out, discreetly, in public. They even held hands in the street. That was also part of the Khatami effect. But these young lovebirds were pushing it a bit far.

"Iran is a time bomb! More than sixty percent of the population is under twenty-five years old. Khatami made a breach in the wall that today's youth dream of toppling!" Sepideh insisted.

Saying these words, she couldn't help throwing a mischievous glance toward the counter, where a portrait of the Supreme Leader, Ayatollah Khamenei, was featured prominently. He, "God's representative on earth," always had the last word in Iran. But for how much longer?

"For years, the conservatives wanted to control everything. They imposed archaic dictates on us: no hair outside your veil, no makeup, no tight jeans, no relationships between girls and boys before marriage . . . Today, the reformers understand our desire for change. They're more in tune with our generation. They want to shake things up. It'll take time, but our ideas will win out in the end."

Sepideh paused. I used the time to switch on my recorder. I wanted to ask about her childhood memories. Her face tensed. Had I been too intrusive?

"You have no idea how lucky you are not to have been born here. My generation is a sacrificed generation!"

A sacrificed generation. I didn't really know how to respond. Sepideh was a true "child of the revolution." The eldest of three children in a middle-class family, she had the misfortune to be born in 1980, just after the fall of the shah and three months after the beginning of the Iran-Iraq War. While I, in my Parisian comfort, was writing you letters and playing hopscotch, she was living at the whim of power outages and food rationing. At night, she woke to the sound of sirens warning of imminent bombardments. Everything she told me that day was something from which you had spared me.

"My childhood was steeped in mourning. When Saddam Hussein attacked Iran, not long after the revolution, my father was sent to the front. He was a commander in the air force, a post he had occupied under the shah and kept under Khomeini. So we followed him to Dezful, not far from the battlefield. One day, my best friend, Leyla, was cut up by shrapnel. What a shock! Staying there had become too dangerous. My mom and I went back to Tehran. Before saying good-bye to us, my father said to me, 'Don't worry, soon we will be back together again. Peace is around the corner.'"

But the war dragged on. Sepideh's father's furloughs were so infrequent that she had a hard time recognizing him on the rare occasions he managed to escape from the front.

"At home, I called my grandfather 'Papa,'" she continued.

Eight years went by. Eight long years during which her neighborhood kept filling with little *hejlehs*, funerary monuments strewn with mirrors and sequins, erected in honor of soldiers killed by enemy bullets.

"I remember faces in tears, neighbors in mourning who had to hide their sadness, because, officially, you had to be proud of having offered up a 'martyr' to the homeland. With the war, the Iranian religious leaders had found the perfect excuse to stifle the population beneath a patina of propaganda. At school, it felt like we were being brainwashed. Girls had to drape themselves in a black chador as a sign of mourning. Quran lessons were obligatory. Every day, the teacher would recount the 'exploits' of the young heroes, such as Hossein Fahmideh, a thirteen-year-old schoolboy who set off a grenade under an Iraqi tank . . . And Khomeini would repeatedly say to the Iranian people, 'Make more children so they can go defend our country!'"

In 1988, a chorus of ululations invaded Sepideh's street. Iran and Iraq had finally signed a cease-fire agreement. Her father had returned safe and sound! His military base had been attacked with chemical gas by Saddam Hussein's army, but he had made it out unscathed. Or so it seemed.

"He was tired, but everything was fine. And then, after a few months, my father started to feel his arms stiffen. He started to visibly lose weight. As soon as he spoke a bit too much, his voice would get hoarse. We went from hospital to hospital trying to figure out the cause of these astonishing symptoms. After numerous exams, the doctors concluded that he had developed Parkinson's disease because of the negative effects the gas can cause in the long term. Can you imagine, ten years later!"

After all these hardships, Sepideh came out stronger and more determined. They had stolen her childhood; they would not steal her youth. She confided in me that between two preparatory courses for the university entrance exams, she would devour Persian translations of Jürgen Habermas and Hannah Arendt. After being banned for nearly twenty years, these works were finally available in the libraries again. At night, to escape from the wooden, official newspeak, she would listen to the Persian programs of the BBC on an AM radio and flip through foreign TV channels thanks to a mini satellite dish hidden on the roof of their building. News reports, wildlife documentaries, Western music videos—everything interested her, as long as it didn't have anything to do with Islam. Her hunger for knowledge impressed me. When I complimented her English, she explained that she had learned it from American TV. Her mother dreamed that she would become an engineer, *mohandes*.

In Iran, more than a sign of success, "engineer" is a title that sticks to your skin until the end of your days. But her true passion was politics—and journalism.

"You'll see. One day, I'll be a reporter, too," she declared.

The more I listened, the more I was struck by the paradox of contemporary Iran: by encouraging a baby boom in the '80s and advocating for free education, hadn't Khomeini ended up digging the Islamic Republic's grave? Because these same young people, who were nourished with propaganda from infancy, now filled the universities and dreamed of breaking free from the straitjacket of religion. In twenty years, the number of students had doubled. With more than two million enrolled in universities and a literacy rate of 80 percent, the new generation constituted the primary threat to a regime that had given rise to it.

I had no trouble getting Sepideh to speak about Khatami. She was a die-hard fan.

"That man is the only hope for escaping the dead end that is the Islamic Republic!" she asserted.

When he came onto the scene in May 1997, she had just celebrated turning sixteen, the voting age. Before going to the ballot box, she had plunged right into the electoral campaign. Each day, she walked through the capital sticking posters of the smiling mullah on all the cars. Countless undecided parents, like her own, were influenced by their children and also voted for Khatami. With characteristic spontaneity, Sepideh had hurried to send a handwritten congratulatory letter to him as soon as she learned of his victory. "And he wrote back to me!" She laughed, recalling the anecdote. She always kept his letter on her desk, like a precious treasure, and hasn't missed any of his speeches since. Listening to her so delicately articulate the name of this Iranian Gorbachev, I felt as though I were with a teenager in the throes of her first love. Furthermore, she told me that, to seduce girls, multiple boys had started wearing a *firoozeh*, a ring with a blue stone like the one adorning Khatami's hand.

"Do you know what his nickname is?" she asked me.

"No."

"The Angel."

The Angel. After the corrupt monarch and the cruel sorcerer, the Angel . . . Would he have the power to move mountains, to continue to enthrall his female admirers? Or was he merely a political mirage?

I glanced around. The café had emptied. The young couple had vanished. Other faces, even younger, had taken their place. Outside, the street lamps shone endlessly in that sprawling capital of more than twelve million inhabitants. Absorbed in Sepideh's story, I hadn't seen the moon enter through the window. But the hour had come, and her studies called. She quickly gathered up the pile of books from the table, downed her cooled coffee in one go, and stood up, readjusting her messy locks of hair beneath her headscarf. Before leaving, she pressed me against her chest, hugging me with that unfailing spontaneity. Then, in her little heels, she disappeared into the night.

A MONTH LATER, another corner of your city's veil would be lifted. This time, in the intimacy of a secret party.

When the door half-opened onto the apartment whose number was on the invitation, I immediately stopped short. Had I gone to the wrong floor? Or country? Niloufar, one of my new acquaintances, had invited me to her birthday party with the warmth that comes completely naturally to Iranian women. "A small convivial party among friends," she had said on the telephone. I didn't expect to find myself in a nightclub. As soon as I walked in, I felt the floor pulsing beneath my feet. A deafening sound system reverberated through the apartment. The walls were shaking. Corks were flying. Heels were clacking on the floor. All around I saw bloodshot retinas, cigarette butts trailing out into the stairwell. In the entryway, the floor was strewn with scarves. Abandoned by the beauties of the night, they lay like wreckage next to empty bottles of illicit alcohol. I had to elbow my way to the living room. In the hallway, a daisy chain of veiled women was lined up in front of the bathroom. They came out transformed, hair curled, wearing striped dresses and glittery false eyelashes. And I had hesitated to wear a low-cut top.

The living room was unrecognizable. The armchairs shoved against the walls, the rugs rolled up to the side. A bowl of pistachios forgotten on a coffee table vibrated to the techno beat.

In a flash, a laser beam pierced the cloud of cigarette smoke that enveloped the room. There emerged a chest, then an arm, then a Marlboro held between two manicured fingers. A ghostly vision in the blur of the Iranian night.

"How's it going?"

It was Niloufar. She was wearing a miniskirt and holding a glass of arak. With her crimson lipstick, she tattooed her lips onto my left cheek.

"Happy birthday," I said clumsily, handing her a garbage bag.

She gave an amused, complicit smile. She could guess by the wrapping that it was a forbidden beverage. And she couldn't wait to see if the little French girl had succeeded in finding Russian vodka or black-market gin.

"Champagne! What a find! But where did you unearth this?" she asked.

"A 'suitor' who works at the French embassy."

"Bravo!" she conceded, as if I had just passed an initial hazing test with flying colors.

And she burst out laughing, revealing a dimple in her left cheek—her only wrinkle, she used to say. At forty years old, this unconventional, beautiful, shapely woman had lost none of her freshness. Perhaps thanks to her company. Nicknamed the "godmother" of the youth, she was always surrounded by an assemblage of young men and women. Day or night, they would knock on her door, eagerly seeking someone to whom they could confide their problems. Always available to help, she had a solution for everything: the high-end surgeon who restores the hymens of deflowered young women, the multi-visa consulate for express immigration, the feminist lawyer who separates couples as quickly as he marries them . . . Divorced herself, Niloufar lived alone. Ever since she discovered Spanish sperm banks on the

Internet, she dreamed of having a baby on her own. Her neighbors were unquestionably offended by her lifestyle, but she didn't care what other people said about her. For her, her lifestyle was a form of redemption. A former opponent of the shah, she bore the guilt of a backfired revolution. To compensate for the blunders of the Iranians of her generation, who had really believed in Khomeini, she had given herself over to the mission of helping young people. And sharing in their nocturnal escapes.

Magnum of champagne between her legs, Niloufar let out a piercing cry before popping the cork. Amused, I watched it land in the pile of scarves that had doubled in volume since I arrived. The glasses of champagne started to fizz.

"You know the famous Iranian joke? 'Under the shah, we used to drink outside and pray inside. Today, in the Islamic Republic, we drink inside and pray outside!'" she exclaimed.

A crowd had formed around Niloufar. The magnum was a success. Above the fray, I recognized Leyla, a mutual friend. Late, as usual, she was stumbling around in stilettos. She must have gone to at least three parties before joining us.

"I have to tell you!" Leyla roared, leaning on my shoulder. "The other day, I was driving my car, with Siamak—you know, the guy who was hitting on me at the university? We were listening to a Madonna tape—I had just bought it on the black market. A few yards farther on, we found ourselves at a police roadblock. It was the morality police! You should have seen their faces. Madonna! They weren't pleased at all. We tried everything to sweet-talk them; we ended up at the police station. Seventy lashes of the whip for him. And for me, you can't even imagine, the ultimate hu-mil-i-a-tion: a virginity test. Lucky for me I'm a virgin! Otherwise, I would have found myself with a ring on my finger pronto!"

Listening to her made me shudder. Mischievous down to the bone, she always had incredible stories to share. This one was particularly traumatic. In her place, I would have shut myself up at home and drawn a clear line against going out. But no! It was incredible to see how nimbly she went from one misadventure to another, as though racking up trophies. The hesitant political overtures had only sharpened her sense of defiance and provocation. Each day, her scarves shrank more and more. Every weekend, her boozy parties ended when the sun rose. This prima donna night owl was an expert at zigzagging between the *biroon* and the *andaroon*, the "outside" and the "inside." As if that back-and-forth between the hidden self and the public self had become her raison d'être.

"Welcome to the kingdom of schizophrenia!" she said, desperately trying to make me smile. "You know, this is how we grew up; it's our way of life. Here, starting in kindergarten, you learn only one thing: to lie. That's your key to survival. At school, when the teacher asked us questions, we would immediately reply, 'Yes, my mother wears the chador! No, my father doesn't play cards, and he hates wine!' Sometimes I feel like a chameleon; I change skin depending on the circumstances. During the day, I put up with the veil. At night, I have a ball forgetting about it."

"But . . . isn't it risky?" I asked her, skeptical.

"Risky? Of course it's risky. But what choice do we have?"

She emptied her glass of champagne in one go and rushed to the dance floor. The DJ had just put on her favorite song: "La Isla Bonita." Hands stretched toward the disco ball hanging from the ceiling, Leyla's body started to undulate—her stomach, her fingers, her eyelids, everything! She laughed with drunkenness and audacity. Her bursts of laughter drowned out by Madonna's lyrics.

"You don't want to dance?"

In the half-light, I didn't immediately recognize Ardeshir, his thin face, his bowl cut. We had met the week before, at a rehearsal for *The Blacks*, by Jean Genet. It was in the basement of the City Theater of Tehran. A dark room with a few rugs on the floor and wooden bleachers. After being banned for twenty years, the play was about to be staged for the first time in the Islamic Republic, and he was the assistant director. "Ardeshir" was the name of a king from Ancient Persia. Ardeshir's parents had deliberately chosen the name, as opposed to one of the Arab names the mullahs adored. Ardeshir was a fan of the absurd. His way of resisting. Between the lines.

"It's like we're in the middle of one of your plays!" I said to him, contemplating the carnival of guests.

"Well, yeah, our life is absurd!"

He stopped talking to grab a bowl of olives. Then, signaling for me to sit down, he continued:

"In the end, we're all puppets who—"

He stopped short. The ringing of the intercom had stolen the end of his sentence. A sudden ring, unexpected, intrusive. It was after midnight. All the guests had already arrived. Niloufar wasn't expecting anyone else. Unless . . . I saw her, armed with a candle, scurrying around and imploring the guests to be quiet. Her eyebrows formed two circumflex accents. Her face was ashen. A mask of panic. I had never seen her like that. "*Shhhhh!*" she begged again. Instinctively, the DJ straightened behind his sound system. With an expert hand, he unplugged the speakers. There were a few bursts of laughter, a murmur of indignation, then worried whispers. Niloufar was gripping the intercom handset, pale. Her body was frozen. She took a big breath and, in her sweetest voice, said in a perfectly collected Persian, "Hello!

Who's there?" A long silence confronted the question. A lifesaving long silence that invaded her living room.

"Phew! False alarm!" she said, hanging up the phone.

And the music started up again right away.

Ardeshir let out a sigh of relief. He swallowed, then turned toward me again, faking a smile.

"So, I was saying, in the end, we're all dislocated puppets who flail around wildly—"

The bell rang again, with even greater intensity. And this time, continuously. A flash of panic went through the smoky living room. Instantly, the dancers froze in their high heels. Champagne glasses, placed hurriedly on the table, teetered. Then, silence again. I heard what sounded like the crackling of a walkie-talkie coming from the street. With a nervous gaze, Niloufar walked toward the window. With one finger, she discreetly pushed the curtain aside.

"*Komiteh! Komiteh!*" she shouted at the top of her lungs.

The officers of the "Committee," the morality police, were at the door! In the living room, muddled words started to fly in every direction. I was nailed to my chair. I understood one word out of every hundred. I had no idea what might happen to me. To us. Sweating, Leyla grabbed me by the sleeve.

"Don't just stand there!"

What came next was like a hastily edited film. With one firm hand, Leyla gave me a makeup-removing wipe. With the other, she rapidly pulled on her "emergency outfit," buried at the bottom of a backpack: blue jeans and a shawl to hide her hair. On the run, the guests were shuttling back and forth between the living room and the bathrooms to empty all the bottles. Mint chewing gum was passed from hand to hand. Niloufar had also transformed in a flash; she was unrecognizable. She looked like a black bat hidden in her thick chador, not even an eye visible! Index finger over her mouth, she signaled to the guests a hidden door in the kitchen before rushing into the main elevator. I caught hold of her arm, anxious.

"Don't worry! I'm going down to negotiate with the cops," she said while pushing me toward the others.

I followed the crowd.

The back stairs were dark. In single file, we hurtled down the five floors and ended up in an underground parking lot. A putrid odor inundated the space. In the darkness, a hand grabbed onto me and forced me to crawl under a car, the only hiding place left. I was shaking. I could barely breathe. Head flattened to the ground, I tried to get a grip on myself. What was going to happen to Niloufar? Where had Leyla and Ardeshir gone? And what might happen to me? In Iran, nationality is passed down through the father. In the eyes of the authorities, I was therefore Iranian, and a "criminal" like the others. Guilty of wanting to have fun. But I didn't have their courage. Would I have the strength to endure the lashes of the whip? Carried away by the naïve curiosity that had spurred me on since my arrival in Tehran, I had neglected to imagine the possibility of an arrest. A minute passed, two minutes, three minutes. Time seemed to stretch on for eternity. Sometimes a sob broke out. And then silence again. We were condemned to wait.

An hour later, perhaps more, the creaking of a door woke us from our semi-coma. Had our hiding place been found? Clicks of heels resounded on the parking lot pavement. I pricked up my ears. They were a woman's heels. Was that a female cop? The clicks, more and more pronounced, drew closer to the cars. In the shadow, I could make out a pair of dainty black leather slippers. Niloufar's slippers! I lifted my head out from under the

Renault 5 that had served as my shelter. Our hostess was safe and sound.

"That was a close call," she said in perfect French.

Dozens of other heads emerged. Blackened with grease but reassured! Niloufar caught her breath, leaned against one of the cars, and proudly addressed the assembly:

"There were three of them. Three young cops. They said that the neighbors had heard music, that they suspected an 'indecent' gathering, and that they had authorization to enter the apartment. I grimaced, acted utterly outraged. I told them that it was a women's gathering, that it wouldn't be 'moral' to let them enter my home. One of them snickered; he didn't believe a word I was saying. So I risked it all. I slipped some money out from under my chador and handed it to one of the cops. At first he hesitated. Then, encouraged by the elbow of one of his sidekicks, he took the bills, slipped them into his pocket, and said to me, 'You're lucky. The next time, it's prison, guaranteed!' I didn't say anything. I quickly closed the door behind me. When I heard their car engine, I exhaled and told myself, 'I did it!'"

What courage! And what nerve. Playing the part of a good "godmother," Niloufar invited us to stay the night at her place. She said that she had enough mattresses to put on the floor of the living room. She was worried that the drunkest among us would be stopped at a checkpoint on the way home. Still in shock from the incident, I wanted to take off as soon as possible. A friend who lived not far from there invited me to spend the night with her. The next morning, I woke with a start: What about Ardeshir? I hadn't seen him in the parking lot when Niloufar came to get us. Worried, I dialed his number right away. After a few rings, he picked up.

"You'll never guess what happened to me!" he said on the phone.

He told me that, afraid of getting caught, he had hidden in the building's backyard. An acrobat in his spare time, he had scaled the outer wall. A good ten feet of gray cement. On the other side, the street was dark and deserted. A tunnel. When the first shared taxi passed, one of those old orange Paykans that you can't find in Iran anymore, he waved down the driver and shoved himself into the car.

"It turns out I wasn't the only passenger. The backseat was already filled with a few women! They smelled of alcohol. In fact, I quickly understood that we were all in the same boat: survivors of police raids from two different parties!" He chuckled.

I let out a hollow laugh. I had come out of my first Iranian party petrified. In the days that followed, I declined invitations, saying I had hurt my back or had temporary fatigue. When the sun went down, I prudently stayed at home, impatiently awaiting the next day. My friends didn't understand. They thought I was too serious. They laughed to see me so careful. I didn't share their boldness. I secretly envied them. And then, one night, I ended up giving in. Reluctantly, I accepted an invitation to a secret alt-rock concert. It was in a Russian Orthodox church, not far from the former U.S. embassy. A redbrick building empty of any occupants since the hostage crisis. To foil the police patrols, I got out of the taxi on an adjacent avenue and tiptoed to my destination. I had learned my lesson.

The streets were deserted. Tehran was sleeping, and I felt like a tightrope walker. In front of the door, I murmured the name of the group, O-Hum, like a password. In Persian, *O-Hum* means "Illusion." When I entered, I was immediately seized by the unusual spectacle unfolding before my eyes. The church was jam-packed with young people, crosses around their necks, candles in their hands. The nave smelled like altar candles and vodka. The girls were wearing low-cut tops and the boys black T-shirts. It was really something to see how they danced with such ease, no holding back, in the forbidden space. In the middle of the improvised stage, four musicians in blue jeans strummed their electric guitars and recited poems. The meaning of the verses eluded me. But the tempo seemed familiar. In the shadows, someone said to me that it was Hafez. Hafez! I shuddered. It sent me back immediately to the "wave." To my first Persian lesson. To you, Babai, my grandfather departed too soon.

It was at that moment, I believe, that my fear fell away. In that sacred building transformed into a musical forum, I began to feel as if I were on familiar ground. Your Iran was changing behind closed doors, and I was changing along with it. I wanted to seize the tiniest nuances, let myself be guided by the unexpected. After a few other similar parties, I had to face facts: flirting with risk was a little intoxicating, and I was beginning to like it. I attended underground screenings of banned and pirated films. I memorized the addresses of the best private art galleries that were sprouting up like mushrooms. Between filing two reports, I even posed in a blue dress with my hair down for Khosrow Hassanzadeh, one of the first local artists to dare to paint women without headscarves.

In June 1998, once my reporting on Tehran youth was finished and I'd returned to Paris, all I wanted to do was talk about Iran. A headline on Iran in any paper was enough to make me buy everything in sight at a newspaper kiosk. Listening to the CDs of Googoosh, the former diva of Iranian pop, gave me goose bumps. On weekends, I devoured the works of Henry

Corbin, Dariush Shayegan, Sadegh Hedayat . . . I was enraged not to be able to read *The Shahnameh: The Persian Book of Kings*, by Ferdowsi, in the original edition. I binge-watched films by Abbas Kiarostami, incapable of getting up from my chair. I even stopped drinking coffee; I preferred Iranian-style tea. Addicted to the unexpected, I grew bored of Parisian parties. My city suddenly seemed so calm and bland. I no longer understood my friends, their orderly lives, their daily routines, their planned vacations, their outings to restaurants, and their dinners scheduled months in advance. The concept of seating arrangements, of the perfectly calculated number of guests, was unbearable. And not a mouthful left for the latecomers. In Tehran, there was always an extra setting at the table. A smile to offer to the new arrival. A song improvised at the end of the meal. A few guests who began dancing.

My French half started to agitate me. I understood that my generation in France had nothing more to prove. At the same age, our mothers had fought for the legalization of the Pill, for abortion, for more socioeconomic rights, for better professional opportunities. And we rested comfortably on these laurels. Did we even know how to appreciate them? Our freedom was not a struggle; it was a way of life. It was the opposite for young Iranians. Like athletes, they slalomed daily between obstacles that cropped up in their way, despite the reforms. From morning to night, their lives were a skillful arbitration between the licit and the illicit. In their twenties, they braved the forbidden as one braves the waves. With panache.

On June 21, 1998, the French city of Lyon hosted an event that was unprecedented for Iran: a soccer match between the Iranian national team and that of the United States. A historic encounter. The two countries had not communicated in nearly twenty years. I wasn't a sports fan, especially not of soccer. But this time, the occasion was too good to pass up. Without a second thought, I bought a train ticket to go support the Iranian team from the bleachers of the Lyon stadium. I had never been to a soccer match in my life.

When Iran won 2–1, I jumped for joy. I dialed Leyla's number in Tehran on my cell phone as quickly as I could. "We won!" she raved at the other end of the line. Behind her, I could hear ululations, cries of ecstasy, car horns . . . "Iran! Iran!" the fans were yelling. I had tears in my eyes. I was enraged not to be over there, with them, to share in this moment of euphoria. On the phone, Leyla described the emotional crowd for me, crammed in the streets: men in pajamas, babies on their shoulders, teenagers with their faces painted in red, green, and white, the colors of the Iranian flag. "There are even Iranians dancing with the police. Now, that's a first!" she said. And I, too, started to scream at the top of my lungs, "Iran! Iran!" I couldn't help myself.

YOU SHOULD HAVE seen Papa's face. I had just announced that I would be going back to Tehran, this time for good.

"Are you sure about this decision?" he forced out in an irritated tone of voice.

That afternoon in August 1998, we sat opposite each other in the living room of our apartment in Paris. Since your death, Papa hadn't been the same. Your loss cut the last cord tying him to Iran. And now everything to do with your country was a source of irritation.

"Absolutely!" I replied, hurt by the question.

Never before had I felt the need to justify my decisions. At home, independence was sacred. A Western way of life inculcated by my two parents. And here was Papa trying to oppose my desire to move to Tehran.

"You can't understand," he said to me.

How many times had I already heard that refrain? That was exactly it, I *wanted* to understand. And to do so, I had to dive in headfirst.

I gazed at your photograph. Ever since you left us, the photo sat on the top of the living room bookcase. Seated in your Persian garden, you were smiling at the camera, with that mysterious smile that suited you so well. Your face speckled with sunspots and your hairless head made you look like Picasso. Papa lit a Gitane and sank into the sofa. He had never been very talkative. His silences often spoke for him. For once, he wanted to express himself.

"Iran is constantly churning out problems. You'll never be able to adapt! It's impossible to negotiate with the regime. If you knew what his henchmen put your grandfather through for all those years . . ."

"I thought he was apolitical," I shot back, surprised by this detail that had been kept from me until now.

"It's a long story. Let's just say that he wasn't pro-shah. In fact, that's what saved him after the revolution, even though he had been a diplomat under the old regime. But don't think that he got out of it so easily! The Islamic Republic doesn't only punish its opponents. It's obsessed with controlling everything: private life, extramarital relations, property . . . That's how the authorities seized some of your grandfather's land, by sticking him with accusations of 'bad morals' . . . Professional racketeers! You can imagine the rest: the summons to appear before the judge of the Revolutionary Court, who believes he's the messenger of God; the humiliation; the bribes squeezed out of him by so-called judges; the ban against leaving the country . . . It went on for nearly twenty years. That business nearly finished him."

"And how did he get out of it?"

"The day before his death, he won. The court announced that they were finally going to return his assets to him."

Papa paused and took a drag from his cigarette.

"As if that were all he had been waiting for so that he could die in peace."

So that was it, that mask of fatigue plastered to your face during your last visit to France, just before your hospitalization? For that occasion, you had dug up your old dark blue suit that smelled of mothballs and livened it up with an elegant striped tie. As if to cheat time. And to protect us, as well, from the collective suffering that millions of Iranians were enduring in silence. For you were not the only one to bear, for so many years, the burden of a revolution that had gone awry. How many poignant testimonies did I hear during my first Tehran immersion: all those stories of summary executions, of teenagers forced to enlist in the army, of dissident families who had to flee the country over the mountains of Kurdistan for having been opposed to the fundamentalism of the new leaders . . . I didn't doubt that mullah-run Iran was a country of maniacs trying to cripple their people by making them trust in nothing but divine law, but I was convinced that things had changed. New political players were emerging, others were questioning themselves. Indeed, Papa knew it: for the first time in his life, he had been invited to a reception at the Paris residence of the ambassador of the Islamic Republic of Iran. The occasion coincided neither with the anniversary of the death of Imam Hossein, the emblematic figure of the Shiites, nor with the umpteenth commemoration of the "Islamic Revolution." That night was about investments, calls, offers, and encouragement to thousands of Iranian expats to return to their country.

"Papa, Iran has changed!" I insisted.

But my father didn't see things that way; he was entrenched in the past. His response was categorical:

"I have just one piece of advice for you. Beware of Iranians. As the Persian saying goes, 'When they slit your throat, it's with cotton thread.'"

What was he trying to say? That they open the door to you so they can better stab you afterward? His rusty proverbs exasperated me. If he chose to wear blinders, that was his problem.

In my head, I had already crossed the border. My suitcases were packed. I wanted to leave as soon as possible. Make my pilgrimage to Iran, that land that was yours and that was whispering for me to come back. I was impatient to plumb the past so I could better understand the present.

Back in Tehran, Emadeddin Baghi, a former revolutionary, taught me the best lesson about modern-day Iran, one that neither you nor Papa had given. At thirty-six years old, Baghi was one of those ex–Che Guevaras of Islam, one who had swapped his Kalashnikov for a pen. That autumn of 1998, I hurried to knock on the door of the daily *Tous*, the latest addition to the reformist press, for which Baghi wrote articles denouncing the very system he had helped put in place twenty years earlier. The building was understated, lost in the haze of traffic jams on the Haft-e Tir Square, in the heart of the capital. In the lobby, a young receptionist signaled for me to follow her. Framed by the customary headscarf, her nose was covered in a bandage, the sign of a nose job—or merely her way of faking rhinoplasty so she could seem up on the latest fashion.

The wooden door opened onto a pretty room encircled with a crystalline light. The room had also clearly had a quick face-lift; it smelled of fresh paint and wallpaper paste. Positioned around a large table, the chairs were still in their plastic slipcovers, their price tags hanging from the armrests. Around the table, a dozen young reporters were tapping away on brand-new computers. Their articles broached subjects that had been taboo until now: gender equality, greater freedom of speech, a revision of the Constitution. In the absence of real political parties, the newspapers had become the spillway for all demands, the forum for discussion. An older man, his head bent over a screen, was proofreading, commenting out loud as he read the articles. He had a helmet of brown hair and was wearing an elegant white shirt and linen pants. "That's Baghi," the secretary whispered in my ear. Amid his exchanges with his young colleagues, I managed to make out a few familiar words, directly borrowed from a Western vocabulary: *laïc, démocratie* . . . Unfamiliar jargon had been springing up recently in the new papers.

"Welcome," Baghi said to me politely, lifting his head.

His voice was warm, at once gentle and controlled. I sat down in a chair at the other end of the table. Watching him disappear into the kitchen and come back with a steaming cup of tea, I had a hard time imagining that this same man was one of the people who had "kidnapped Iran," as my father used to say. Questions were piling up in my notebook. Who was he really? Why had he chosen the path of radicalism twenty years earlier? Did he regret it? And most important, what had made him switch sides? Baghi seemed almost amused by my astonishment. I must not have been the first journalist to subject him to this kind of questioning. In a friendly tone, he responded to me enthusiastically:

"I was only seventeen years old when the revolution happened. I was young and full of illusions. My friends and I formed a guerrilla group that we baptized Maysam. We went from university to university, we forced the students to scream slogans against the shah, we passed out Ayatollah Khomeini's cassettes. We thought we could change the world. We wanted to create the first Islamic Republic on earth, and we believed in it one hundred percent."

Islam had rapidly become Baghi's raison d'être, which was

understandable, because he had bathed in it since early child-hood. Born in the holy Iraqi city of Karbala, he descended di-rectly from a family of religious dissidents. His grandfather was a cleric who was very respected in traditional circles. Upon the family's return to Iran in 1962, his father was immediately ar-rested and tortured by the SAVAK, the shah's secret police. From then on, Khomeini became, in his eyes, the only way out.

"He was the only one who dared to say no to the shah, no to corruption, no to excessive Westernization! He promised to give Iran back its dignity and independence. He was a spiritual leader. And so charismatic! A sort of savior fallen from the sky. When he spoke, we drank up his words without even thinking."

At the time, the zealots weren't the only ones to make Aya-tollah Khomeini their new hero. As soon as he returned to the country, on February 1, 1979, he quickly assembled a motley crew: Islamists, secularists, nationalists, Communists. Seduced by his promises of equality between the sexes, many women took a chance on this new kind of leader. They would quickly be disillusioned. As the sacred Supreme Leader, he became the key figure of the state, the source of all political legitimacy. He even appropriated the title of imam, like the Mahdi, the messiah the Shiites have been awaiting for centuries.

During these first months of collective euphoria, the revolu-tionaries attacked the symbols of the former regime: statues, vil-las of important civil servants, administrative buildings. Baghi chose as his target the infamous Evin Prison, where a number of his close friends had been rotting away for so many years.

"When the doors of the prison finally opened, I was as giddy as a child! I wanted to go see, scour the cells, understand the horror of torture—saying to myself: Never again! I thought: We need to turn this place into a museum, so we never forget, so it never happens again."

Speaking these words to me in that moment, Baghi was far from imagining that he would end up, years later, behind those same bars. But we weren't there yet. Submerged in his memories, he continued his story:

"Infected with Islamic fever, I left to go live in Qom, the Vatican of Shia Islam, where I enrolled in theological school. For years, the Quran was my only companion, my road map."

Disillusionment wouldn't arrive until ten years later, in 1989, with the death of Khomeini and the end of the Iran-Iraq War. Religious ecstasy, which had been spurred on by the Supreme Leader's speeches and by the battle in the name of Shia Islam against the Sunni enemy, began to peter out. Previously bonded around the Supreme Leader, the actors from the various factions started to tear one another apart. Those who had monopolized power were advocating an outrageous conservatism. The others, left in the margins, took refuge in philosophical and sociological studies. They were Saeed Hajjarian, Abdolkarim Soroush, Akbar Ganji . . . Former members of the security apparatus and the Revolutionary Guard, these previously powerful, shadowy figures became the new architects of political change. It was this same group that would later give rise to the reformist wave.

"So I decided to follow the stream," Baghi continued. "I went back to Tehran and enrolled in Allameh Tabataba'i University, to study sociology. Then I started to write."

Listening to him, I was reminded of Abbas Abdi, another of Khomeini's disciples. While Baghi was studying the Quran, Abdi was participating in the attack against the U.S. embassy in Tehran. After years of hard-core militancy, that former hostage taker had become one of Khatami's closest advisers. At the end of July 1998, he even crossed the line by accepting a face-to-face with Barry Rosen, one of the American hostages.

The historic meeting took place in front of the cameras of the entire world within the safety of the UNESCO headquarters in Paris. I remember closely following that exchange, which unfolded, coincidentally, in the same place of dialogue and culture where you used to work. That was the first face-to-face of its kind in twenty years. A thinly veiled mea culpa.

And Baghi? Did he regret shouting all those anti-imperialist slogans, thinking he was forever closing the door on a tyrannical system?

"You know, even Michel Foucault, one of your greatest thinkers, sang the praises of the Islamic Republic. Today, the most important thing is to admit our mistakes and listen to the demands of the people. It's our Iranian Thermidor."

This parallel with postrevolutionary France, when liberals kept their distance from the Terror enacted by Robespierre, captured my full attention. Baghi had read widely, had gathered information to better understand his country in a historical context. From then on, he wanted to take advantage of that new forum, the press, to help his country overcome this period of change. Leaving *Tous*, I knew immediately that we would see each other again. His candor, his analytical method, would guide me for years through the inextricable labyrinth of Iran.

On the way home, I stopped at a newspaper kiosk in the neighborhood where you used to live with Grandmother, a daily ritual since my return to Tehran. From seeing me hang around his stand so often, the vendor had learned my habits. Each day, he saved me the best articles, gleaned from reformist publications, whose summaries he translated for me with the help of a small English–Farsi dictionary wedged between the packs of cigarettes and the boxes of chewing gum. That day, it was a satire by Ebrahim Nabavi that had caught his attention. Nabavi, a confounding character, had gone from anti-shah militancy to anti-mullah satire. Now that journalists could breathe again, he had started writing a scathing chronicle that was published daily in *Tous*. It was called "Fifth Column," a mockery of the conservative claim that behind every journalist is a potential "spy"! It shamelessly ridiculed the extremists. The column was such a big success that the best of Nabavi's articles made their way around the universities, where they evolved into jokes that people told in lecture halls. I plunged into the small text meticulously circled in red by the newspaper seller. Dripping with irony, the satire of the day mimicked a conservative speech: "We are against the politics of the Taliban, except where it concerns women, youth, politics, and war."

His irony read like prophecy.

TO RESEARCH YOUR country's history was to uncover your own story, too. The story of a scholar whom I knew almost nothing about. On the top of the list of important figures I couldn't wait to meet, I had underlined the name Dariush Forouhar. At seventy years old, he was an intellectual of your generation. Since that crazy party, Niloufar had often talked admiringly of him. "A man with integrity, a true secular democrat who has always fought for his country . . . My spiritual father . . . I'll introduce you," she had promised me. His old age had instinctively caught my attention. I said to myself that he alone would be able to talk to me about your Tehran, the Tehran of your youth. I was thrilled to speak with him.

And then, a few days before our meeting, the news of his death dropped like a bomb.

It was an autumn morning in 1998, the time when the trees begin to lose their first leaves. Grandmother had gone out to run an errand. I was eating breakfast when Niloufar called:

"They killed Forouhar! They killed Forouhar!"

She uttered these few words in a broken voice. Then her voice transformed into a metallic buzzing, before being swallowed up by silence.

"Hello? Hello?" I repeated, with no response but a succession of beeps.

I immediately redialed her number, but the line was always busy. Nestled against the window, I stared for a long time at the mountains, lightly covered with snow, before finally putting down the phone. Dariush Forouhar had been assassinated! Confused, I turned on the TV in search of a news bulletin. "In the name of God the Almighty and Merciful," said the newscaster in a voice as monotone as the rumble of a dishwasher. Impatient, I flipped through the channels. On the TV: a Quran lesson, an episode of the German TV series *Derrick* dubbed in Farsi, and a piece on the Iran-Iraq War . . . Not a single word about Forouhar. Seda va Sima (Voice and Vision)—the official name of the state broadcaster—neglected even to mention the controversial thinker's name. I knew from my journalist friends' stories that this mouthpiece of the regime was used to target writers and opponents on a program called *Hoviyat* (Identity), broadcast in the '90s. A dark age that everyone now believed to be over.

I decided to call my friend Leyla, the queen of the night. Hardly had I spoken Forouhar's name when she curtly replied that she was in a rush. She who usually spent hours glued to the phone didn't have a single minute for me. Hastily, I tried another number. On the phone, another friend immediately changed the subject: "Now that I think of it, the next time you go to France, don't forget to bring me back a copy of *Elle*." Her reaction was odd. Why such paranoia?

Worried, I left to go question an Italian colleague, Nadia Pizzuti, one of the few female news correspondents in Tehran.

"Something's not right," she said to me, opening her door.

She had guessed right away the reason for my visit.

"Do we know anything else?"

"Apparently, he was stabbed to death . . . His wife, too . . . It happened in their home . . . One of the family friends found their bodies . . . disfigured, bloody . . ."

A few hours later, the information was confirmed bit by bit. With even more sordid details: the couple had been brutally stabbed dozens of times and mutilated before the killers dumped their bodies facing Mecca. The evidence showed that the crime had been premeditated and that it bore the signature of a religious fanatic. But how to justify such an inhumane act in the name of Islam? And why Forouhar, of all people? I clearly knew very little about the elderly dissident.

Nadia, who had lived in Iran longer than I had, explained to me that he was one of those men who never renounce their ideals. Under the monarchy, he had already paid a high price for his fight for freedom of speech, spending fifteen years behind bars. Then, with the fall of the former regime, he briefly held the post of minister of labor before switching again to the opposition. Since then, he had been the leader of a party that was illegal but tolerated: the National Front, a democratic movement. But to turn him into a target for that . . .

"He wouldn't have hurt a fly," Nadia continued. Apart from distributing among his acquaintances a newsletter on human rights violations, he wasn't very active anymore.

"If his ideas displeased certain extremists, why weren't they content to put him in prison, like they usually do?" I asked my colleague.

A thick silence pervaded Nadia's office. Since the beginning of the '90s, the Islamic Republic seemed to have renounced assassinating its opponents. The last time it had happened was in 1992, when four Kurdish dissidents were killed in a restaurant in Berlin. Neither of us could find an explanation for this sudden resurgence in violence.

"Clearly, I'll never understand this country," I murmured, distraught.

However, I persisted. The day of the funeral, I didn't hesitate. I picked out the longest of my black coats and paired it with a raven-colored shawl. In my go-to uniform, I hopped onto a public bus. It was packed. Without saying a word, I climbed into the rear compartment, the one for women. At the stop closest to the Fakhr al-Dawla Mosque, where the services were being held, I disembarked along with the crowd. With slow and solemn steps, the passengers poured into the street, which was already filled with a dense, silent crowd. The Forouhars had lived modestly for years in this neighborhood south of Tehran.

The atmosphere was heavy with sadness. Eyes on the alert. No one dared say a word, as if fear had once again muzzled every mouth. Then, after a few minutes, indignation gained the upper hand. Shattering the sober melody of footsteps on pavement, a man in his sixties started chanting to the glory of the deceased. Carried by the rhythm, he raised his hands toward the sky, brandishing portraits of Dariush Forouhar, mustache smoothed and pointed, and of Forouhar's wife, Parvaneh, locks of gray hair flowing out from under her scarf. The couple had been inseparable, Niloufar told me. While he was fighting obscurantism, she would write poems. Back hunched, leaning over his cane, an old supporter let a tear escape his eye. He was wearing a tie and a small beret. "Long live freedom of thought!" hummed a frail voice. I turned around. It was an Iranian woman of about thirty, Forouhar's party button pinned to her black coat. I was immediately moved by the scene. Before my eyes, two generations were defying the forces of anti-enlightenment. I thought of you, Babai, of the duo we could have formed. That impossible tandem.

In a flash, the procession transformed into a protest, carrying in its wake hundreds of other young people, who had discreetly assembled on the sidewalk. "I had never heard of Forouhar," one of them admitted to me. "But when they killed him, they turned him into a symbol of our resistance!" Behind him, students were sobbing, heads lowered. "Do you see this crowd?" one of the organizers exclaimed. "This is the sign that our battle for freedom is still alive. They can't snuff it out!" And then something unexpected happened. Instead of piling onto the buses parked along the avenue to go directly to the Behesht-e Zahra Cemetery, where the couple would be buried, the procession went first toward the Majlis. With a determined gait, the crowd approached the headquarters of the Iranian Parliament, created after the 1906 constitutional revolution against the Qajar king. A vital symbol of a long fight—still being waged—for democracy.

The police were there, on the lookout. They formed a barrier around the Majlis, ready to draw their guns at the slightest provocation. The Forouhar supporters continued their march nevertheless. They advanced cautiously, hand in hand, carried along by their stubborn desire to honor, to the end, the memory of the deceased. They weren't there to provoke; they just wanted to get their message across. "The killers think, in vain, that through atrocious acts they can discourage the Iranian people from pursuing the fight for democracy and justice," a pamphlet being discreetly circulated warned in black letters; I kept a copy of it for myself.

Apparently, the killers hadn't received the message. In the following days, other victims would fall, one after another. Like autumn leaves, noiselessly. Majid Sharif, Mohammad Mokhtari, Mohammad Jafar Pouyandeh—what these intellectuals all had in common was that they had advocated for freedom of speech. Initially reported missing, they were later found dead in the middle of the street. Lifeless. Strangled. The criminals didn't leave a trace. Not a fingerprint or a statement. Gratuitous acts, cowardly, without apparent motive, apart from wanting to sow confusion and alarm among writers and defenders of democracy. Who was behind the death squad decapitating the intellectual community? And why such savagery?

One afternoon, I visited Amir Hassan Cheheltan, a writer friend. Since this deluge of assassinations, he had shut himself up at home. With a trembling hand, he showed me a document. "It's the list of people to be killed," he murmured, devastated, as if the walls had ears. I glanced at it. His name was right in the middle. In black and white. I didn't dare ask him how this paper had wound up in his hands. "And to think I had recently stopped shaking each time I heard footsteps at my door," he murmured.

When I first met him, a few weeks earlier, he had been a different man. With a smile on his lips, he had signed one of his books for me, one that had been banned for years. The work had just been published, at last! Then he had confided in me about a new project: to relaunch, with his writer friends, the famous Writers Association, an outlawed organization that had fought against censorship. They thought that with the tentative liberalization of the regime, the future once again belonged to them. "Now I'm crippled with fear again, day and night," Amir Hassan Cheheltan confided, accompanying me to the door. Shaking hands, neither one of us had the courage to say goodbye. We knew all too well that it might ring of a final farewell.

Later, I learned that Amir Hassan and fifty of his colleagues had dared to break the silence by writing a letter to Khatami in which they implored him to get to the bottom of these heinous murders. In a surge of unprecedented courage, the president joined their side. At his explicit request, an investigation was opened. It revealed to the public something that in other times would have been silenced: these crimes bore the mark of powerful secret police. A finger was pointed at the minister of intelligence, Ghorbanali Dorri-Najafabadi, who resigned. A major victory for reformist politicians. But although the assassins had been stopped, they were never exposed—or punished. After a few months, the case ended with the mysterious death of the prime suspect, Saeed Emami, who had allegedly swallowed depilatory cream in his prison cell. Iranian intellectuals struggled to turn the page, to continue their course toward a more glorious future. Did they suspect that these murders were just the macabre prelude to a series of even more malicious attacks against advocates for change?

IT WAS AROUND that same time that I began frequently waking up in the middle of the night. I was used to sleeping like a baby, lulled by the continuous murmur of the *jub*, the little canal that flows through Tehran, fed by the melted snow of the mountains and passing beneath the windows of your house. But then, sporadic noises started to disturb my sleep. One morning, I almost had a panic attack. When I opened my eyes, my heart was pounding furiously. It must have been five in the morning. I was soaked. I sat up in bed and listened. The noises sounded like furtive steps on the tile. They were coming from the living room, at the other end of the corridor. But before going to bed, I had padlocked the gate of the building. The windows were closed, too.

"There's nothing worse than sleeping in the grips of paranoia," I had been warned by Nadia, my journalist friend, fifteen years my senior. A few days earlier, she had tried to reassure me when I confided in her that objects were mysteriously vanishing from my bedroom. Some women's magazines, brought from Paris. One or two tops. Nothing important, but still . . . In the end, I blamed fatigue and stress. Sometimes lack of sleep can lead to confusion.

One night, I had an absurd idea: What if your ghost was watching over the family home I was sharing with Grandmother, the last building on a cul-de-sac bordered by majestic trees? I was living at the top of your two-story white brick house. Tucked in the back and to the right, the house was number 12 + 1—probably to avoid the dreaded number 13—the numerals inscribed in black paint, just below the front door.

That night, the noises were definitely real.

"Who's there?" I asked, cautiously approaching the door to the living room.

The footsteps stopped. I slipped my head through the small opening.

It wasn't an optical illusion; there was actually someone there! A thin silhouette, hidden behind the sofa . . . In the chiaroscuro, I was gradually able to discern a few particular characteristics: waxen face, curly hair dyed brown with henna, a frail body enveloped in a long nightshirt. It was a feminine, strangely familiar figure.

"Mamani!"

Grandmother was standing there in her slippers, a duplicate of the second-floor keys hanging from her neck!

"What are you doing here? You scared me!" I snarled at her, angry.

"I . . . I couldn't sleep . . . So I came up here to stretch my legs," she murmured sheepishly.

So it had been Mamani: the discreetly disappearing magazines, the fingerprints on the dresser, the half-closed drawers, the tubes of cream mysteriously emptied. The odor of fresh herbs left in her wake should have given her away. Clearly, your wife had a knack for surprising me.

Ever since my move to Tehran, our acclimation to each other had turned out to be a perilous undertaking. The divide between us was twofold: generational and cultural. According to the

Iranian codes of the time, I had no other choice but to move into the family home. Grandmother had taken advantage of that fact to lay the groundwork.

"Here's your apartment," she had announced to me upon my arrival, pointing to the second floor, just above her living space.

The area she had reserved for me was crumbling under a carpet of dust. Everywhere were old trinkets and boxes sealed with packing tape. But it had the merit of being separated from the first floor by a door that double-locked. As soon as I had finished cleaning, plans materialized in my head. The quiet room would become my office. The kitchen's faded walls would be repainted yellow. The balcony would conceal the satellite dish that allowed me to access foreign channels illegally. The large living room would welcome my new acquaintances. I didn't suspect for a second that in becoming the upstairs "neighbor," I would lose my independence. It took only a few days for that to become clear.

Very quickly, I became the object of all her attention, the subject of all her discussions. "Abandoned," she used to say, by her three children corrupted by the virus of Western freedom, for years she had wound the clock of her life to your service: breakfast, lunch, dinner, time for medicine, tea, visit to the doctor . . . Everything was perfectly scheduled, to the minute. You squabbled all the time, but that was how it was: you were her reason for living, her backbone. I always asked myself if you two had ever been in love. In your time, love meant something different. You had given her a ring when she was only sixteen years old. An arranged marriage, according to tradition, she had told me. She was the daughter of bazaar merchants. You were the descendant of a family of intellectuals. With time, you grew accustomed to each other.

After the 1979 revolution, Grandmother built an imaginary fortress at your side. In taking power, the clerics had robbed her of her points of reference. First, there was the veil that crushed her hairdo. All those streets that changed names, too. On the white-and-blue metal plaques, squares adopted the names of ayatollahs, of martyrs of the Iran-Iraq War . . . It was then that her memory, which was actually very good, became selective. For her, Pasdaran Avenue (referencing the notorious Islamic Revolutionary Guard Corps, Iran's elite military force) would always remain Saltanat Abad Avenue, a long strip of pavement that leads to the posh neighborhoods in the north of Tehran and that runs perpendicular to your cul-de-sac. Not that she was nostalgic for the old regime, but from a pure instinct to contradict, a character trait whose reasons I would come to understand only much later.

When you died, the void left behind turned her daily habits upside down. Disoriented, she closed all the curtains of the two-story building. In her vast living room, the armchairs were back in their nylon covers. Your house was her last refuge. For her, the *biroon* didn't exist anymore. There was only the *andaroon*. While those walls thickened from day to day, her daily routine shifted to revolve around the samovar, ever ready to pour tea for passing visitors who were too few for her liking, and the daily feeding of the goldfish, the only Islamically correct inhabitants of what had been, in another time, the pond in the backyard. Sometimes she spent entire weeks in her pajamas, shut in her "gilded cage," as she called it, for which she alone possessed the keys: for the padlock of the entrance gate, for the main entryway, for her living room, for her bedroom. In her home, even the refrigerator was double-locked.

Over time, Mamani transformed into the heroine of her own

tragedy. The window that separated the kitchen from the outside world served as the curtain for her Greek theater. Nose glued to the glass, she often hid herself there to spy, suspiciously, on what took place on the other side: the comings and goings of the neighbor's son, straddling his bicycle; the clinking of the junk dealer; the beggar's accordion. Her favorite pastime. Beneath her shutters, the regular flow of the *jub* drowned out the distant murmur of a city where the dream of democracy was painfully giving birth. Nothing in that house brought us together, except for a photo of you placed in the middle of her collection of plastic butterflies, which she dusted daily. Ironically, you were our only common denominator.

One day, I dared to ask her why she didn't go live in France, where you were buried. After all, she would feel less lonely.

"So they can throw me in a retirement home? No, thank you!" came her reply. "And now that you live in Tehran, I'm not going to abandon you. A young woman living alone—that won't do. Our family's reputation is at stake."

Widow at seventy, without her bearings, she naturally began to organize her new daily routine around this granddaughter who had made a sudden intrusion into her life. Animated with a renewed maternal instinct, she wanted to control every single minute of my life. And wasn't afraid to use trickery to achieve her goal.

Immunized by her eternal complaints concerning her legs, which were "no longer good for anything," I had believed her incapable of walking up the fifty steps that separated us. That day, at five in the morning, I discovered, stupefied, her talent for climbing stairs and her art for breaking open doors. Worse, my aggravation when faced with her nocturnal appearance only sharpened her nosy, castrating instinct. After that unfortunate episode, every single distant cousin's unannounced visit became an excuse for making me run down to the kitchen as quickly as possible to help serve tea and cakes. Often, these summonses happened through the intercom, to the bewilderment of the neighbors. From a distance, they observed with obvious amusement as this petite woman who looked like a Scout leader, chador thrown over her pajamas for appearances' sake, called her granddaughter by pressing the intercom button at the building entrance. To establish her parental authority even further, she started to complement my outings with a fitting ritual. When I vanished for more than a day, she would hurry to hold the Quran above my head and to make me spin around endlessly while whispering a few verses she knew by heart. She who'd practiced religion as she pleased now saw it as a way to protect me from the evil eye. A way, also, to secretly pray for me to return to the right path.

For, in her eyes, everything about me was wrong: single at the age when she had already had two children; not very sociable, because I had refused to greet one of her visiting friends (never mind that I was in the middle of a live radio broadcast); prone to burying my head in a book as soon as she started spreading the latest neighborhood gossip. I was "too French" for her liking. Too independent, too secretive, too cold. Too, too, too. Worse: I made the mistake of revealing my boredom during family dinners. "In the West, they raise you with a stone where your heart should be," she would say to me at every possible opportunity. And always the same refrain: "If you wait too long to get married, you'll be too old and too wrinkly. Men won't want you anymore." Sometimes I asked myself how you had managed to put up with her for so many years, you who were the opposite, an expert in the art of extreme discretion.

One day, when Khatami was speaking on TV, I tried to talk to her about politics, hoping to find potential common ground. In vain.

"The shah, the mullahs—they're all the same! Corrupt leaders who try to suffocate us," she said to me.

"Yes, but they say Khatami's different."

"So they say! You know, I've never voted in my entire life."

In fact, her only relationship to politics was Radio France International's Persian programs. She often listened to the nightly news bulletin, an old transistor radio on her knees, secretly picking up AM broadcasts. It was her way of pulling herself out of isolation and being close to her three children, scattered between France and the United States. When the radio crackled at full volume all the way up to my floor, Mamani let herself be carried away by the dream that one day, *inshallah*, they would all be reunited in Tehran, and she would finally take out the old oilcloth for the dining table, free the sofas from their nylon covers, slide flowers into the big white vase, and dust off the family photos sitting atop the living room chest of drawers.

Only the ringing of the telephone was able to wrest her from her thoughts and bring an end to that racket. Barely two rings and she already had her hand glued to the phone, making sure she never missed a call—including those meant for me. In my absence, she would even take the liberty of screening my callers. If it was a man, she had to know if he was from a good family—you never know! If the call was from Paris, she found it the perfect occasion to dust off her French. When the playwright Pari Sâberi would leave a message inviting me to her latest play, Mamani always managed to get a ticket for herself, too. One morning, she almost had a heart attack when she recognized the voice of Abbas Kiarostami on the phone! The world-renowned Iranian filmmaker was calling me back about an interview. For the next week, Grandmother could talk about nothing but him. Kiarostami! She told everyone. And I was suddenly an object of admiration for the entire neighborhood.

Exasperated by these successive intrusions, I was going stir-crazy. The Iran that Mamani wanted to impose on me didn't resemble the Iran you had sparked my interest in. The more she tried to lock me into her daily routine, the more I wanted to emancipate myself. To avoid a palace coup in my own family, I absolutely had to leave. Rediscover my wanderlust as quickly as possible.

BANDAR ABBAS! I circled the name of the port town in red ink on an old map I found in one of your boxes. With its toes dipping into the Persian Gulf on the southern tip of Iran, that multicultural city had always intrigued me. The large distance separating it from Tehran made it all the more enticing. In February 1999, I finally found the ideal pretext to go: the municipal elections, the first in the Islamic Republic. While the capital was hibernating beneath its blanket of snow, struggling to heal from the trauma of the "Chain Murders," I grabbed my backpack, donned my trusty headscarf, and hailed a taxi on Pasdaran Avenue.

The road to the Tehran airport offered me the best introduction to the electoral campaign. Banks, bus stops, gas stations—no space had escaped the rapid pasting of candidates' posters, many of which broke with tradition. They signaled the desire to overcome obstacles, to pursue the steep road of reform at whatever cost. In black chador and crimson boots, Faezeh Hashemi, the daughter of former president Rafsanjani, multiplied as far as the eye could see. Plastered to her photo was a slogan advocating for gender equality. Struck by the extent of this political competition, unusual for the Islamic Republic, I had my taxi stop so I could buy some newspapers. On the centerfold of *Salam*, the customary ad inserts for "laser hair removal" and "miracle diets" had been taken over by the numerous candidates. Tempted by the benefits of Photoshop, some were posing with Khatami, the reformer; others with Khamenei, the conservative. Flipping through *Iran*, I happened upon a surprise: an independent candidate from the holy city of Mashhad, Jamal Sanat Negar, declared in an interview that he scoffed at the *mostahabbat*, those good, pious deeds prescribed to the faithful for salvation. Breaking the traditional barrier between public and private, he proudly listed his guilty pleasures: sandwiches, movies . . . and pop music, which gets him "all worked up!" Not to mention this controversial detail: his desire to connect with America.

This climate of political détente made things easier for me. At the Foreign Media Department, once again under the control of Ershad, the powerful Ministry of Culture and Islamic Guidance, I was granted press credentials right away. I didn't have to justify my motivations or my movements or the fact that I was traveling alone, without a "chaperone"—that is to say, a male family member. Taking a bus from Bandar Abbas to Bushehr, a charming fishing port that would later be at the heart of a nuclear crisis, didn't elicit objections from any officials. "Beware of the shrimp; they're really spicy," said a smiling Ali Reza Shiravi, one of the ministry's civil servants, wishing me a safe journey.

I landed in Bandar Abbas full of curiosity. Nothing in that colorful city collapsing under the heat reminded me of the capital's cold and pollution. When I disembarked from the plane, a young man with skin leathery from the sun was waiting for me on the tarmac. It was Moussa, a young photographer who was to be my guide for the trip. Dropping me off at the hotel, he invited me to meet him a few hours later, for a gathering of friends. I accepted the impromptu offer. The driver at the hotel didn't share my enthusiasm. Reading the address scrawled on a scrap of paper, his eyes widened with terror. As if I were going to meet an axe murderer.

"But that's the black ghetto!" he exclaimed, and implored me not to go.

I understood that I had struck a raw nerve: that of cultural diversity and the many prejudices it engenders in Iran. The driver, who refused to accept the fact that only half of Iranians were Persian, had nothing but contempt for the small black community that made up part of the population of Bandar Abbas. "Concerned," he said, for my security, he made a point of accompanying me to the door and waiting there, "just in case."

That night, another Iran revealed itself to me. The Iran at the edge of Iran. The Iran of the Persian Gulf. The Iran that Mamani, barricaded in her "gilded cage," would probably never know. We spent a good half hour weaving around modest adobe houses before arriving at the edge of an abandoned beach. Suddenly: the odor of fish, then the noise of the waves and the caress of a melody. When I stepped out of the taxi, a small light welcomed me: it came from a simple oil lamp, hung on a limestone wall. Moussa was there, waiting for me in front of the small window that acted as a door. "*Salam*," he said, signaling for me to follow him. In the central courtyard, a colony of shoes had been meticulously arranged along the wall. Once I had taken mine off, I let myself be carried by the rhythm of the music. A voyage outside time: in one of the rooms accessed through the courtyard, a chorus of men and women, dressed in white tunics, tan pants, and colorful scarves, lent an air of enchantment to the space. Above the fray, a cloud of incense made it hard to breathe. These "black" Iranians, untrustworthy characters to my taxi driver, were incredibly elegant. They were beautiful: singing, dancing, drumming on jugs, reciting poems from another shore.

I had shown up in the middle of a *zar* ceremony, the exorcism ritual that Moussa had briefly told me about, which in 1969 had inspired the Iranian filmmaker Naser Taghvai to make his very poetic documentary *Bad-e Jenn* (*Wind of Jinn*). In this little "ghetto" at the edge of the water, it was a woman, "Mama Zar," who set the rhythm. She was wearing a pearl-colored dress embroidered with violet flowers. Square shoulders, a round face—she brightened the atmosphere with a warm, sulfurous voice. Standing in the middle of the room, she moved her arms in waves above the head of a child covered in a long sheet. At the same time, the other participants banged sticks red with the blood of sheep, sacrificed for the occasion. "This is our way of warding off the evil eye," Moussa whispered to me, putting two wooden sticks in my hands so I could participate in this spell-lifting ritual. The child, they would explain later, was suffering from migraines. In their eyes, he had been "bewitched."

Fascinated by this small community made up of a few hundred souls, I decided to share in their daily life for a few days. These people lived off almost nothing. During the day, the women would smoke hookahs in the shade of trees while the men went fishing in the sea aboard small wooden rowboats. The most resourceful of them risked trafficking contraband TVs with Dubai, on the other side of the Strait of Hormuz, a dicey enterprise that allowed them to earn a little extra money, and to feed their families. Isolated from the rest of the city, they were light-years away from the debates about Islam and democracy that were igniting Tehran's intellectual circles. They lived, they survived daily, by re-creating rituals passed down through generations. They didn't know a lot about their origins, except that their ancestors had arrived from Africa more than four centuries earlier. Immersed in a unique syncretism of Persian Gulf traditions and ancient, esoteric African customs, they were the distant descendants of slaves who had arrived in Iran at the time when Portuguese traders established their trading posts in this strategic region.

Moussa wasn't black. A musician in the making, he had an incredible fascination for these hidden customs. He even wanted to promote them. For years, he had fought to organize small, semi-secret concerts, mixing pop and traditional music, at the Dolphin Youth club, one of the rare places for young people in Bandar Abbas to meet up in this town where the only entertainment was drinking Zamzam, the Iranian Coke, and watching the sun set over the mostly abandoned beach. In an unexpected windfall, his band, made up of local prodigies, had just landed official authorization from the famous Ministry of Culture and Islamic Guidance to perform in public—which was probably one of the reasons he had invited, without fear of reprisal, a foreign journalist to this private ceremony: to shine a true spotlight on the cultural diversity of his country, of which he was so proud.

"Iran for all Iranians," Khatami had said. Here, in the heart of the country, I truly understood the significance of that slogan. Two years after his victory, the expression had transformed into a leitmotif, not only for the youth and for women, but for all minorities—ethnic, cultural, social—who had, until now, been resigned to live in the shadows of others. A rapid survey of the surrounding villages allowed me to measure the importance of the municipal elections. For friends of Moussa, but also for the forgotten populations of the Hormozgan and Bushehr Provinces, a page was turning: excessive centralization, in the guise of both Islam and authoritarianism, was suddenly giving way to real local concerns. In this remote south, the electors didn't vote for or against constitutional reform, nor for or against a few additional locks of hair being allowed to escape the headscarf. For them, what was important was an acknowledgment of their differences, access to running water, more recreational activities for the youth, cleanup of the roads . . .

From village to village, I saw this same desire to be heard on the national level. In Bandar Dayyer, a small, lost village of twenty thousand inhabitants west of Bandar Abbas, where I followed Moussa and his friends, the local elections were provoking an unprecedented frenzy. Throughout the campaign, the main road was overrun with a kitschy decor of garlands, bright paper lanterns, and mini-flags sporting the national colors. From morning to night, the fifty-five candidates, of whom four were women, distributed leaflets and stuffed their potential electors with pistachio and rosewater candies. Between two meet-and-greets, the most organized candidates presided behind the counter of a local bakery transformed into a campaign headquarters. There was something for everyone: from the bearded Basij militiaman who brandished his boombox disseminating the praises of war martyrs; to the champion of reforms, in a flannel jacket, extolling the virtues of dating before marriage; to the thirty-year-old teacher proudly supported by her husband.

On election day, I went around to polling stations. Joyous crowds jostled in front of schools and mosques requisitioned for the occasion. The next day, upon the announcement of the initial returns, waves of ululations broke out throughout the south. They confirmed that unbridled desire for change: across the country, the independent and reformist candidates had won in a landslide, with 80 percent of the votes. Even better, women attained an unprecedented political breakthrough. In certain towns, they were even the winning candidates. Moussa was ecstatic. His enthusiasm contrasted with the doom and gloom that had contaminated Tehran since the Chain Murders. Thanks to him and his friends, I had rediscovered hope for your country, Babai. But I had no idea how fleeting this respite would be.

BLOOD, BLOOD EVERYWHERE. And all those shouts of anger escaping from chadors. "Down with despotism!" a protester screamed. "Liberty or death!" a student continued, forehead encircled by a headband. Your city was unrecognizable. July 14, 1999, Tehran was plunged into chaos. On Enghelab Street, around the university, tires were on fire, garbage was spilled across the pavement. All that was left of the red flowers of the previous year was a muddled memory, smothered in a thick cloud of black smoke. Hidden behind dumpsters, the protesters clung to their slingshots. Huddled beneath a porte cochere, I watched them defy those in power, carried along by a spirit that had awakened them. The capital had been shaking with anger for five days straight. Twenty years after their elders, the youth had had enough. The first spasm since the revolution. The Basijis came pouring in from a street corner. I recognized them immediately by their black beards and Honda motorcycles. They drove in a tight formation, zigzagging between the barricades. On edge, they had taken out their chains. They lashed them against the university gates. Alarmed by this metallic noise, the protesters rapidly dispersed. Then, once the raging pack of Basijis had taken off, they reappeared—in even larger numbers.

On July 14, 1999, the unimaginable was unfolding before my

eyes. In the middle of a swarm of protesters, a fist pierced the sky. Then a scream shot up from amid the chaos. "Death to Khamenei!" Had I heard correctly? In the tear gas fumes, I searched for the face of the person who had just signed his own death sentence by cursing the Supreme Leader. In Iran, insulting him was blasphemy. Guaranteed capital punishment. No one, to this day, had dared to rise to the challenge in public. In the crowd, the call rang out once more, even clearer. *"Marg bar Khamenei!"* Death to Khamenei! This time, there were more than a dozen challengers to the untouchable guardian of theocratic and revolutionary legitimacy, the successor to Khomeini, Ali Khamenei himself.

With that one rallying cry, the lid had been blown off. But at what price? I didn't know it at the time, but this was only the beginning of a long history written in blood. That of a jeopardized autocrat who would do anything to regain his power. A man faced with a society that sought, if not to overthrow him, then at least to change him. That of a dangerous decade when, torn between democratic and Islamic values, the heirs of the revolution would wage a merciless battle. My eyes stung and my head was spinning. Drowning in the crowd of protesters, I witnessed, mesmerized, the igniting of the University of Tehran campus, the first act in a violent shadow play of which I was to become an inveterate spectator. "Death to Khamenei! Death to Khamenei!" Your country was faltering. And I felt as if I were faltering right along with it.

It all started with a common newspaper story. On July 7, *Salam* received an order to close its doors. The liberal newspaper had been accused of publishing a top-secret letter in which an intelligence agent urged a toughening of Iran's Press Law, amendments that had just been voted on that same day in Parliament. This wasn't the first time the intelligentsia had faced crackdowns. In one year, the conservative Ministry of Justice had already shut down dozens of new papers, including *Tous*, where Baghi, the ex-revolutionary, worked. With each closing, new, smaller papers immediately took up the torch. But with *Salam*, the hardliners of the regime had struck hard: they were attacking one of the most popular news sources among intellectuals, one of the pillars of Khatami's reformist project.

Like a shockwave, the news of *Salam*'s silencing immediately made its way around the universities. The following night, a sit-in took place at Amir Abad, Tehran's main student dormitory. After the rally, the students calmly went back to their rooms. A few hours later, they had a brutal awakening. Armed with iron bars, the Basijis barged in during the night. The day after the assault, Mehdi, a nineteen-year-old student whom I met near campus, told me all, right down to the smallest detail. He had seen everything, lived everything. He wanted to bear witness. That night, he had been in a deep sleep when the regime's thugs broke into his room. Without a word of warning, they yanked open drawers, tore down posters of Khatami, smashed windows that looked out onto the courtyard. Then, like vultures swooping down on their prey, they pummeled the students until they bled. Mehdi lost consciousness. When he came to, the assailants had fled. His body covered in bruises, he crawled into the hallway to see the extent of the damage. Scattered on the floor were ripped-up mattresses, demolished walls, smashed chairs. Mehdi was a survivor. In a trembling voice, he confided in me that a few feet from his bedroom, a young resident had been thrown out a window. For no reason. The body of the murdered student had swiftly been carried away by the Basijis, and his friends didn't know what had happened to it.

The dorm raid had stirred up a hornet's nest. Wound up by this savage act, thousands of students like Mehdi flooded the streets of Tehran. A spontaneous movement, apolitical, propelled by a feeling of injustice and above all disgust for a system that was renewing its appetite for violent repression.

First confined to Tehran, the protest rapidly bled out into other cities: Shiraz, Tabriz, Isfahan, Mashhad. Each day, new protesters filled the ranks of the rebellion, a helium balloon ready to pop. At night, ambulance sirens reverberated through the city as clashes broke out between protesters and militia. For the first time since the rise of the Islamic Republic, passions were being unleashed in public. The pact between *biroon* and *andaroon* had been broken.

That July 14, more than a thousand protesters had poured into the area between Valiasr Square and the university campus. In response to cries of "Death to Khamenei!" the barrage of gunshots resumed with greater intensity. "Hide! They're coming," shouted a student on the run. In a fraction of a second, a group of militiamen appeared from within a cloud of black smoke. The protesters vanished immediately. Pressed against a pharmacy's security gate, two students signaled for me to join them, to protect myself. I crossed the street as quickly as possible, stepping on shards of glass. On the wall adjacent to the shop, someone had scrawled FREEDOM in blood red. The blood of someone wounded, maybe. Or someone dead.

"Delphine! Delphine!"

At the sound of my name, I turned around. I immediately recognized Sepideh, the young student from Café Shouka. She was gasping for air. Temples soaked with sweat, she started yelling:

"They're killing students! They're killing students!"

Her eyes were filled with tears. Her mouth contorted with panic. I brought her into a neighboring back alley, where we took shelter beneath a porch.

"Why? Why?" she repeated, bursting into sobs.

Sepideh was lost. She had put all her hopes into the reforms; she couldn't accept such a brutal backlash. I was helpless. I couldn't find the words to console her. This battle wasn't mine. "You can't understand," she had said to me before. Instinctively, I took her in my arms. Nestled against each other, we waited for the gunshots to stop before taking a breath. Students approached us, signaling to us that the Basijis had set off down another road. It was time to leave, before the pack returned. I glanced at Sepideh. Before leaving her, I asked awkwardly:

"Do you think we're headed for another revolution?"

"Definitely not!" she exclaimed right away. "We can't repeat the mistakes of our elders. Look at this country. It went back a century in less than twenty years! Back then, our parents were blinded by their revolutionary utopias. When they climbed on the roofs, at nightfall, they thought they saw Khomeini's face in the moon! We're more realistic. God can't do anything for us. It's up to us to take our destiny into our own hands."

"How?"

"I don't know . . . I don't know. The most important thing, right now, is not to give in to violence. Maybe I'm wrong, but I still want to believe in the possibility of reform."

That night, I walked home. Going down Valiasr Street, a long road bordered with plane trees that runs perpendicular to

Enghelab Street, I didn't recognize a thing. The front window
of a bank lay smashed to pieces on the sidewalk. A bus shelter
was in embers. Farther on, a Wrong Way sign was lying in the
charred asphalt. Abandoned wreckage. Behind the carcasses
of cars, dogs were howling like wolves. Where had the red
roses of the Iranian Spring gone? Into what abyss was your
country sinking? For the first time, I questioned my enthusiasm. Maybe Papa was right: What if the Iran that I had come
looking for was only an illusion? How could I have been so
naïve? How could I have sung the praises of a country in the
throes of change, as if we were living in a new era, irrevers-
ible? Carried by the wave, I had been hooked by the charm of
headscarves that looked like handkerchiefs, by the boom of
Internet cafés, by the extravagance of ski slopes where golden
youth strutted around, sheltered from the gaze of the morality
police. Each weekend, the threat of a police raid had spiced up
rather than poisoned my nightly outings. Fascinated by the
very Persian art of transgression, and filled with optimism, I
hadn't seen any of this coming.

With aching feet, I crossed the Seyyed Khandan intersection. Walking through it, I felt the silence enveloping the north
of Tehran. Reality had a different face there. An entire population
was living far from the tremors of the city center. Behind the
doors of posh villas where the Westernized bourgeois gorged
themselves on Britney Spears videos on MTV, the capital smelled
like Chanel perfume and vodka.

When I pushed open the door of the house, my grandmother's
voice wrested me from my thoughts.

"Someone called for you!"

Obsessed by the student riots, I had almost forgotten about
her. Eyes still irritated by the tear gas, I walked toward the

bathroom. Agitated that she had not commanded my attention, Mamani followed on my heels.

"Someone called for you!" she repeated.

I let the tap water run so I could cool down my face. Used to the familiar noise of her babbling, I didn't react to her comment. I was mad at her for caring more about me than about her country. For refusing to see beyond the limited scope of her house. Of her street. Of her life. Shut up inside her protective bubble, as thick as an armored door, she didn't suspect for a second that her city was boiling over.

Unflappable, Mamani continued:

"And he wasn't even polite. He didn't even leave his telephone number, or his name!"

I lifted my head toward the mirror. Her hair curlers invaded my field of vision. She was sulking because some guy hadn't deigned to respond to all her questions, while next door, her city was sinking into chaos.

"There's no need to make such a big deal out of it! If it's important, he'll call back!" I replied, irritated.

Then I gathered my things to shut myself up in my space on the second floor. I needed to breathe, to recover from the storm. I had no more patience for her complaining. As for the unknown male caller who hadn't deigned to reveal his identity, he was the least of my concerns. Except that, a few days later, the mysterious, anonymous man did call back. And that time, when the telephone rang, I was the one who picked up.

THERE WERE TWO of them. Two men with brown hair, haggard features, squared shoulders, backs glued to their chairs. When I arrived, they didn't budge. They just stared at me. I lowered my head, mechanically readjusting my headscarf. The palm of my hand on my chest, I let out a faint "*Salam.*" They didn't reply. Their eyes spoke instead. They dissected my movements with an inquisitive gaze. The walls of their office were an immaculate white. So white that you could hear the echo of silence in them. On the ceiling, an insipid fluorescent light. The thick curtain hanging in front of the only window emitted a musty odor. Outside, a young soldier in uniform stood guard at the door. As if we were in a courtroom.

"Sit down," the taller of the two ordered me.

I immediately recognized the voice of the anonymous man on the telephone by his timbre. This was the man who had refused to give his number to Mamani, the strange caller who had insisted on seeing me. I had imagined he would be smaller, or maybe fatter. In the middle of the large wooden desk that separated us lay a thick folder. I saw my name inscribed in Latin letters. What did he want from me? He hadn't explained over the phone the reason for my summons. He had simply given me this address: "Department of Foreign Nationals, Villa Street, downtown Tehran." I didn't ask anything else, thinking it was a simple administrative formality. Now I regretted that. In that cramped room with no natural light, I felt like a small mouse cornered in a trap.

"State your name," he commanded.

"My name?"

"Yes, your name."

"But . . . you know it already," I replied, looking at the thick folder.

"State your name."

I remained silent. I didn't see what he was getting at.

Unperturbed, he raised his voice:

"Your name! It's part of the proceedings."

"What proceedings?"

"State your name! We're the ones who ask the questions here, not you!"

His voice turned shrill. He was speaking in an English tinged with a strong Persian accent. Back bolted to my chair, I didn't know how to react.

"So, *Khanum* Minoui, cat got your tongue?" he sneered, opening my file.

I said nothing. What right did he have to speak to me like that? I stared at his hands as he flipped through the documents. One detail struck me immediately: his left hand was atrophied. He was missing two fingers. Lost in the war? Or in a street fight? This single detail made him even more menacing.

He continued:

"What do you think of Khatami?"

"Of Khatami?" I replied, unable to tear my gaze away from his hand.

"Yes, you heard me. Khatami!"

What did the new president have to do with this conversation? Flabbergasted, I replied:

"The youth seem to like him."

"And you?"

"Me? . . . I don't really have an opinion on the matter."

"And the Supreme Leader, what do they think of him?"

"Uh . . ."

"You went to the protests. You saw things, you reported about them on French radio."

I didn't know how to respond. The man with the missing fingers was annoying me with his questions. His accomplice didn't say a word. I searched his eyes, hoping to find a sign in them, some comfort, if not an explanation for my summons. He stared at me with a neutral, insipid smile. I stayed silent.

"So, you've decided not to respond? You're much more talkative in your reports!" my interviewer continued.

At these words, I understood. I saw what was playing out. The two men seated opposite me had nothing to do with the "Department of Foreign Nationals." They weren't there to verify the validity of my passport. Nor to see whether my stay in Iran was going smoothly. These two shady men were interrogating me. They worked for the intelligence service! The same service that had beheaded the liberal intelligentsia leadership the previous year. I shuddered. My Iranian journalist friends had often spoken to me about these men of the shadows. They were used to receiving this kind of summons as soon as their reporting crossed a line. But why me, still a novice in this country where I was only just taking my first steps? How had my name ended up in their files?

Curt and aggressive, their questions increased in intensity. Did the youth have a reason to protest? Why had my father left Iran? Did I feel Muslim or Christian? Who were my friends, my interpreters, the activists I hung out with? With each evasive response, the interrogation sped up, the questions becoming even more specific, more cutting. Did I have a French passport or Iranian? What had I studied in school? Why the hell had I returned to Iran?

To this last question, I replied without hesitation:

"Because of my family. The desire to connect with the country of my grandfather."

I thought this a noble reason, an explanation that would appease the one who'd asked it. But this type of personal account held no interest for him. He looked me right in the eye before launching into a deluge of "advice" given in an indifferent tone. I shouldn't believe what the young Iranians told me. They exaggerated when they said they were disillusioned by the regime. Contrary to appearances, the population was "proud" of its Islamic Republic. Each year, more and more Iranians commemorated the anniversary of the revolution. Isn't that right, *Khanum* Minoui? You were there. You were able to see the situation, the real situation.

Yes, I was there. And I hadn't observed that at all. In February, when the Iranian theocracy had celebrated its twenty-year anniversary through organized parades, I had been able to observe with my own eyes that the onlookers who had shown up revealed themselves to be more interested in the street vendors selling slippers and bras than in the speeches by the leaders of the regime. The youth, conspicuously absent, instead chose to attend the concerts of the first pop music festival, sponsored by Khatami's reformist friends. I wondered what expression the man with the mutilated hand would have made upon seeing the superstar Khashayar Etemadi, in an imitation leather Perfecto jacket and dark sunglasses, set the cardboard stage on fire, guitar glued to his blue jeans, his fan club of starry-eyed girls at his heels.

"Perhaps you were too busy with your report about satanic music?"

It was as if he had read my mind! Clearly, this man was up to speed on everything: my outings, my meetings, my interviews. He knew the smallest details of my life. He had read and listened to all my reports, knew I was obsessed with Iranian cinema. He even knew about my quarrels with Grandmother. From a list that he rolled out on the table, he started to read aloud the names of my new acquaintances, of my best friends.

How had he found all this out? Was my telephone tapped? Were my comings and goings under surveillance? Who had spoken to him about me? Was it Masoud Dehnamaki, one of the leaders of Hezbollah, the regime's enforcers, suspected by the students of having organized the dormitory clampdown? During the riots, this elderly veteran of the Iran-Iraq conflict had agreed to see me despite his hatred for the Western press. In an office filled with sandbags and cases of mortar shells, an atmosphere of war that he cultivated like a garden, he extolled to me the virtues of the "Islamic Revolution." In his eyes, it was in danger. It had to be saved. For him, Khatami was in the process of selling off the imam's sacred legacy. He was a pawn of the Great Satan. The enemy within had replaced the enemy without. We had to get back on the right path. Squash the protesters. Stop the revolt before it was too late. The message was clear. And I had left the interview perplexed.

As the man with the missing fingers continued to run through the list of my acquaintances, he stopped at a name.

"Niloufar," he said, distinctly pronouncing every syllable.

Niloufar! The echo of her name ricocheted off the white wall.

"Your friend Niloufar," he continued. "How did you meet her?"

I frowned. I was starting to get fed up with this little game of riddles.

"You know very well whom I'm talking about."

Of course, I knew whom he was talking about. But what did he want? And why her? Was it because of the cannabis she grew on her balcony? Her brazen lifestyle? The numerous admirers who attended her clandestine parties? No, the private life of the "godmother" of the youth was the least of his concerns. What he was interested in were her political affiliations, her role in the protests, her foreign contacts . . . In the end, I didn't know all that much about Niloufar. She had always put others first and was rather discreet about herself. And even if I had known her CV by heart, it wasn't my place to tell. He insisted; I resisted. He kept insisting; I mumbled a few words. He insisted once more; I clung to my silence. He raised his voice; I tried my best to keep calm, but anxiety started to take over. I couldn't stop thinking about the sinister practices of the secret police: mysterious disappearances, torture, assassinations. Was I also at risk of ending up at the bottom of a hole?

Suddenly, silence. Probably in accordance with one of their old intimidation techniques, they abruptly stopped their questioning. Silence, another form of psychological torture. I glanced at my watch. I had been there for two hours. The other interrogator still hadn't said a single word. That's when he started to speak.

"Don't worry, *azizam*—my dear—we're not going to eat you. You're like a sister to us. After all, you're Iranian. And Shiite. With us, you can feel at home."

He snickered. Then he continued in the same friendly tone:

"*Basé, digé,* that's enough for today. Your turn now, if you have any questions for us."

"With whom do I have the honor of speaking?" I asked naïvely, still stupefied by the deluge of questions.

"That's top secret!" the lead interrogator cut me off before pointing to the door with the index finger of his atrophied hand.

The door! And so the ordeal was over. I hurried out before they could change their minds, avoiding looking at that hand that so disturbed me.

LEAVING THE INTERROGATION, I immediately felt how much I missed you. Disoriented by the avalanche of prying questions, I felt like an orphan. In that moment, I wished I could talk to you, nestle in your arms. Outside, Villa Street was drowning in sunlight. I had to squint to readapt to the natural light. I blindly cleared a path for myself through the traffic. Someone yanked on my sleeve. I jumped and turned around. It was a kid, hands black with grime, angelic face, a canary on his shoulder. He was holding out small envelopes like party favors. They were Hafez poems. How extraordinary! In Iran, Hafez was everywhere, even in the middle of traffic. So present that he had the singular gift of creating rainbows in the darkest moments. I rummaged in my pocket and held out a small bill to the young beggar. Then I chose an envelope at random and opened it.

But I was completely incapable of deciphering the poem's verses. I had been running after the news so much that I still hadn't found time to improve my weak Persian, to go beyond the few words that you had belatedly taught me from your hospital bed. Overwhelmed by my reporting, I relied on an interpreter to conduct interviews, to help me hastily write articles in university bathrooms, to do live radio broadcasts. Like an automaton, I jumped from protest to protest without taking the time to digest the information unfurling at full throttle. How many students had disappeared? Dozens, hundreds, thousands? Pressured by the pace of news, I could not get all their names, their ages, the color of their hair. A dead person with no name is easier to deal with.

I hadn't liked the way my interrogators had so insistently mentioned my friend Niloufar. Where was she in all this chaos? We hadn't spoken since Forouhar's assassination. I had to find her, clear up this mystery. Once at home, I tried to call her. No answer. I refused to think the worst. I clung to an image of her in Nice, sipping cold soda water and mint syrup on the shore. The city of her student years, where in 1992 she had defended her thesis on sex-based discrimination in Iran. I said to myself that maybe she had decided to go back there for summer vacation. Spur of the moment, that was her way. But the mint syrup scenario rang false.

One morning, I decided to jump in a taxi and head toward the mountains in the north of Tehran. Once past the ancient palace of the shah, I showed my driver the side street that cars had to sneak down to get to Niloufar's place, one of those rare winding alleys where the traditional two-story buildings had survived the real estate development frenzy of the Niavaran neighborhood. I had walked down that path so many times, day and night, that I could have done it with my eyes closed. Kids were playing soccer in front of the white building. A fleeting sign of life rapidly snuffed out by the thick, leaden silence that came, suddenly, from beyond the large gate. In a last surge of hope, I pressed the intercom button. Once. Twice. Three times . . . I looked up at her window. The second-floor curtains were drawn. On the balcony, the pots of geraniums were empty. The cannabis leaves had dried up. I felt terribly alone. Niloufar, like Forouhar, had probably paid the price for that ferocious war being waged by reformists and conservatives with daggers drawn. She had disappeared. Without a trace.

A few days later, the campus uprisings were nipped in the bud, crushed by the security forces. The official numbers were three dead, three wounded, and fifteen hundred arrests. Unofficially, the numbers were more alarming: at least five killed and hundreds wounded. Not counting the many anonymous people who, like Niloufar, had disappeared in utter silence, and of whom there was no news. At the start of the school year, the situation grew even darker. Accused of being *moharebs*, enemies of God, four protesters were condemned to death. Among them, Ahmad Batebi, a young man with medium-length hair whose "crime" was having made the cover of *The Economist*, a bloody T-shirt in his hands. The first symbols of an ever-expanding Iranian revolt, the four would eventually be liberated after long and painful years of imprisonment.

The protests hadn't mobilized every student; far from it. There were a few thousand rebellious students out of the million enrolled in the universities. However, they would forever transform the campuses. As a result of the revolt, the protesters secured the resignation of the chief of police. The minister of culture and higher education, Mostafa Moin, quit in solidarity with the movement. In the following months, universities, although under strict surveillance, became the new epicenters of demands. Each decision by the Ministry of Justice led to a new sit-in. Roundtable discussions were held in the auditoriums. In the cafeterias, pamphlets circulated under the tables. Deprived of their favorite newspapers, the students launched their own zines. A press agency made up entirely of students, ISNA (Iranian Students News Agency), established its headquarters behind Enghelab Street, a short distance from the University of Tehran. Between classes, the youth would take up their pens to unleash their anger. A few months later, in February 2000, members of Daftar-e Tahkim-e Vahdat, the main student association, launched into politics by running in the legislative elections. Along with the reformists, they won the February 18 elections in a landslide.

For the conservatives, the defeat was hard to swallow. After Khatami's accession following the presidential election of 1997, and after the municipal elections of 1999, won largely by his partisans, Parliament was slipping away from them. Their vengeance would be even more formidable. And merciless. Two weeks later, Saeed Hajjarian, one of the closest advisers to the president, narrowly escaped death. Hit in the middle of the street by two bullets from an assassin on a motorcycle, this central figure of the reformist faction fell into a long coma and later woke half-paralyzed. The participation, at the beginning of April, of about twenty journalists and distinguished intellectuals at the German conference "Iran After the Elections" only exacerbated the anger of the regime's henchmen. Upon their return from the Berlin conference, the participants felt the hammer of conservative justice descend upon them. The unluckiest among them received several years in prison after a sham trial aimed at shutting up liberal voices. In the coming days, I would also learn of the arrest of Emadeddin Baghi, the journalist for *Tous*. At issue were articles pointing the finger at certain leaders of the regime for the Chain Murders of autumn 1998. In fact, the extremists had it out for Baghi in particular. For them, he wasn't only a dangerous dissident, but above all a "traitor" to be brought down. He had outraged them by renouncing the religious ideology that he had once gobbled up, like so many others, in the sacred city of Qom, the "cradle" of the revolution, where a wind of change was also ruffling turbans.

QOM, CURSED CITY . . . Qom, capital of mourning and tears . . . Qom . . . A name easily breathed in a single syllable, like a powerful mantra. Its avenues, which run perpendicular to one another, are dull and monochrome. Its alleys, narrow and dusty, make it seem like a medieval city. Its buildings, with their flat, badly maintained roofs. Nothing filters through from behind the closed doors of the madrasas, the Quranic schools. Their thick facades keep in the tiniest sound, the slightest murmur. In that impenetrable city, even the inhabitants carry their own walls. Walls not of stone but of fabric. The netting of turbans, of cassocks, veils, and chadors. Appearing out of nowhere, around the bend from a mosque, women draped in black are half shadows, half phantoms. Silhouettes of invisible humans: no shoulders, no arms, no legs, no chest, no backsides. As if they are wearing their own premature deaths. Their chadors like sarcophagi. Their bodies shapeless, asexual burdens they drag through the maze of alleyways . . . Qom . . . Never had a city inspired so much aversion in me.

That morning in April 2000, I followed the decrepit walls of the holy city, starting at dawn and sweeping the dust of medieval sidewalks with my black veil. I groped through this maze of mosques. I had come to question the religious scholars about the political crisis, but upon my arrival, I collided with one more wall: that of Ayatollah Mesbah-Yazdi, the bête noire of Iranian students, the man who, a few years later, would throw a caricaturist friend of mine in prison for depicting him as a crocodile. I was particularly interested in his role in the repression. The muzzling of students. The assassination of intellectuals. He was known for advocating for violence to "punish" those who "didn't respect Islam." For being the mentor of ultraconservatives. I absolutely had to meet him. Yet the interview was canceled at the last minute. Despite the persistent efforts of his secretary, Mesbah-Yazdi refused to see me. He didn't like the press, let alone the Western media. Condemned to wander around while I waited for my next meeting, I roamed from neighborhood to neighborhood. Around the corner from a religious school, I went down a back alley swarming with people. Always the same shadows. Veiled women. Turbaned mullahs. The same closed doors. The same faces, a hue of sadness . . . Qom, a tomb with no way out.

In this great labyrinth, I took refuge in the words of the journalist Emadeddin Baghi before he wound up behind bars: "Don't trust appearances." He was the first one to have encouraged me to come to Qom. He said that it had become a hotbed of dissidence against the very theocracy that the city had bred. He said that you had to take your time, circumnavigate the facades to unveil the enigma. For it was there, in the shadows of the minarets, that the real duel between the reformists and their conservative adversaries took place. One side called for tolerance; the other wielded the sword of obscurantism. A war of religion, or, rather, of interpretation of religion. Islam against Islam.

Ironically, the cleric best positioned to talk to me about all this was also behind lock and key, under house arrest. Forbidden from having visitors. Cut off from the world. His name was

Ayatollah Hossein Ali Montazeri. This high-ranking religious man possessed the prestigious title of *marja' taqlid*, "authority to follow," the highest level in the Shiite religious hierarchy. Though I was unable to meet with him, his son, Ahmad, a friend of Baghi's, granted me the discreet privilege of an interview in his office, which was attached to his father's home.

Nestled in a cul-de-sac, guarded by plainclothes cops, and under surveillance, the residence of the old cleric was bleak. As if the city's moroseness had bled into its walls. Head lowered, face half-covered, I passed through the barrier incognito. Ahmad opened the door at the first ring. He was wearing baggy pants and a white shirt. He knew exactly why I was there and dispensed with the customary greetings. His office served as a reception area. Antiquated decor, strictly minimal: a library, a table, two chairs. Hardly had I sat at the table when Montazeri's son immediately began the conversation. He clearly wanted to talk.

"Our country is veering toward religious fascism!" he exclaimed straightaway, a clear allusion to the most recent events.

Now I better understood why this man was so close to Baghi. With shameless sincerity, he expressed himself without affectation. A man of conviction, one who had learned the price of words so many times that he no longer scared himself into self-censorship. While talking, he let his gaze linger tenderly on a photo of his father. A small man with a round face split by thick, black-rimmed glasses, Ayatollah Montazeri was smiling. What a contrast with the austere portraits of Khamenei. And to think that a single partition separated this modest office from the family apartments where, cloistered, the dissident cleric lived. And to think that he was probably there, not far from us, behind the thick wall that constrained him to complete silence.

Could he hear us? What did he do with his days? Did he regret this Islamic Republic after being one of its principal architects in 1979? It was a strange feeling to imagine this religious authority, former heir apparent to Ayatollah Khomeini, today a prisoner of a system that he had contributed, body and soul, to conceptualizing.

Ahmad Montazeri handed me a cup of tea. Then he continued in the same determined tone:

"My father thinks that we have to change with the times. Modernity is an intellectual defiance. Not a test of strength. For him, we can't continue to use an archaic interpretation of religion; in doing so, we destroy its original meaning . . . The only way for the religious to save their reputations is to get out of politics."

Hearing this, I understood that no other person better symbolized the evolution of postrevolutionary Iran in the making than Montazeri. A native of Najafabad, twenty-seven miles west of Isfahan—they say he still has a bit of an accent from there—Hossein Ali Montazeri studied theology in Isfahan before heading to Qom, where Khomeini became his mentor. A real bond rapidly formed between the two men. The faithful disciple, once a prisoner in the shah's jails, would even make a detour through the Parisian suburb of Neauphle-le-Château during the exile of the man who would become the icon of the Islamic Revolution. Together they would write the constitution. It defined Iran as a rule-of-law country, with a parliamentary system. Democratic in appearance, with its legislative and presidential elections, the Islamic Republic as they envisioned it was also ambiguously overseen by a divinely inspired authority: the famous concept of *velayat-e faqih*, or "Guardianship of the Islamic Jurist," which, until the reappearance of Mehdi, the Twelfth Shiite Imam, grants the Supreme Leader responsibility over matters concerning the faithful. According to the legislative text, the exercise of *velayat-e faqih* had to be entrusted to "the just and pious faqih who is fully aware of the circumstances of his age; courageous, resourceful, and possessed of administrative ability; and recognized and accepted as leader by a decisive majority of the people." But it was this redundancy in conformist adjectives that ultimately made abuses possible. According to varying interpretations, the power of the leader was, for certain people, absolute. For others, elective.

Named "Friday prayer imam" and president of the Assembly of Experts, Montazeri was first presented as the intended successor of Imam Khomeini. The son of peasants, a man of the people, speaking simply, in common parlance, he had the skill to draw crowds and shared his mentor's vehement hatred of "Western imperialism." But over time, the honeymoon fizzled out. While the Iran-Iraq War was dragging on, Montazeri was the first to denounce the authorities' justification for it. Too many lies, too much propaganda, too many deaths provoked by a conflict that, according to him, should have been brought to an end much earlier. Then, once the peace treaty was signed—once "the cup of poison" had been drunk, in Khomeini's own words—Montazeri had dared rise up against the mass liquidation of thousands of the regime's opponents. "Your secret police are no better than the shah's were!" he wrote to Khomeini. It was one criticism too far. His mentor would never forgive him.

When the Supreme Leader died, in 1989, another cleric would be named successor: Ali Khamenei, the president of the Islamic Republic since 1981. However, this mid-ranking religious man did not possess the attributes the post required. He hadn't drafted the famous *Risalat al-Huquq,* the Treatise on Rights that permitted him to attain the title of "ayatollah." His nomination quickly created unease among clerics. For many of them, Ali Khamenei had neither Khomeini's aura nor his skills. An unprecedented debate on the essence of the role of Supreme Leader, taboo until then, had begun to rise quietly in certain Qom seminaries—progressively undermining Khamenei's authority.

Fallen from grace and ousted from power, Ayatollah Montazeri did not lay down his arms. After a brief silence, in 1997 he harnessed the winds of freedom roused by Khatami's election to attempt the unimaginable: to call into question, through his writings, the arbitrary origin of the Supreme Leader's absolute power. This was the ultimate offense in the eyes of his adversaries. A few months later, they pillaged his library and put him under house arrest.

"According to my father," Ahmad continued, "the *velayat-e faqih* has no divine legitimacy." The faqih, or Islamic jurist, "must be democratically elected for a limited, revocable term. Election or divine authority? That's the whole debate. For those at the center of government, this questioning was seen as a declaration of war. That's why Papa was condemned to isolation."

The man may have been confined within four walls, but he had opened a breach. His ardor would rapidly inspire a whole new generation of mullahs. Without the zeal and support of Montazeri, who was idolized by the youth, the protesters in July 1999 might not have dared to chant publicly, "Death to Khamenei!" For, as hated as he was by the extremists, his status as *marja' taqlid* gave him carte blanche to give advice, or fatwas, to his numerous followers.

"If my father dares to criticize the system so fiercely, it's because he has all the necessary legitimacy to do so . . . Because of his cultural and religious knowledge, he knows how it all works. He is thus able to reveal its paradoxes better than anyone else. Therein lies his danger to those in power," his son continued.

When viewed under a magnifying glass, the contradictions in the Iranian system are numerous. On one side, the democratic institutions, such as municipal councils, a parliament, and a president elected through popular vote (albeit one preselected by the Guardian Council, one example of the regime's control). On the other side, a Supreme Leader with unlimited power. His direct control over the justice system, the police, and the powerful Army of the Guardians of the Islamic Revolution made a "potential tyrant." Which of the two sides will end up winning out?

"We are in an unprecedented period of debate, but also of uncertainty. The foundations of the regime have never been so contested. The diversity of viewpoints is exploding in broad daylight. It's a new experience. For now, the powers that be get by with the semblance of a vote. But could they stand up to a truly democratic election? In other words, can the *velayat-e faqih* coexist with democracy? "I really fear that if this situation arises, our leaders will favor force over the ballot box," Ahmad whispered.

Ten years later, in June 2009, his words would come back to me after the almost certainly rigged victory of Mahmoud Ahmadinejad, supported by the Supreme Leader against the will of the people. Meanwhile, at the first signs of a discreet closing of conservative ranks, Ahmad Montazeri persisted in spreading his father's progressive ideas. He was devoted, through thick and thin. Baghi was right. You had to look past appearances. Now that cracks had started to appear in the wall, it suddenly felt easier to breathe in the holy city.

With the echo of the midday muezzin, I took my leave of Montazeri's son. Before letting me go back to Tehran, he asked me to wait a second. I saw him disappear behind the door and return with a giant envelope.

"These are my father's 'memoirs,'" he said, handing me the packet. "In them you'll find the essence of his ideas."

The voluminous collection, thick with more than two hundred photocopied pages, had been censored, strictly forbidden from being published. But Montazeri's followers distributed it secretly. I thanked his son with a nod, immediately making the imposing document disappear beneath my black veil. Then, without anyone noticing, I rushed into a taxi.

Sometimes, the chador has its advantages.

YOU, WHO VENERATED poets more than God, would have made fun of me: after my trip to Qom, I developed a fascination with mullahs.

I wanted to know everything about them. I had every last one of their lectures translated. I kept an eye out for their gatherings. I memorized the names of the most progressive among them. One day, when I confided in a Swiss colleague about my new obsession, she gave me the contact information for a young cleric in Shahr-e Rey, a working-class suburb of Tehran. At twenty-six years old, Mehdi J. had just graduated from a religious seminary. Perfectly Anglophone, addicted to new technology, he had the incongruous dream of opening an Internet café right near his mosque.

"Come see me before the hour of the prayer," he had suggested in a jovial tone when I called.

I hurried to my meeting without worrying about what would happen next.

His modest brick-and-cement mosque was thick with people. The faithful arrived in scattered clusters from the four corners of the neighborhood. I immediately recognized Mehdi J. in the crowd by his white turban. He waited for me at the entrance, palm on his heart by way of welcome.

"I'll let you join the women upstairs," he announced right away, gesturing toward an outside staircase.

Surprised, I nodded my head. I had thought I would have time to speak to him before the prayer. Now I had to go join the women's prayer room, on the upper floor, sheltered from male gazes. In single file, a dozen young girls quickly climbed the steps. The call of the muezzin had just started. Before disappearing to the men's side, Mehdi J. simply added:

"I told them you were Shiite. I hope that is okay with you?"

Shiite? I was irreversibly Shiite. In Iran, religion is passed down through the father. Impossible to free yourself from it. From the moment I was born, unbeknownst to me, I had inherited that denomination, a branch of Islam that had broken away from Sunnism in the seventh century over a difference of opinion on the succession of Muhammad. Better, I was *sadat*, daughter of *seyyed*—in other words, a descendant of the Prophet. It was written in my Iranian passport. In black and white. Raised in a secular household, I had never questioned it. In France, God had deserted the schools a long time ago. Maman, raised by the nuns of the Couvent des Oiseaux, had distanced herself from religion after an overdose of Catholicism. For me, religion was just a game. As a young girl, I thought only of the "chips" eaten in church during the interminable communions of my French cousins. Or the sessions of leapfrog when, passing through Paris, Mamani occasionally unrolled her prayer rug in our living room to bow down toward Mecca at the hour of the *azan*. That day, in the middle of a Tehran suburb, even a little bit of religious background would have saved me from embarrassment.

I followed the young Iranian women up the stairs. At the top of the steps, a wall hanging served as a door. On the other side was a narrow room, illuminated by a yellow lightbulb hanging from the ceiling. The women were wearing ornate prayer veils. Like dragonflies clustered in tight formation. "*Allahu Akbar, Allahu Akbar.*" A concert of deep voices rose from the floor below. The echo from the women followed. "God is great, God is great." A hand escaped from a veil to stroke my arm. A woman handed me a chador and a prayer stone. I had been invited to join the collective prayer! Without warning. Impossible to withdraw. I smiled and positioned myself behind the unknown woman who had invited me to participate in this ritual. I didn't have a choice. "*Allahu Akbar, Allahu Akbar . . .*" Caught off guard, I tried my best to follow the rhythm. Both eyes on the back of my hostess, I started to imitate her. On my knees. Head to the ground. Upright. Arms toward the sky. A real exercise. I was soaked with sweat. Eaten away by the fear of committing the tiniest faux pas.

"Is your throat sore?" one of the worshippers asked me at the end of the prayer.

"No, I pray to myself," I responded, hoping to conceal my ignorance of the Quran.

As I was leaving, Mehdi J. was already at the bottom of the stairs.

"You did very well!" he exclaimed, winking.

I was enraged at having been trapped. It was the first time in my life that I had prayed. And in Iran! The young mullah owed me an explanation. As soon as the door of his office was closed, he apologized profusely.

"The fanatics keep an eye out for even the slightest irregularity. Many times, the neighborhood Basij has tried to block access to my mosque. They accused me of blaspheming Islam, of presenting a skewed image of it. A young mullah who speaks English—they don't like that. So imagine if they learned that

I had a meeting with a Western female journalist in my mosque."

Mehdi J. signaled for me to sit down before sitting down himself.

"Are you upset?"

"Uh, no," I replied, still breathless from the tedious improvised exercise.

I had a hard time masking my embarrassment. He could have warned me at least.

"You know, here, it's not just the extremists who keep an eye on me," he continued, as if to excuse himself. "When I started preaching, only one man and a young girl came for the prayer. The teenagers sulked at me. They would cross to the other side of the street when I passed. The taxi drivers refused to take me in their cars because I wore a turban."

"That's not surprising. Everyone knows that mullahs are unpopular," I replied, quickly regretting my directness.

He continued:

"It's true that these days, the religious aren't very well liked. But rest assured that I am the first to criticize the religious zealots. People are sick of this joyless Islam that's been imposed on them from on high for years. They're right! Religion isn't just about restrictions."

I said nothing. I waited for him to back up his words.

"I know that in France, you lump us all together," he said. "For you, Shiites, Sunnis—they're all the same! In reality, Shiite Islam is a lot less rigid than it seems. At least, assuming it's followed correctly. That's the principal of *ijtihad*, the interpretation of the sacred texts. We even have a term for it: *sacred doubt, shak-e moghadas*. We doubt everything. We question everything. Is smoking halal? Is polygamy legal? Nothing is fixed. We even have a principle called *osroharaj*, which means 'the one that is the exception to the rule.' For example, if you are lost in the desert and you only have wine to quench your thirst, it's not a sin to drink it!"

My frown did not escape him. His examples had piqued my interest.

"It's true, it's true! I promise you!" he insisted. "In Shiite Islam, each believer has a *marja'*, an ayatollah, to whom he can ask any question that comes into his head. No matter what your concern is, he will respond to you by mail."

"And how does your Internet café factor into all this?"

"Oh, that, that's my baby," he said. "For a little while now, they've had me do public relations for our four thousand mosques. I'm also working on the computerization of five hundred places of worship. Doing all that gave me the idea to open a small center near here. The youth would be able to access the Internet. The problem is that there's not a lot for them to do. So they're tempted by drugs, alcohol . . . I believe in the principle that we, the religious community, should be there to help them, not to terrorize them."

I took careful notes. Amused by my ignorance of Shi'ism, he replied to my questions with enthusiasm.

"If this continues, you're going to become a real Shiite!" he laughed.

I smiled. I didn't know that a mullah could be so sarcastic. Was it his youth, or his excellent English? After an hour-long interview, my respect for him had been restored. I started to feel more at ease. In the following weeks, each time I confronted an arduous question about the Quran, I called him to ask his opinion. At each religious festival, he picked up the phone to wish me a good day. When I was studying the place of women in Islam, naturally I turned to him.

"I'll come to your house. It'll spare you from sitting through traffic," he offered.

I said yes, seeing his offer merely as a sign of pure politeness. Before receiving him, I made sure to cover my hair with a headscarf, as a gesture of respect for the clerical institution. When he arrived, he was unrecognizable. Apart from his thin brown beard, everything about him was different—his slippers, his cassock. There he was on the doorstep of the house, straight as a rod, squeezed into blue jeans and a leather jacket.

"It's so I don't embarrass you in front of your neighbors," he said with a funny expression on his face.

And he stuck out his hand! According to the codes of conduct of the time, it would have been inappropriate to shake his hand. Even if he had swapped his clerical clothes for an ordinary outfit! Disconcerted, I discreetly extended mine to show him the living room.

"Women's issues, especially when it comes to relations between men and women, is a subject close to my heart!" he began, taking a seat on the small sofa.

He was in a rush to speak. This topic, he said, was of the utmost importance. He wanted to use his family as an example: married to a woman older than he, "like Khadija, the first wife of the Prophet," he was also the happy father of two little girls.

"Never would I let their future husbands raise a hand to them. A man does not have the right to be violent with his wife, even if she has misbehaved. The Quran is actually very clear on this. If the man wants to punish his wife, he can hit her with a bunch of basil. That's it. And if he hurts her, if her skin turns blue or pink, he has to pay a fine. The wife even has the right to ask for a divorce!"

It was incredible to see his passion for the subject. For him,

a woman was a "delicate flower" to be respected, a being to protect. The discussion then inevitably turned to the veil. From
his perspective, which I shared, Iranian women should be able
to choose to liberate themselves from it. He even confessed his
surprise at seeing me wearing the veil in my home.

"Even if it suits you so well," he added.

Then his eyes scanned every last detail of my face. Seated
next to me, he placed his hand on the armrest of my chair. Preferring to give him the benefit of the doubt, I got up to serve
him a cup of tea. He blushed. His hands were trembling lightly.
There was a silence. To fill it, I resumed the conversation, asking for his opinion on the possibility of a woman aspiring to the
presidency.

"You're not married?" he asked.

I didn't see what my private life had to do with the question.

"You . . . You're not married?" he repeated.

"No."

"And you have no intention of getting married?"

"One day, maybe . . . I still have time."

He paused, observing my face, my eyes, my hands.

"Have you ever thought about a *sigheh*?" he continued.

"A what?"

"A *sigheh* . . . You know, the temporary marriage that allows
you to have sexual relations for a determined period of time. Ten
minutes, a day, three months . . . Or ninety-nine years . . . A
made-to-order relationship, if you will."

I was astounded. I didn't know how to react. He continued:

"In the time of the Prophet, it was commonplace among travelers and pilgrims. Especially when they stayed away too long
from their families. They would marry a second wife for a limited time. A way to . . . satisfy their needs."

Listening to his description, I understood it to be nothing more than a form of prostitution or adultery. Clearly, I still had a lot to learn about Shi'ism.

"But I thought that the entire principle of religion was to protect the household. Isn't that all . . . a bit hypocritical?"

"No, not at all! It's also in the interest of women in need of affection. Because, officially, only widows and divorced women can have a *sigheh*—"

He cut himself off again, hesitated for a moment. Then he carried on:

"At least, that's the general rule. Beyond that, there can always be exceptions."

"What are you trying to say?"

"I'm going to tell you a secret: let's say that it can be a sort of secret pact between two people. No need to inform their families."

A secret pact! When he said these words, Mehdi lifted his head in my direction, looking me straight in the eyes. I lowered mine. I now understood perfectly well what he was getting at. I was mad at myself for having opened my door to him, for having once again been trapped by my own naïveté. How could I have imagined that a twenty-six-year-old married mullah would ask me to . . . "marry" him? I felt his gaze weighing on me. I remained silent, staring at the coffee table, then at my feet, then at my watch. I was running out of ways to divert my attention. So I got up. I adjusted my headscarf, tightly plastered against my temples. In a dry tone, I simply told him he had to leave. That I had another meeting to get to.

"Already?" he said.

"Yes, I'm very busy. But it would be a pleasure to see you

again," I added clumsily, hoping to get rid of him as quickly as possible.

Mehdi J. looked disappointed. With a clammy palm, he shook my hand again, before turning on his heels. I opened the door for him. Then I watched him go down the stairs, in his leather jacket, still baffled by his behavior.

"See you soon," he said, before disappearing into the street.

"Good-bye," I replied, hoping never to run into him again.

A few days later, the telephone rang at one in the morning.

"Hello?" I answered in a sleepy voice.

"It's Mehdi."

Mehdi! I couldn't believe his audacity.

"I hope I didn't wake you?"

"You did," I replied drily.

"I'm going for a hike on the mountain this Friday. Would you like to come with me?"

The mountain! One of the favorite pastimes of young Iranians in search of escape was to climb the trails of the mountain, less than an hour from Tehran. Those young people are, in fact, trying to get as far away as possible from mullahs. After getting a hold of myself, I clumsily replied:

"Oh, as you know, I'm very busy."

He insisted.

"If it's because of my mullah outfit, don't worry, I'll ditch the turban for my leather jacket!"

"No, no, really. No, thank you," I replied, thinking again of the "secret pact."

Silence on the line. This time, he was the one who kept quiet. Voice on edge, he finally responded:

"I thought you were different from the others. I thought you weren't prejudiced against mullahs. I thought you had come to Iran to better understand its nuances. But, the truth is, if you don't want to see me, it's because I'm a man of God!"

"No, not at all. That's not what I'm trying to say—"

He had already hung up.

THE DEAD ALSO have their secrets. I thought yours would be buried forever. Never would I have imagined that I would unearth them one day, let alone that it would be thanks to an unexpected visit.

It was a summer night in 2001. At around ten o'clock, a surprising chuckling suddenly lured me from my computer screen. The laughs were coming from Grandmother's part of the house. At that hour, Mamani was usually already deep in her pill-induced dreams. Since the "phantom" episode, she had never shown herself again in the middle of the night. Where was this surge of energy coming from? I didn't take the time to turn on the light. In the darkness of the stairwell, I hurled myself down the stairs four at a time. Halfway down, a sliver of light guided my last steps. It was coming from the front door of her apartment. On the mat, blue shoes gleamed in the darkness. Mamani had company.

"Ahaha! Heehee! Ahahaha!"

The snickers started up again, even more intensely. High-pitched, irregular. This explosion of joy was unusual for Grandmother. I don't think I'd ever seen her smile, she who could launch into jeremiads with the same ease as some recited Hafez's poetry. I rang the doorbell. The shrill "tweet-tweet" of an imitation canary rang out in the stairwell. The laughter stopped. The gate creaked. The door opened a crack. A blinding light flooded the landing.

"*Salaaaaaaam!*"

I didn't have time to identify the origin of this piercing cry. I had already bounced headfirst into the softness of an opulent chest. Insistent hands embraced me firmly, then ran up and down my back frantically. I struggled against her bold cleavage as it crushed my nose. I sneezed, recognizing the peppery scent of counterfeit Coco Chanel. The embrace loosened, revealing two large green eyes framed by bleached hair.

"Your grandmother and I were just talking about you!" exclaimed the garish woman standing in front of me.

She spoke to me with such familiarity that it was as if she had known me since I was a child.

I had no idea where she was from. Her porcelain face, run through with subtle wrinkles, didn't give me much to go on. Eyebrows waxed to perfection, a perfectly redone nose, outrageous lipstick matched to her taffeta dress . . . Was it because of her portliness or because of the plastic surgeon that it was difficult to guess her age? It was clear that she had been beautiful in her youth. In a burst of outrageous affection, she covered my face in kisses. Then, nonchalantly, she crouched on the floor to pick up a ball of fur. A dog! At my grandmother's house! According to Mamani, anything with four legs was *najes*, impure, and thus strictly forbidden to enter her gilded cage. Scarcely had the pooch been nestled in the arms of its owner than it started to lick her lips. I had a hard time hiding a grimace.

"Follow me," she said, scampering to Mamani's bedroom.

She seemed quite at home for a guest. Through what sleight of hand had this exuberant creature found herself here? Walking through the living room, I noticed small teacups with the

Qajar pattern that Grandmother brought out only for important guests. The covers had even been removed from the sofas, revealing a pretty blue-and-white design. On the coffee table, half-eaten pieces of chocolate cake melted in the heat. I tripped over a chicken bone in the hallway. The furry pooch, too, had marked its territory.

"Delphine! *Bia beshin!* Come sit down!"

My grandmother was calling to me from her bed, eyes wide open. She was casually snacking on pistachios in a nightshirt and black stockings. A rain of shells poured onto the Persian rug. Placed on her night table, right next to a large box of cream-filled pastries, her "Sandman" pills sat, ignored, next to a glass of water. She had neglected to take them that night. Reading between the lines of her relaxed face, I thought she might have taken a Xanax instead. Once the dog had jumped to the floor, that night's visitor dug a crater for herself next to Grandmother. She must have been double, maybe triple, Grandmother's weight. The two women didn't really have anything in common. Neither physically nor mentally. Nevertheless, they seemed like such good friends behind the closed door of this bedroom.

"Marie is a friend . . . of the family," Mamani said in a mysterious tone. "She's going to sleep here tonight."

"Marie" wasn't a very Iranian name. She probably chose it to give herself the air of a *farangi* (a foreigner). Watching her take out a fake Christian Dior face powder from her imitation Louis Vuitton bag, I noticed that her gluttony manifested itself even in her excessive use of cosmetics. In a cloud of blush, she redecorated her face, and gave a few playful brushstrokes to her dog. Then she turned to me and exclaimed:

"Hey, since you seem to travel to Paris often. I'll have to place an order with you next time!"

"Uh, I—"

My grandmother cut me off right away. She had leapt from her bed. Her face had abruptly darkened.

"How's that? What about the makeup I brought you back from my last trip to France? Was that for your dog's beautiful eyes?" she cried.

"No, that was junk from a convenience store, barely good enough for a teenager!" Marie chided.

"And the leather pumps I bought you on Rue de Rennes?" Mamani grumbled, visibly offended.

"Don't get me started on the pumps! They're too big, and on top of that, they're fake leather!" Marie quacked.

In Iran, passion often surpasses reason. Especially among women. Behind closed doors, nothing is held back. But this was overkill! It was like a fight between scavengers. Marie paused, gave herself another stroke of the blush, swallowed another cream puff. Then continued: "Your husband, Hossein, God rest his soul, had much better taste! He pampered me with costume jewelry and real ladies' perfumes brought back from Paris."

Hossein. You, my Babai? What on earth did you have to do with this? A silence cut through the night. Mamani's face tensed. All it took was one word, one sentence, for her to put her Iranian Medea mask back on, her tragic gaze, and her frown. I remained glued to my chair, like a paralyzed referee, overwhelmed by the tempo of this incongruous duel. Her pooch at her heels, Marie suddenly disappeared into the kitchen. Sulking, my grandmother curled up under the covers. The creases in her forehead revealed not only vexation but also the sad expression of a disowned wife.

"Your grandfather always had a harem around him. In the end, his straying got the better of him. By opening to too many women, his heart atrophied, before quitting on him entirely! It cost him his life!"

I sat down on the edge of her bed. She cleared her throat, then grumbled a few inaudible words. As if to preempt the question I didn't dare ask, she continued:

"Marie was his favorite . . . But I had never heard about her . . . When he died, she suddenly appeared. As if she had fallen from the sky! Her name had been written in black and white in Babai's will. He had left her a plot of land . . . That's how she turned up in my life one day: to claim what she was owed. Strange way to meet, isn't it?"

So you, too, enigmatic Grandfather, gave in to the temptation of a secret temporary marriage . . . Mamani had refrained from pronouncing the taboo word, *sigheh*. I didn't need it spelled out for me. For so long I had put you on a pedestal, raising you up as an invincible hero of all humanitarian causes! Half philosopher, half poet, always inclined to spread goodness. In reality, you weren't all that different from everyone else. You, too, had your secrets, your weaknesses. I felt as if I had just swallowed a bitter pill. And yet I knew about your early penchant for women; according to the rare memories evoked by Papa, you were breastfed by different wet nurses until you were five years old. At that time, the practice was commonplace. Also, as a young girl, I walked in on you several times when, during your rare trips to Paris, you were greedily flipping through a magazine filled with photos of naked women. On the cover, I read *Playboy* in pink letters. "This isn't for someone your age!" you declared each time, chasing me from your bedroom. When you went back to Tehran, you always had a suitcase filled with blouses that Maman, unwitting accomplice to your conquests, thought she had bought for your "students," as you told her. Later in life, you even used your charms on the nurses at the Paris hospital where you spent your final days. From the day you arrived, you made it a principle to learn all their names by heart. They were your "sweethearts," the "light of your eyes." But to go from that to leading a double life with Allah's blessing, especially an erudite and secular man like you . . .

I watched Mamani nervously shell her pistachios. Eyes plunged into the patterns of the Persian rug, she continued in a monotone voice:

"I detested Marie from the moment I met her. I found her too exuberant, too talkative. I was in mourning and couldn't stand for her to come knocking at my door unexpectedly as soon as she needed a photocopy or a signature. However, I had no choice but to respect Babai's decision . . . And then, with time, we ended up growing closer. After all, I told myself, she hadn't done anything wrong in this affair. The real culprit was your grandfather!"

"And you've seen each other regularly since?"

"She comes to see me twice a month . . . Sometimes she even sleeps here, when it gets too late . . . The truth is, she keeps me company. I forget that I'm alone. Plus, she's funny—except when she taunts me with the list of gifts your grandfather gave her, when he was so stingy with me! And then I can't help it: I fly off the handle."

"How long did their secret affair last?"

"I have no idea. In fact, I prefer not to know . . . The past is the past."

Poor Mamani! I had given up trying to understand her, infuriated by her random intrusions into my private life, but now I felt stupid for having judged her so quickly.

"And it never alarmed you to see him flirting all the time?" I asked.

"You know, in those days, we accepted everything without asking questions. We settled for acting happy with what we had been given . . . I have to admit that I was naïve . . . When I got married, at sixteen, I almost felt lucky: my older sister had been promised to her husband when she was only ten . . . On top of that, Babai was a rather good-looking man. He wore elegant suits, he was respected in society for having written a thesis on archeology, he spoke several languages. I have to say that, from the beginning, I even found him quite charming."

Mamani had certainly benefited from being your wife. As soon as she was married, she inherited the title of *Khanum* Doctor, "Madam" Doctor, even though her own studies had stopped after the baccalaureate. In Iran, where the family name and curriculum vitae are one and the same, everything is transmitted through marriage. Thus, it was enough to marry someone with a doctorate to be able to call yourself "Madam Doctor," or an engineer to become "Madam *Mohandes*." To be "the wife of" was better than nothing, she told herself. But the beautiful brunette with the pretty dresses that showed off her perfect hourglass figure would quickly become disillusioned. At dinners, her husband's eyes roamed from woman to woman, from cleavage to cleavage. Very busy with "his work," he often came home late. When she became pregnant, two years later, she found a measure of comfort in motherhood. But her first baby, Nasrine, died of a bad case of dysentery at the age of two. At the end of the 1940s, that was commonplace. Hygiene and health conditions left much to be desired. The young monarch, Mohammad Reza Shah, had other concerns: buying private jets, flirting with Americans, making a name for himself on the international scene. It would take until the sanitary and scientific improvements of the current Islamic Republic—a success the mullahs can be proud of—to see a rapid drop in infant mortality.

"I cried a lot . . . I was alone, faced with my sadness . . . And then your father arrived. Then your uncle and your aunt . . . At that moment, I switched roles, from spouse to mother. Hossein and I had started sleeping in separate bedrooms, and I turned a blind eye to his secret life."

So that was the reason for her constant bitterness. Deprived of happiness, she couldn't help herself from systematically destroying it in others. Maybe because she thought that, in any case, it didn't exist. Listening to her, I understood her wounds, her flaws, which reminded me of those of other Iranian women. Islamic law, in effect since 1979, was a convenient scapegoat. People blamed it for all the evils of the earth. But the suffering of women didn't begin with the revolution; it had long before been sealed with the mortar of patriarchal traditions.

A high-pitched barking tore me from my thoughts. The furry pooch had just made a new interruption into Mamani's room, preceding Marie, who had a large lollipop in her mouth and a colorful cake in the shape of a hamburger in her arms. She was cheery, as if nothing were wrong.

"Dessert!" she cooed.

Still riled up about Marie's insensitive wisecrack, Mamani's eyebrows were on alert. I had never seen her with such incandescent eyes. She pushed back the covers, sat on the edge of the bed, scornfully stared down her adversary from head to toe. Then said, with a mischievous grimace:

"Look at you, with your fat belly! You eat so much you'd think you were pregnant with triplets."

What a comeback! Your secret wife spat out her lollipop — to the immense joy of her dog, who immediately seized the sugary gem. Bewildered, I observed this little game of Ping-Pong, worried it might end badly. But, the game at a tie, the opposite happened. After a brief pause, Marie swallowed, and broke into an enormous fit of laughter. I turned toward Mamani. Her body had been taken over by convulsions that transformed rapidly into little high-pitched cries: she couldn't stop laughing!

"That was a good one!" Marie guffawed.

Outside, the moon was round. Their chuckling petered out in a singular nocturnal melody. There was something cathartic about their way of laughing until they were in tears.

Also, in the following weeks, I started getting used to Marie. With each visit, the same merry-go-round. Arms full of sweets, she perfumed the air with her asphyxiating eau de cologne, her dog trailing behind her. In Grandmother's apartment, there was always a bed and a place setting waiting for her. With time, their complicity grew even stronger. As if in having shared the same man, they were linked to each other, despite the odds.

I observed your two wives, the visible and the invisible, squabbling like sisters and then reconciling right away through the magic of a good joke. They also mocked your quirks: your mood swings or your naps in the middle of meals, when you would pretend to be "thinking." A greater absurdity, Mamani soon became an adviser to Marie. When your "second wife" was on the lookout for a contractor or mason for the construction of her villa on the land she had inherited, Grandmother always found a way to unearth a telephone number or a name. For the duration of the work, Marie would always visit, making sure we didn't forget about her.

While the villa was taking shape, her visits started to spread out. Three years later, once her house was finished, she disappeared for good—along with her pooch, her hamburger-shaped cakes, and her lollipops. No doubt about it, that woman was exceptionally brazen. But I had a hard time being mad at her. She had deserted our life as suddenly as she had invaded it, but I almost missed her, so much had she spiced up Mamani's morose daily life. In fact, I was grateful to her. In revealing a part of the shadow of your past, she had achieved the impossible: she brought me closer to Grandmother.

"*SOKOUT . . . HAREKAT . . .* SILENCE . . . Action!" Pitched on the rocks, our camera zoomed in on the face of a Persian Castafiore. "Daughter of the sea, it's morning! Wake up! Open your eyes!" crooned the young actress, impersonating Googoosh, the timeless pop diva from before the revolution. Her words ricocheted through the gully. Her doe eyes lit up the jagged ridges. Thumbing her nose at the prohibition against women singing in public! Gathered around her, boys and girls repeated the refrain in unison. "Wake up! Open your eyes!"

At the end of September 2001, I was working as an assistant on a Belgian documentary, *Iran Behind the Veil*, about your country's ongoing changes. We walked for hours in the hills, filming some novice actors along the hiking trails. Lungs swollen with oxygen, they darted about like mountain goats, sending imaginary monologues down through the clouds. Far below, Tehran had disappeared under a blanket of pollution as thick as a theater curtain. That day, the Darakeh Mountain, accomplice to defiant teenagers, revealed its secrets to us: unmanageable headscarves, unleashed words, backpacks pouring out their hidden treasures (cassette players, guitars, tambourines).

At the first whistle, the mini-Googoosh froze on the spot. Index finger on her lips, she signaled to her partners in crime to be quiet. The whistling was intermittent. It disrupted the gurgling of a neighboring spring. Intrusive, piercing.

"Who's there?" she asked.

Thinking it was an ad-libbed sketch, we continued filming.

"Shut off the camera!" shouted an unknown voice. "Right now!"

We turned around. Eyes bulging, a stocky bearded man came charging out of the bushes. Fists clenched, he plowed straight into our small group. He must have been twenty, the same age as the young actors. A walkie-talkie was affixed to his belt, a black shirt stuck out of his khaki pants—there was no doubt about it: he was a Basij militiaman! Since the summer of 1999, I had been able to spot them easily, but this was the first time I had been confronted by one of them directly.

"Hijab! Hijab!" he screamed, glaring at the girls.

As in synchronized choreography, we all put our headscarves back on. The budding singer had swallowed her voice. She was petrified. Her friends looked mummified. In their pale faces, I read the same question: What was this militiaman doing on "their" territory? The morality police almost never ventured up so high. Normally they limited their patrols to the teahouses nestled at the foot of the hiking trails. Furthermore, summer— "hunting" season for uncovered heads, when the heat prompted women to lift their veils—had already passed.

"Your documents!" the bearded man continued, furious.

We were stupefied. We let a few seconds go by in utter silence. These young people weren't related to one another. If the militiaman checked their IDs, he would have reason enough to arrest them. With a slow, prudent step, one of the actors approached the intruder and handed him his backpack, empty.

"What did we do wrong? Go through my things. There isn't even any alcohol!" he said with a nervous laugh.

"As if *this* weren't already enough! Half-naked girls in front of a camera—you've already crossed the line! This isn't America!" the Basiji ranted.

"Hey, watch what you say!" The young man was beside himself.

"Listen, *sousoul*, daddy's boy, hand over your papers and shut your mouth if you want to stay out of trouble!"

"You think you're better than us? If you don't like us, just go back to your barracks. It's because of people like you that Iran has regressed a thousand years since the revolution."

The bearded man's face hardened. Cut to the quick, he puffed out his chest, straightened his chin. With his right hand, he pointed to a nearby hill and continued:

"Have some respect! 'Brothers' of the war rest beneath the soil of this mountain."

I wasn't sure what he was implying. One of the girls whispered in my ear that he must have been referring to the bodies of soldiers who fought in the Iran-Iraq War. The Basij militia had recently made the controversial decision to bury them here, out in nature. As if to mark their territory.

"Right, right, the war again . . . It's a great scapegoat! As if there weren't a more appropriate place to bury the dead. Haven't you heard of cemeteries! An ideal pretext for spying on us and stealing one of the rare spots where we have freedom," the young actor said, angry.

"'Freedom'? What do you mean 'freedom'? Smoking and drinking . . . like in the United States? How decadent!" the militiaman shot back, snatching the actor's bag from him.

The pitch had been dialed up a notch. Up till this point, the camera crew had remained in the background, but with that, the Basij had gone too far. I slid my hand in my bag to retrieve my press pass. After all, we had the proper authorization from the Ministry of Culture to film on the mountain. I handed the pass to the militiaman.

"Foreigner?" he asked me, suspicious, examining my credentials.

The press pass didn't impress him at all. It was as if, on this mountain overlooking Tehran, he had outsize power, was above the law.

"Foreigner?" he insisted.

"Half," I replied.

"Another Iranian woman who was all warm and cozy in Europe while our soldiers were getting their brains blown out defending our country against Saddam!" he growled.

While he spoke, he nervously fingered the beads of a rosary wound around his wrist. His arrogance baffled me. It was obvious that we were not cut from the same cloth. But I had to find a way to appease him at all costs.

"Uh, no. Not at all," I replied. "Actually, I recently did a report from a mosque."

"To better humiliate us afterward?" he snarled.

I didn't see what he was getting at with his dirty look.

"All you have to do is watch CNN or BBC to see how Muslims are demonized! Ever since the kamikazes crashed their planes into the towers in New York, we're all Islamist terrorists in your eyes. You Westerners have such short memories. Not only has Iran never attacked any country, but on top of that, when Saddam Hussein invaded us in the eighties, he was backed by the West!"

So that was the source of his anger. I was starting to better understand . . . A few weeks earlier, the attacks of September 11, which bore the mark of Al-Qaeda, had devastated the international community. Mohammad Khatami, reelected in June 2001, had been one of the first heads of state to condemn the attack on the Twin Towers in New York City, lamenting the fact that the horrible crime had been committed in the name of Islam. The people of Tehran had also expressed compassion and their solidarity with the families of the victims. The following Thursday, hundreds of people lit candles on Mohseni Square, exclaiming loudly, "Down with terrorism!" and "Death to the Taliban!" But in the West, anything the least bit associated with Islam was reviled like the plague.

"The reformists are fools if they think that by smiling at the West, they'll be accepted as equals by your leaders. You'll see, the West will use us in order to better take advantage of·us afterward. This will end badly."

I was still perplexed. I thought he was giving in too easily to conspiracy theories. That's often the case in this part of the world. Ironically, what came next would prove him right, in light of the paroxysms that would shake Iran and the region. In October 2001, when the United States decided to attack Afghanistan to drive out bin Laden, a common enemy, Tehran would immediately demonstrate unprecedented cooperation with Washington, D.C., offering humanitarian and logistical aid. With the fall of the Taliban regime in Kabul, Tehran would reiterate its support, helping the West form a transitional government in Afghanistan.

But on January 29, 2002, the American president, George W. Bush, chose to include Iran in his "axis of evil." Later, the Islamic Republic would even be accused of plotting with Al-Qaeda. In Tehran, this would be a hard pill to swallow. Many Iranians felt betrayed, stigmatized—which only helped the conservatives, who were quick to accuse the reformists of letting themselves be hoodwinked by the White House. It also served to feed the bitterness of the Basijis, like this young militiaman. Looking back, you had to ask if the United States' so-called war on terror hadn't contributed to heightening Islamist extremism at the expense of more moderate voices. Was the dialogue Khatami so dreamed of sparking at risk of turning into a clash of civilizations?

That afternoon, trapped on our rock, our concerns were more practical. How to save our film and keep our videotapes from ending up in a police dumpster? How, most importantly, to stop this young self-proclaimed leader of Darakeh Mountain from calling in his "troops" to put us behind bars pronto? Seeing his resentment, I was imagining the worst.

The Basiji stopped talking. Once he had spat out his litany on "international arrogance" and the Western media, it seemed like a burden had been lifted. Then, pen in hand, he wanted to write down the names of the girls and boys. He said it was for his own records, that he didn't want to cause us any harm; he simply wanted to ensure that we respected "Islamic virtue" and the "values of Imam Khomeini." With these words, the young actor started to sputter. He determinedly snatched up his backpack, which was sitting on a large rock. He had heard too much; he wanted to leave. The militiaman grabbed him by the sleeve.

"You're not getting out of this so easily. Did you know that I could keep you out of university? And that I can get you sent directly into the military?"

The young singer hurried to stand between the two men, trying to create a barrier. The militiaman abruptly retreated. According to his backward beliefs, he was not allowed to touch a woman. He was stuck.

"Go on, get out of here before I call my superiors," he retorted. "You got lucky this time. But rest assured, it's the last time!"

We gathered our things at once, before the Basiji could change his mind, and started our descent, hightailing it down the path that ran along the gully. Jumping from stone to stone, we felt his gaze following our shadows. He disappeared behind a bush. At the foot of the mountain, Tehran was lit up with a thousand lights. From that angle, the capital seemed deceptively peaceful. A little farther down, in front of the traditional teahouses, we crossed paths with other young people who were climbing upward, to camp under the stars. With a complicit wink, we signaled to them that the hills were compromised. In Iran, solidarity is a mode of survival.

I COULDN'T LOOK away from the frozen expressions, on faces barely old enough for a shave. Their smiles were fixed, stoic, timeless. They stared solemnly into space, "Allah" stitched into their headbands and guns on their shoulders. Not a single wrinkle, not a hair on their chins, not the least trace of fear. Looking at these hundreds of black-and-white snapshots on the walls at a neighborhood exhibit on the Iran-Iraq War, one could have imagined that this army of beardless adolescents might rise again at any moment. They were thirteen or fourteen, maybe younger. Too young to go to the front. Too young to die.

"Is that really you?"

I jumped. Was I on edge because the photos of these young martyrs had heightened my emotions? Or because the voice that tore me from my contemplation was strangely familiar?

"What a surprise to see you again!" continued the mysterious person standing behind me.

I turned around, squinting. I couldn't make out the silhouette in the darkness of the temporary exhibition hall. Squared shoulders, prominent facial features . . . I let a few seconds go by, at first thinking I must be mistaken. Meanwhile, my eyes acclimated to the lack of light. The militiaman from Darakeh Mountain was standing there, next to me! He seemed as surprised as I was by this unexpected reunion only a few weeks after the incident on the mountain.

"And what brings you to our neck of the woods?" he asked with a hint of irony. I could have asked him the same question. The exhibition was in my neighborhood, far from his mountain. On my way home from running an errand in town, I had stopped in by chance, intrigued by the gigantic camel-colored tent set up temporarily on a small soccer field. At the entrance, hanging from an old rusty tank that stood guard, a sign, black letters on a blood-red background, read "Sacred Defense Week," commemorating the eight-year war. Out of curiosity, I had lifted the thick covering that acted as a door, and entered.

"They're beautiful, aren't they?" the militiaman continued, even more absorbed than I was by these photos decorating the walls.

"They're . . . so young," I answered.

"Only the best die on the battlefield. God chose them!" he said.

I detected an astonishing mix of respect and envy in his voice.

What a unique way to evoke the memory of these child soldiers, these colonies of "mobilized volunteers"—the literal and original meaning of the word *basiji*—who had served as cannon fodder for the regime. In 1980, at the beginning of the hostilities with Baghdad, they had rushed, heads down, over Iraqi minefields thinking they would go to Paradise . . . I remained silent.

"Shall I give you a tour?"

"Excuse me?" I asked, taken aback.

"A guided tour—would you like one? I work here part-time, as a volunteer guide," he continued in a soft, calm voice that contrasted with the arrogance of our first encounter.

"Uh, sure, why not."

I followed him over a ramp. Loudspeakers crackled out a

children's song praising the bravery of the volunteers. *An army, one man, all equal before God, all equal before death!* In the buzzing melody, the *shahids*, the "martyrs," were compared to Imam Hossein. The decapitation of the Third Shiite Imam by the Umayyad Sunni army, in Karbala in 680, was one of the foundational events of Shi'ism. Then we entered a second room, with unbearable scenes of carnage. Unperturbed, the Basiji continued:

"These martyrs are the pride of our country! They sacrificed themselves for Iran and for Islam. Some had only their hands to defend themselves with. But they knew that in dying, they would attain purity."

His eyes lit up when he spoke about the war. As if he dreamed of being in their place. Until now, the young people I had spent time with had never shown any interest in that violent conflict that claimed perhaps a million victims on both sides. At most, like Sepideh, they expressed a pronounced disgust. For my "guide," the Basiji calling was sacred. The war, an obsession. He told me that his father, from the working-class area of Tehran, and a revolutionary to the bone, was a war veteran who survived the trenches. But, for him, the real hero was his uncle. Having died during the conflict, he now rested in Behesht-e Zahra, the "Paradise of Zahra," named after the daughter of the Prophet Muhammad, the gigantic cemetery adjoining the mausoleum of Imam Khomeini on the road that leads to Qom. Over there, the tombs of *shahids* stretch as far as the eye can see.

"My parents and I visit him every Friday. We bring flowers, fruit, and cookies. In Iran, Friday is dedicated to the dead. We clean his tomb, we spray rosewater, we picnic there, we talk with the other families. We read the Quran and recite prayers. We also pay tribute to the memory of Imam Khomeini and the revolution. We recount the exploits of our 'heroes,' those who had the courage to defy, with the help of God, the powerful army of Saddam Hussein. It's an important moment of reunion, of fraternity . . . of wellness."

This young man seemed like a stranger to me. His account peddled the same ideology that had lured so many adolescents to join the front line. Raised on propaganda, they had charged toward death, a gift from the heavens. And their friends and families celebrated them with pride. From morning to night, the television honored them with syrupy videos. In Tehran, most of the streets bore their names. At intersections, one saw their faces covering building facades. Even the schoolbooks were full of stories of the victories of Allah's valiant soldiers, written in the style of the great epics of ancient Persia.

What a contrast with the way we French are taught about the two world wars. A more restrained instruction, more individual, markedly less exhibitionist. Listening to this young militiaman, I thought again of my French grandfather, Jean Hubert, a resistance fighter during World War II. A prisoner of the Germans for four years, with an atrophied lung, he had dropped the military uniform as soon as the conflict ended and made an effort to forget about those dark years. He died before I was born; I didn't have the chance to know him. But when my grandmother talks about him, it is primarily to tell us how he had asked for her hand in marriage once he was back in Paris. "He wanted to settle down, have children. It was his way of turning his back on death, of recovering his zest for life," she once told me. They had six children together. Three girls, three boys. And none of my uncles has ever showed much of an interest in the army.

The constant crackling of the loudspeakers pulled me from my thoughts: *An army, one man, all equal before God . . .* Intoxicated by the patriotic songs that followed us from room to room, the militiaman didn't notice my bewilderment. He was still set on proudly recounting the battlefield feats of this soldier, the bravery of that. He knew by heart the stories hidden behind each photo. As we neared the exit, he handed me a book. I looked at the cover. It was decorated with red tulips, the symbol of martyrs. It was a collection of all the snapshots of the war.

"Consider this a modest gift."

"Thank you," I replied awkwardly.

"Thanks to you for taking the time to listen to me."

After some hesitation, he continued:

"My name is Mahmoud, by the way."

"Mahmoud . . . Nice to meet you."

Mahmoud blushed. He started to rifle in his pockets to take out another photo. A young woman with gray eyes seated in front of the camera. She must have been younger than eighteen. A female martyr?

"This is . . . This is my wife," he murmured, blushing even more intensely. Her name is Fatemeh."

"Oh . . . *Moborak!* Congratulations!" I exclaimed, surprised that he would shed this small light onto his private life.

"We just got married," he said, lowering his head.

"She's very pretty," I continued out of politeness, even if it was quite difficult to appreciate her beauty through the thickness of her chador.

"I would really like to introduce you to her. Would you accept an invitation to come for dinner at our house one night?"

His suggestion stopped me short. He, the Basij militiaman of Darakeh, the man who had terrorized my young friends up on the mountain, was inviting me to share a meal at his home!

"It's just that . . . I wouldn't want to be a bother," I replied according to the *ta'arof*, that very Iranian art of politely declining an invitation.

To tell the truth, I was torn between a fear of crossing the border into the Iran that frightened me and an insane desire to enter the impenetrable world of these shadowy forces.

"No trouble at all. Fatemeh will be thrilled!" he insisted.

In that moment, neither of us could have suspected that our paths would end up closely intertwined.

When Fatemeh opened the door for me, I couldn't help staring at the long, silky hair that brought out the gray in her eyes. She was so much more beautiful in person than under her chador in that photo! Though the intimacy of her home and the absence of a male guest spared her from wearing the veil, I, on the other hand, had to keep mine on.

"Welcome," she said in a frail voice, motioning for me to enter.

I hadn't had any trouble finding their home. The young couple lived in a modest ground-floor apartment nestled in a back alley in Darakeh, at the foot of the same hiking path where Mahmoud had questioned us. Fatemeh invited me to follow her into the living room. The walls were decorated with verses from the Quran. A few cushions on the floor acted as a couch. They had been placed around a *sofreh*, a traditional tablecloth, on which the young woman had laid out place settings.

"Mahmoud went to pray at the mosque; he'll be back in a few minutes," she murmured timidly, playing with her shirtsleeves.

Following her, I wondered which of the two of us was more uncomfortable. Hoping to lighten the mood, I congratulated her on her marriage, wishing, *inshallah*, that she would have children. She gave me a faint smile. Then she explained that the nuptials had taken place a month earlier. An arranged marriage, by the book. I was curious to know how the two had met.

"Our parents have known each other a long time," she said. "One of my uncles was a martyr in the war. Mahmoud's mother noticed me at a memorial reception for him. She was looking for a good wife for her son. One day, their family came to visit us. I served tea, offered cookies. Then, after a few minutes, they left us alone, Mahmoud and me. My hands were trembling under my chador. It was the first time I had looked a man in the eyes . . . I liked him!"

"You mean you fell in love right away?"

"He didn't smile much, but he seemed nice. During our time alone, we found out we had a few common interests: walking in the mountains, religious festivals, anti-Americanism . . . That's what's most important! Praise God, it was a good match! We decided to get married."

So, for her, love was that simple? A cup of tea, a few cookies, common deaths to mourn, and just like that, ring on the finger! Not even a handshake . . . Hadn't she ever felt attracted to another man? Hadn't she ever imagined herself as the princess in *The Thousand and One Nights*? Hadn't she dreamed, as a teenager, of a Prince Charming coming to win her heart?

"In my opinion, love before marriage opens the door to every kind of debauchery," she continued, as if she had guessed my questions. "Look at those girls who run away. It's always because of a love affair. At night, they find themselves sleeping in parks. To survive, they end up prostituting themselves . . . Some of them even take drugs! I have to say that I'm very lucky—"

She cut herself off. The front door had just creaked. Mahmoud was back.

"Sorry to be late . . . But I see that you two are already hitting it off!" he exclaimed, hanging his jacket on the coatrack.

Once Mahmoud was sitting cross-legged on the opposite side of the *sofreh*, Fatemeh hurried to fill our plates with *khoresh bademjan*, with *fesenjan* and *ghormeh sabzi*. Seeing these huge, succulent dishes on the tablecloth, I gathered that my hostess had made a great effort to impress her husband. But he was interested only in the preparations for the festivities of Ashura, which he tended to every night. In a few days, Iran would be in mourning for forty days to commemorate the death of Imam Hossein, who had died more than thirteen hundred years ago.

"A real event! Every year, I wait impatiently for this day. My Basiji friends and I always manage to get to the front of the processions. Together, we lash our chests with metal whips. It's a very special moment, a moment of collective fervor. We're almost in a trance, we learn to surpass suffering, and we think of all the soldiers who had the strength, like Hossein, to defy death—"

Mahmoud cut himself off to serve me a glass of *doogh*, a cold drink with yogurt and dried mint. Taken aback by his account of suffering, I took advantage of the pause to ask the question that had been gnawing at me since our first encounter: Since he seemed so fascinated by the war, why hadn't he gone to fight at the front?

A silence crashed down upon the *sofreh*. Mahmoud put down the carafe. Crossing his arms, he let out a large sigh. A shadow of melancholy crossed his face.

"If only I could have gone . . . If only . . ."

Plunged into his memories, he continued:

"I was a restless, daredevil child. I wasn't afraid of anything.

I celebrated my tenth birthday in 1988, a few months before the end of the war. My father was on leave in Tehran. I begged him to let me go fight with him. He refused. He said I was too little. So I cheated. I faked an ID, changing my date of birth, and I joined the Basij. My father found out. He was furious. He lectured me, and blocked me from leaving! I was condemned to stay in Tehran. I never recovered."

Kept from the battle against the outside enemy, Mahmoud the martyrophile started to seek out enemies inside Iran: the young hikers of Darakeh, daddy's boys who listened to punk rock in secret, improperly veiled girls, children of adversaries . . . He spent his free time collecting everything that had to do with the war. Once a week, he went to the Mahestan Shopping Center, a Mecca for young Basijis. Located in the south of Tehran, it was home to a plethora of stores selling trinkets dedicated to the memory of the soldiers.

"And where do you keep it all?" I asked him, looking around the living room, which was almost empty.

"In the bedroom!" replied Mahmoud, as if it were obvious. "Come, I'll show you!"

I followed him, intrigued. Printed on large tiles, two gigantic turbaned portraits presided above the queen-size bed. To the right, Khomeini. To the left, Khamenei. Was *this* where the young couple had spent their wedding night, under the impenetrable gaze of these two icons of the Islamic Republic, whose star continued to fade? The idea seemed absurd, but it was certainly the case. In a solemn gesture, Mahmoud opened the door to a closet. Small, meticulously dusted objects were lined up on a shelf. Shoelaces, plastic "keys to Paradise," license plates, bullet casings, newspaper clippings yellowed with time . . . A real miniature museum! On the shelf below was a collection of films by Morteza Avini, a war correspondent who died a martyr's death stepping on a land mine at the front. Mahmoud's idol.

"If Iran had to wage war against another country one day, I would be the first to offer myself as a martyr!" he exclaimed.

In fact, Mahmoud was a living *shahid*, a half-martyr. Death was his reason for living. A divine objective. A refuge where he could shut himself away. He ate, he slept, he dreamed of death. However, since the end of the war, life had smiled upon the Basijis. Taking good care of them the better to use them once the opportunity arose, the state had offered them a multitude of privileges. They could shop at a discount in specific cooperatives. They received favorable bank loans. They were granted a quota for spots at the university. At the end of the war, Fatemeh's father had been promoted as a Basij commander in a suburb of Tehran. Mahmoud's father had joined a small, partly state-sponsored business where he worked part-time. The Basijis had their own summer camps, their own networks of mosques, of clinics. And a certain social prestige.

"Everyone in the neighborhood respects Mahmoud. If he were to run in the elections, he would win by a landslide!" Fatemeh proudly proclaimed, having followed us into the bedroom.

But clearly that wasn't enough for Mahmoud. His daily life remained haunted by a double frustration: that of living in a country at peace, and feeling out of step with his own society. In his eyes, he was the victim, not the liberals.

"The youth call us every name. They laugh too loudly, they listen to 'cool' music. They have no respect for traditions, or for their elders who defended their country. It's not fair—"

Fatemeh interrupted him. She had something to show me, too. I watched her plunge her head into a chest of drawers.

From between two tubes of red lipstick, which I'm sure she wore only for Mahmoud, she pulled out a laminated document.

"This is my nursing diploma!"

"Nursing?"

"Yes, each year, with the girls from the Basij Corps, I take part in vaccination campaigns. Abroad, they always depict us as a group that terrorizes the population. But violence is a weapon that we use only when national security is at risk. Since the Khatami years, we've become increasingly involved in social work. If there's an earthquake, we assist the victims. We take disadvantaged children to the countryside for summer vacation. We distribute free meals during religious holidays."

I hadn't known about this facet of the Basij. Listening to Fatemeh, I realized that this group was more complex than it seemed. Lost in his deathly dreams, Mahmoud had disappeared into his closet of trinkets. Fatemeh took me by the hand to lead me back to the living room. She whispered to me:

"The other day, up on the mountain, I think Mahmoud got a little carried away. Forgive him. Please, don't write lies in your articles. As you can see, we're Iranian like everyone else; we deserve to be better understood. Here's my cell phone number. Call me whenever you like, we can go shopping together. I know some good places."

This young woman was especially sensitive to the image she was projecting. I found it almost touching that she wanted to convince me that the Basijis were respectable people. Despite their preconceived notions about the West, Mahmoud and Fatemeh had opened their door to me. They had served me their best dishes, had confided their dreams and resentments to me. But in the end, what had I done to deserve this hospitality? On the way back, I started to have doubts. Had that been a tactical ambush? Had the two young lovebirds been ordered to get closer to me in order to better spy on my daily routine? Or were they simply stirred by the same curiosity about me that had drawn me to them?

I DIDN'T RECOGNIZE her at first. She was wearing a blouse with thin gray stripes. Her face was as white as porcelain. Her empty gaze was lost in the crowd of uptight guests at a society dinner at the end of February 2002. One of those old Iranian intelligentsia soirées, the kind you would certainly have attended, Babai, where people sit around until the early morning sipping whiskey from crystal glasses and dreaming of a better world. When I arrived, I walked among the tables, complimenting the women on their elegant '60s dresses, which still carried the scent of mothballs, and discussing the day's news with their husbands.

So much younger, she stood out from the crowd. But her eyes were what first caught my attention. Eyes at once soft and icy, as if frozen by the cold breeze blowing through Tehran that night. At first there was silence. Then a smile. "Delphine?" murmured the intriguing woman in the striped blouse. "Niloufar!" I responded immediately. My dear Niloufar! Two years had passed since my search had dead-ended at her apartment, after the interrogation by the intelligence service. Two years of imagining the worst, even her definitive disappearance. She was there, standing in front of me, in the flesh. But so different! Her beautiful brown hair, thick and silky, had turned completely gray. Her features were drawn. Bags hollowed out her eyes. She had lost at least twenty pounds. "You've been missed," I said to her awkwardly, embarrassed to ask where she had been all these months. She glanced to her right, then her left, as if to reassure herself that no one was eavesdropping.

"They arrested me during the protests of July 1999," she murmured in one breath.

"They" . . . Hardly had she said the word when the face of my interrogator, the man with the two missing fingers, reappeared in a rush of dizziness. *They*—that had to be the secret police. Or else Mahmoud and Fatemeh's Basiji comrades.

"And after?" I asked her, teeth clenched.

"They threw me in prison and sentenced me to five years."

"Five years!"

"But, you see, I was lucky. I was out after two," she continued in the ironic tone she had not lost.

Niloufar had come back from the dead. I could see that she was trying to reassure me. I wanted to tell her how worried I'd been, tell her about the void left by her prolonged absence. But the hostess's invitation to be seated for dinner quickly brought us back to more practical concerns.

"I have to tell you about it," whispered Niloufar. "It's a long story, but I'd prefer not to talk about it while I'm in Iran. The walls have ears."

NICE, FRANCE, two months later and almost twenty-five hundred miles away. A sunset-pink sky caressed the Promenade des Anglais. Sitting at a table on the terrace of a small café at the edge of the sea, Niloufar blew rings with her cigarette smoke. After her ordeal, she had chosen the sun of the South of France to treat her inner wounds. Until she regained her strength, she would squat on the office couch of a lawyer friend, one of the many Iranians of the diaspora scattered around the world since 1979. On a trip to Paris to visit my parents, I had come to see her for the weekend. Seeing me walk into the café, she smiled. The small wrinkles around her almond eyes had disappeared. She had recovered her normal laugh and put some weight back on. After lighting her umpteenth Marlboro, she took a deep drag and then plunged into the abyss of her memories:

"Everything happened really fast. I was taking photos on Valiasr Square. It was the fourth day of the protests. I had decided to join the crowd out of solidarity with the students. You remember Forouhar, whom I talked about so often? After his death, I threw in the towel. I shut myself in at home. I didn't call anyone anymore. With the campuses ignited, I regained hope. They had killed the thinkers, but they hadn't managed to kill their thoughts. So I decided to join the crowd. A plainclothes policeman saw my camera and yelled at me, asking if I was a reporter. I didn't have time to respond. I felt hands grabbing me, violently. I tried to fight back. No use. All around me, batons and knives were raining down on the youth. Blood was flowing. It was chaos."

I listened attentively to Niloufar. When she described the circumstances of her arrest, I finally understood why my interrogator from the intelligence service had been so curious about her. In the eyes of the regime, she had committed the unforgivable by documenting with a camera those unprecedented riots in which the name of the Supreme Leader had been tarnished for the first time. Obviously, they had tried to shut her up, stifle the testimony.

"And afterward, where did they take you?" I asked her.

"I wound up, a little dazed, with some other protesters in the Den of Spies . . . That's the official nickname of the U.S. embassy. It had been transformed into a detention center. The next day, they blindfolded me and started to bombard me with questions, about religion, politics, my ideas. I had no idea what was in store for me. And then, after some time, they announced that they were transferring me elsewhere. It wasn't until I was released that I realized I was at Towhid Prison—"

Niloufar abruptly cut herself off. Head lowered, she ran her hands over her eyes, her mouth, her forehead. Then she glanced nervously over her shoulder, before reminding herself that she was in France, that there was little risk of being under surveillance here.

"Towhid Prison was a nightmare. They threw me into a minuscule, isolated cell, two meters by a meter and a half. No window to look out of. Thick walls, the void around me. That kind of solitude drives you crazy. With a fluorescent light on the ceiling, just above my head, always on, day and night . . . That light was blinding, it hurt my eyes—it's a current method for getting prisoners to give forced confessions. They call it 'white torture.' I rapidly lost all notion of time. It was a stifling place, haunted by jinns."

"Jinns?" I asked, to be sure she was really referring to the spirits of Middle Eastern mythology.

"Yes, they were everywhere. In the middle of the night, I would hear the voices of the dead, of Forouhar, of my mother . . . They invaded my dreams . . . They were so loud . . . And then they ended up settling into my cell. They lived with me. Sometimes the living came to talk to me, too. Once, it was Khatami, the president, who visited me . . . It's true, it's true . . . He said he had come to help me; he tried to calm me down, pacify me . . . But the guards stopped him. They started to beat him up; they punched him. He was shoved and fell backward. It was horrible! I couldn't stand to see him like that. Since he couldn't get back up, they dragged his wounded body to the bathroom. They sprayed him in the face with jets of water . . . Women were standing around him and laughing . . . I was ashamed . . . I was nervous . . . I cried for all of it to stop. 'Stop! Stop!' I said to them."

Niloufar's face had contorted with horror. Her words were disjointed. Her lips were trembling. Her gaze was lost, elsewhere, disoriented. I took her hand to try to comfort her. Images of her incarceration were bombarding her, pulling her between fantasy and reality. Had they slipped hallucinogens into her meals? Had they inundated her cell with recordings of her own telephone conversations, a well-known interrogation technique used to extract information from their victims? Or was it simply the isolation, the despair, the lack of sleep, that had made her lose her grip during her imprisonment? To the point where she felt as though the "evil eye" had followed her to France?

Her first four months of prison were the most grueling. At irregular intervals, her tormentors would wake her with a start and make her walk blindfolded down a staircase to the interrogation room. How many of them were there? Two, three, four—she had trouble remembering because she never saw their faces. Sometimes the torture lasted more than five hours. Five hours of being inundated with questions, her nose plastered to the wall: Where were you born? What did your parents do? Where are your brothers, your sisters, your cousins, your friends? Why did you write in your dissertation that in Iran a woman is worth only half a man? Why did you go to the protest? What relationship did you have with Forouhar? How did you know him? Did you see him alone, or was his wife there? Obviously, unable to find any concrete proof of her opposition to the regime, they had tried to smear her reputation, accusing her of having sex outside marriage, a "crime" punishable by death by stoning.

When she refused to reply, they assailed her with insults, called her a spy in the service of France, of Germany, of America . . . She was a "traitor." They accused her of trying to overthrow the regime. If only they understood, she said, just how fragile the opposition was, utterly incapable of deposing the Supreme Leader. Her silence irritated them even more. As soon as she refused to cooperate, they resorted to force.

"They would lay me on a bed and handcuff my wrists and ankles. Then they would hit the soles of my feet with cables. The more I screamed, the more I felt like I was suffocating. I would sweat under my chador. To make me suffocate even more intensely, they would roll me up in a wool blanket—in the middle of summer! I'd struggle to pull the blanket back with my teeth, to breathe a little. On several occasions, I fell in and out of consciousness. I could have died like that."

One morning, her prison guards announced that they were bringing her to the Islamic Revolutionary Court. She would finally go before a judge! She told herself that it was over, the rule of the arbitrary designed to make you lose your mind. With a bit of luck, her family would have been informed. But her trial unfolded behind closed doors, with neither lawyer nor witnesses. After a five-minute hearing, the judge condemned her to five years: two behind bars and three out on parole. Grounds for sentencing: taking photos during the protests, insulting the Supreme Leader and the verses of the Quran. Only one relatively joyful bit of news: the charge of espionage had been dropped.

Leaving the court, she ran smack into her brother-in-law. He finally had confirmation that she was alive! "We looked for you everywhere. We even went to the morgue," he said. But when he heard the verdict, he was dumbfounded. "You should have fought it!" he moaned, distraught. Exhausted, poor Niloufar had conceded unconditionally to all the charges brought against her, out of fear that the judge would give her an even harsher sentence.

The verdict had one advantage: she was transferred to the large Evin Prison, in the north of Tehran, not far from Darakeh Mountain, where the young Basiji couple lived. With the right to have visitors for ten minutes every other week. Her aunt was the first to go see her. She told Niloufar how, a few days after her disappearance, without any news from her, she had gone to her apartment. The dresser drawers had been pulled out. The furniture and paintings had been damaged. Niloufar's books had disappeared from the shelves—including her doctoral dissertation on Iranian women. It was as if barbarians had passed through. It took her aunt a week to tidy up each room.

Once Niloufar was at Evin, her life regained a semblance of normalcy. The interrogations, torture, and threats were over. In the women's section, she shared her cell with a half dozen other inmates. She quickly realized that the world of prison was not immune to Iranian paradoxes.

"My cell opened onto a hallway, where there were six other cells. Sometimes we counted up to forty women per cell. During the day, the doors remained open and we could move freely from one cell to another. We even had the right to take off our chadors and walk around in pajamas. In the morning, we had an aerobics class, set to American music! We could watch TV and take courses in sewing, languages, literature . . . In the library, we could get the daily newspapers: *Iran*, *Hamshahri*, *Kayhan*. Toward the end of my detention, I was even allowed to read books my family brought. That's how I read *On Revolution* and *The Origins of Totalitarianism*, by Hannah Arendt. We also had access to a garden, even if it was so small it took only a few steps to walk its perimeter. Imagine: three hundred women crammed into two hundred seventy square feet. The women who had been there a while quickly explained the rules of the game to me: if you have money, you can get anything behind bars—sandwiches, chocolate, cigarettes, alcohol, drugs! There were pros among us. The guards would smuggle things in for a small bribe. Talk about Islamic morality! Such hypocrisy."

Niloufar was a prisoner of conscience. But, in Iran, being involved in politics is a crime like any other. So she shared quarters with common criminals: delinquents, prostitutes, junkies, and drug dealers. The few other political prisoners were members of the People's Mujahedin, an exiled opposition group backing the overthrow of the Islamic Republic.

"The guards called them 'terrorists' or 'anarchists,'" recalled Niloufar. They had been collared before committing an attack on official buildings of the Islamic Republic. Some of them were serving thirty-year sentences; others were in for life.

One New Year's Eve, Niloufar even saw a contingent of teenage girls arrive sporting stilettos and powdered faces. Their New Year's Eve celebration had been prematurely interrupted by a raid of the morality police. But of all those memories, it was her cell mates' executions that haunted Niloufar most.

"In two years, seven of my cell mates were executed. And we don't know how many men suffered the same fate in other prisons. One of them was Mohammad Reza Pedram. He was a former air force officer. Exiled to the United States, he came back in 1996 and was arrested a few years later for spying for the CIA. Condemned to death, he spent ten years in prison before his May 2001 execution. If they wanted to kill him, why had they made him wait so long? To give him false hope that he was going to get out?"

Niloufar paused again. Head lowered, she rubbed her eyes with a weary hand. With the other, she played nervously with the cigarette butts piled up in the ashtray.

"At Evin, the unpredictable gnawed away at us. With each sentencing, death took us by the throat. The inmates asked themselves: Whose turn will it be next? The days of the executions were unbearable; we lit candles and prayed together for the dead. We mourned for more than a week. And then there were also suicides. With my own eyes, I saw girls try to end their lives by swallowing pills and cutting their wrists with bits of broken teacups. One day, one of them even tried to hang herself with her chador."

A woman hanging by the end of her chador! The level of despair you would have to be in to make that choice. I couldn't let go of that image. My tangles with the Iranian intelligence service were trivial compared to what Niloufar and all those women had had to endure in darkness and silence.

"And now that you're free again, what do you plan to do?" I asked her.

To my great surprise, she replied without batting an eye:

"I know that in Iran my hands are tied. Before I was released, they made me sign a document renouncing my political activities. But I plan to go back as soon as possible. My place is over there. I need to stand with my fellow citizens, to feel my country beneath my feet, to visit my parents' grave."

"Really? Even after everything they put you through?"

"Of course!"

"But you have so many friends in France, a residency card. With your diplomas you can teach at a university. You're single. There's still time to start your life over here."

"I know. But I miss Iran. I can't wait to go back. It's hard to explain, but that's how it is."

So her decision was made. Once her vacation in France was over, she wanted to go back to her country. As soon as possible! In her place, others would have preferred exile to the daily war against a system that eats away at your marrow. But nothing would stop Niloufar. Despite the suffering she had endured, she was attached to her country. She forgave it everything, just as some battered women forgive their violent husbands.

"In prison, I developed feelings toward Iran that I had never imagined. All those days, left to my own devices, I did a lot of reflecting. I hate the people who tortured me, I won't ever forgive them, but vengeance is pointless! Our prisons are full of innocent people, our intellectuals have been assassinated, but perhaps that's the price to pay for a better future. We don't want another revolution. We're just fighting for democracy, but not Western democracy, like the Americans want for the Middle East . . . I think it might even be possible to find a happy medium separating politics from religion without actually eliminating the clergy. In my opinion, there are good people in the government, like all those women members of Parliament, for example. Let's give them a chance. Maybe with such people, Iran will evolve."

"So you're still optimistic?"

"Do I have a choice? It's my country."

In saying these last words, her voice started to tremble. Her eyes filled with tears. She burst into sobs.

"You know, when Dariush Forouhar said that he was ready to sacrifice himself in the name of Iran, I had a hard time understanding. He always said that he would die on his feet, head held high. When I think about it, he and his wife taught me to love my country despite all its faults. Yes, I love my country. I'm truly tied to it."

Such steadfast devotion! I watched her dry her eyes and lift her head.

"You know, I would do anything for my country."

I had heard that phrase elsewhere. Her words were mixing strangely with those of Mahmoud, the Basiji. And yet, to all appearances, the two had nothing in common. She, the Westernized polyglot, always meticulous and put together. He, the Islamist in baggy pants, speaking only in Persian and dreaming of becoming a martyr. They would certainly have detested each other had they met. And yet, a profound and invisible thread linked them despite and through everything: an unconditional love for their country, a quasi-carnal patriotism that constitutes the most solid bedrock of Iranian identity, the one that you, Babai, handed down to me and that, as the years passed, has settled into my heart.

AUGUST 14, 2002. Your country was on the front page of every newspaper. From exile in France, the People's Mujahedin had just revealed, with photographs to back it up, the existence of two secret nuclear sites: the uranium enrichment plant in Natanz and the heavy-water plant in Arak. The Islamic Republic was put under the spotlight immediately. No more reporting on civil society, Iranian youth, the future of reforms—anything to do with social issues and politics was old news. In Paris, editors in chief were obsessed with only one question: Does Iran want the bomb?

In the following days, a legion of experts would take over Western televisions, boring viewers with particularly unpalatable jargon: "yellow cake," uranium, plutonium, centrifuges, isotopes, hexafluoride . . . Some cried danger, warning the masses of an imminent risk to the planet. Others, playing devil's advocate, wondered why information already in the hands of Western intelligence services had taken so long to be released. After all, the Iranian nuclear program, momentarily interrupted after the revolution, had been launched during your time, when the shah ruled over Iran. But this turned out to be a happy coincidence for some neoconservatives in Washington, as in that summer of 2002, it validated George W. Bush's infamous "axis of evil."

Iranian authorities reacted swiftly. "Civil nuclear power is our inalienable right," Ali Khamenei hammered away at every opportunity, arguing at the same time that the Bomb was *haram*—that is, "forbidden by Islam." "Why them and not us?" insisted many Iranians (including opponents of the regime), in reference to other nuclearized countries—Israel, India, Pakistan—whose nuclear programs didn't unleash the same passions as Iran's. As a signatory to the International Atomic Energy Agency's Treaty on the Non-Proliferation of Nuclear Weapons in 1986, Tehran claimed it was under no obligation to declare any ongoing work.

Whom to believe in this deluge of contradictory and unverifiable information? Whom to trust? What objective proof was there? Once more, I felt your absence. Your knowledge would have been of precious help to me. In that frantic race for information, there was unfortunately little room for reflection. Or verification. The demand for news reports rained down from Paris. In twenty-four hours, one had to be able to prove that the "mean ayatollahs" of Tehran wanted the Bomb. At that rate, it was impossible to get hold of any expert to try to decrypt the "crisis." I had a friend who was a nuclear engineer, but she wasn't responding to my calls anymore. At yoga class, where we had met, an empty spot had replaced her mat. She'd vanished! Later, I learned that the employees of the Atomic Energy Organization of Iran had been ordered to distance themselves from the foreign press, under threat of serious consequences.

What "saint" to turn to? What "imam"? Did I have to rely, like other journalists, on the goodwill of Tehran? Which is to say, plaster on a smile at the Ministry of Culture and hope to be selected for a guided tour, with a close escort, of one of the nuclear sites? The lucky few scored a permit to access Natanz or

Arak, both under close surveillance. As for me, years later I would receive a consolation prize: the nuclear power plant in Bushehr! The southern port was home to a site whose construction, at first supervised by the German company Siemens, had been suspended after the 1979 revolution, before the Russians took over in 1995. But what could I really hope for from a quick tour, nose pressed to the window of a minibus shuttling us from facility to facility, like bears in cages, under the vigilant eye of uranium guardians? I would have preferred to waste my time eating grilled fish and spicy shrimp in memory of my first trip to the banks of the Persian Gulf. I wouldn't see much of this grand performance except for antimissile batteries deployed along the road leading to the site, the first signs of Iran flexing its muscles against outside threats. And more than anything—yes, more than anything—thousands of burly men with their blond hair and their skin red from the sun, sweating on their bikes: the many Russian technicians who shuttled back and forth every day, in sauna-like heat, between the nuclear facilities and their homes. Once on this gigantic campus, a true city within a city, they had everything within reach: a supermarket, nonalcoholic Baltika beer, a private school for their children . . . Far from prying eyes, their wives even took off their headscarves. Once more, the real entwined with the absurd!

I'd had enough of going around in circles. There was no doubt that Iran wanted to develop nuclear technology. But while Iranians were gradually growing irritated at the entire world trying to make impossible predictions of how many years it would take Iran to obtain the Bomb, another question was gnawing at me: Why? Yes, why was the Islamic Republic so obsessed with the nuclear race?

A few months later, at the foot of the Zagros Mountains,

about six miles from the Iraqi border, I would find a semblance of an answer in an isolated village. Far, very far from Western cameras. A minuscule point unknown to the maps of the world, inscribed like an indelible stain on Iranians' memories: Sardasht. Lost in the depths of the mountains of West Azerbaijan Province, it had been the first city to fall victim to Saddam Hussein's chemical weapons. During the Iran-Iraq War, to complete international silence. That attack, on June 28, 1987, sealed Iran's fate, leading to Tehran's retreat toward nationalism and its determination to protect itself—at all costs.

I took a seat in the black pleather armchair offered by Mustafah Asaghzadeh, a tall mustached man with a Kurdish accent and ebony eyes. His window on the hillside overlooked a landscape imbued with a singular beauty. Thickets of pine blanketed the contours of the mountains. Pomegranate trees heavy with ripe fruit let the morning breeze dance with their branches. In the middle of the fields, farmers wearing *sharwal*, those traditional baggy pants, were busy collecting apples. A village woman in a dress with colored sequins was walking briskly, a stack of *sangak* bread on her veiled head. I noticed a rainbow on the surface of the water flowing between the rocks. Like scenery from a postcard! But the storybook image froze dramatically as, staring out the window, my host started to scrutinize the past.

"There was a time when those who lived here called Sardasht 'Paradise,'" Mustafah Asaghzadeh murmured.

With eyes that had lost their sparkle, he grabbed a photo album sitting on the table and handed it to me with a slow, awkward gesture. In a group photo yellowed with time was his entire family. The women wore colorful headscarves and cheerful faces. The men were carrying the children in their arms. They had happy smiles on their faces.

"This is all I have left of my family . . . It's all I was able to save."

"What happened, exactly?" I asked.

He took a deep breath. And opened his wounded heart:

"It's around four in the afternoon, June 28, 1987 . . . I'm eighteen years old and doing my military service in Tehran. My parents stayed in Sardasht. That day, a friend calls me from Tabriz, panic-stricken. 'There was an attack on Sardasht! There was an attack on Sardasht!' he screams. At first, I'm not worried. Since the start of the war, Saddam's troops had regularly attacked the Iranian army bases and the Kurdish rebels at the periphery of the city. The inhabitants were used to hiding in their shelters. But my friend insists: 'One of the bombs dropped near your parents' house. They were taken to the hospital.' To the hospital? I can't believe my ears. This time, the city center had been targeted! A residential area! I have to get back home as quickly as possible. In a panic, I drive to Sardasht. When I arrive at the hospital, I realize the extent of the damage: masses of the wounded pouring into a courtyard already jammed with people. At least seven hundred heaped there in the blazing sun! Astonishingly, they show no signs of broken bones or scratches. Their wounds are unusual: red eyes, blistered skin. Their breathing, heavy and wheezy. I lower my eyes. In front of me, a woman is suffocating while vomiting blood. Nearby, a man begs a nurse to inject him with morphine to ease his itching. Farther on, a child's body on the ground. Inert. I grope my way forward. Sardasht, my little Paradise, what has happened to you? And my family? Where are they? In the chaos, I search desperately for my parents. In vain. A doctor approaches me. 'Sorry, truly sorry,' he says to me. At first, I don't understand. 'We're all sorry,' I reply. 'No, sorry for you . . . You arrived too late . . . Your father is dead, your mother, too,' he adds . . . My parents! I fall to my knees, wrecked."

Mustafah lowered his head, out of breath. His face was pale, as if he was about to faint. I was stunned by the sharpness of his description, by his way of speaking about the past in the present tense. I wanted to hear the rest, even if I sensed the tragic end to his story.

"In shock, I follow the doctor, who signals for me to come with him. We cross a long corridor; it's like we're crossing through hell. The wounded are leaning against the walls. Their screams echo endlessly. Pale with exhaustion, the nurses brandish razors, saying they have to pierce the blisters. A patient bursts into sobs. Hands to the sky, he implores Allah to help him understand this strange plague that has fallen upon Sardasht. He cries that only eight bombs fell on the city . . . Eight bombs shouldn't cause this much damage! Eight bombs . . . When I try to learn more, he tells me about the strange odor of garlic and apples floating in the air, the city seized in an overwhelming cloud of powder . . . Strange phenomenon . . . Inexplicable . . . The doctor takes me by the hand. He opens a door. Lying on a bed, a young man is suffocating and coughing, a tube down his throat. It's Hadi, my fourteen-year-old little brother! I barely recognize him. His words, incomprehensible, sound like a cat's meowing. I can't hold back my tears anymore. Leaning over him, I promise him that I will find the other members of our family alive. But a few hours later, the body of my older brother Ali greets me at the morgue. I go from the hospital to the free clinic; in the end, I learn that all my other brothers and sisters have died. My grandparents, too! After four months, Hadi also left me. My last family tie, my reason to live . . . I went mad!"

Mustafah stood up, closed the album, and pressed his face against the window. Such a contrast between his cruel memories and this landscape, seemingly so peaceful. A long silence invaded the room. Not wanting to interrupt his thoughts, I remained glued to my armchair. After a few minutes, he turned back toward me before murmuring, his face clouded:

"With time, I learned to accept the curse, live with it, even if the pain will never end."

Mustafah then signaled for me to follow him so he could show me, with a trembling hand, one of the partitions of his house, newly renovated.

"You see this wall? It's still contaminated. A few months ago, when the workers sanded it before repainting it, their eyes started to swell and get red. The gas infected people, houses, the earth, the air, and perhaps the water. An incurable disease."

In Sardasht, stories like his were not isolated incidents. Behind the door of every house lurked another such hidden trauma, each more unbearable than the last.

I met Hossein Mohammadian the same day. A forty-four-year-old farmer, he directed a small local Kurdish association that gave aid to people such as Mustafah. A walking encyclopedia, he knew the tiniest details of this tragedy, having been a victim himself and having only narrowly escaped. The day of the attack, he was on his way to his neighborhood bakery. Flattened to the ground by the impact of the explosion, he had crawled to his house, crammed his wife and their three young children into his old Land Rover, and fled the city as quickly as possible. It was only six hours later that he began to feel an un-settling discomfort. He remembers every single detail of his de-scent into hell:

"I suddenly lost my sight! And yet, I wasn't wounded . . . And then my voice started to malfunction. My skin itched! It was unbearable. At the clinic of a neighboring village, I quickly un-derstood that I was not the only one . . . According to the doc-tors, at least a third of the twenty-thousand inhabitants of Sardasht were suffering the same symptoms. And a hundred others were dead, like Mustafah's parents. The doctors were distraught, unable to arrive at a diagnosis. They evacuated us to Tehran one after another . . . It wasn't until a week later, after they had sent me to a special hospital in Spain, that experts ended up diagnosing me with mustard gas poisoning."

So, Saddam Hussein had used chemical gas. But Iraq had signed the Geneva Convention in 1925, which banned the use of such weapons. How could a crime deliberately targeting civilian populations have been justified? The war had been drag-ging on for years, each day bringing new "martyrs." For years, the Iraqi president had been threatening his Iranian enemies with the worst. But no one had dared imagine that one day an entire city's population would pay the price. Had the Iraqi pres-ident, grown weary of the Iranian capacity for resistance, tried to bring a radical end to the war? Or did he want to impede a secret meeting that he had caught wind of, between Kurdish op-position forces and Iranian officials?

"To this day, all those questions, unfortunately, remain un-answered," Hossein Mohammadian said with a sigh.

"But how is that possible? Surely international inquiries were conducted. Specialists must have looked into the matter."

"No, I swear to you, no."

Then he continued:

"As you know, an investigation into the gassing would certainly have put the suppliers of Saddam's chemical weapons at risk: big European and American companies. So those in the West have no interest in conducting an inquiry. Right after the attack, no one deigned to lift even a finger."

The silence of the West: the second blow to the inhabitants of Sardasht. Less visible, but more perfidious. According to Hossein Mohammadian, the international indifference only encouraged Saddam Hussein a few months later to launch a gas attack against Halabja, a city in Iraqi Kurdistan where five thousand inhabitants were killed, and to continue his chemical attacks against Iran. In total, 360 chemical bombs targeted Iranian military and civilians. The United Nations was the only organization to carry out a semblance of an investigation at the time. Seven fact-finding missions were conducted throughout the war. But the two reports from the UN Security Council didn't lead to any satisfying outcomes for the inhabitants of Sardasht. The first, on May 9, 1988, concluded with a vague warning to the two countries, telling them not to use chemical bombs anymore. The second, in August 1988, specified that "chemical gas was used against Iran" without acknowledging its origin, Iraq.

"Even the UN ended up abandoning us," Hossein Mohammadian continued. "Even the UN."

He stopped talking. His eyes were red. His voice was trembling; his breathing had intensified. With a slow gesture, he rifled in his pocket and took out a tube of Ventolin, the only palliative for "chemical" asthmatics. Once his cough had died down, he explained to me that there were three thousand people in Sardasht (out of a total of forty-five thousand through-

out the country) still suffering the consequences of the chemi-
cals and requiring special care. He and I went to meet other
victims. Words were all they had left for venting their sadness.
I remember an old man lying on cushions. Beneath his shirt,
his chest bore traces of strange burns.

"Did we really deserve that? Iran has never attacked any
country! It's unjust!" he declared.

Another, a woman, whom I met in her modest apartment,
confided in me the pain of not being able to get pregnant. Infer-
tility was one of the numerous side effects attributed to the gas.
"The mustard gas has a delayed reaction. It penetrates into your
tissues, affects the DNA, and can manifest itself many years
later," a doctor whispered to me. Listening to him, I thought
again of Sepideh's father. His tremors didn't appear until ten
years after he had been exposed to chemical gas on the front
lines. One victim among so many others!

Before leaving, Hossein insisted we have another tea together, at the foot of the pretty waterfall that remained the
charming focal point of this scarred city. In silence, we contem-
plated the torrent of water flowing along the rock.

Then he added, nostalgically:

"Behind its bucolic landscape, Sardasht, our little Paradise, will never again be as it was."

❧

For a long time, I kept thinking about these stories. No narrative had ever explained so well your compatriots' propensity for
feeling like victims, and their extreme protectionism in the face
of the major powers. It made me wonder whether the Iranian
nuclear program wasn't, to a certain extent, the legacy of the

chemical gassing perpetrated by Iraq against the backdrop of complete international indifference.

At the end of the war, in 1988, the Islamic Republic did indeed draw two lessons from Sardasht's tragedy: no matter what, avoid finding yourself in a vulnerable position and never again trust in international treaties and conventions. Haunted by paranoia, the authorities wanted at all costs to equip themselves with the means to prevent future danger. "The use of biological weapons may well be inhumane, but we still have to consider developing them for our defense," declared Ali Akbar Hashemi Rafsanjani, then chairman of Parliament, adding, "The war has taught us that international laws are nothing but ink on paper."

In the eyes of the West, the Islamic Republic is often perceived as a threatening power, ready to export Islamic revolution, to support terrorism, to strike Israel with its missiles, and to manufacture nuclear weapons. But after several years in your country, I gradually learned that, for Iranians, their contemporary history was, by contrast, a succession of conspiracies often carried out by the West. In 1906, when Iran's monarch Mohammad Ali Shah crushed the constitutional revolution, it was with the aid of the British and the Russians, who were in a hurry to put an end to an unprecedented democratic experiment in the Middle East. In 1953, the coup d'état against Prime Minister Mossadegh, champion of nationalizing Iran's oil industry and of the country's independence, would not have taken place without the intervention of the Americans. When the 1979 revolution mobilized the masses, it was in part because it carried with it the promise of liberating the country from foreign control.

Years later, in 2005, the specter of foreign conspiracies would be skillfully exploited for political ends by President Mahmoud

Ahmadinejad. In the guise of fighting a foreign enemy, and playing on Iranians' nationalist fervor, he set about strengthening his hold on society while accelerating the nuclear program, which had been suspended during negotiations between Khatami and the West in 2003. But we weren't quite there yet.

In the winter of 2002, the United States turned to Iraq, accusing it (far too late!) of possessing weapons of mass destruction—weapons that, paradoxically, had ceased to exist fifteen years after the attack against Sardasht.

In Tehran, those in power started to tremble. In his war on terror, Bush had first targeted Afghanistan. This time, it was Iraq, the other main neighbor of the Islamic Republic. Iranians asked themselves: When will our turn come? At the sound of combat boots in Baghdad, Iran started to retreat further into itself. In a new surge of protectionism, the authorities in Tehran decided to attack the first target within reach: the Western media.

On New Year's Day 2003, the telephone rang. It was a call from the Ministry of Culture. My press pass had been revoked, without warning. On the eve of the American invasion of Iraq, I became persona non grata in your country.

THE DOOR OPENED. Two men. I recognized them immediately. Haggard features, squared shoulders, backs glued to their chairs. Apart from a few more white hairs, they hadn't changed.

"*Khanum* Minoui! Long time no see," exclaimed the interrogator with the two missing fingers.

Four years had passed since the secret police last summoned me. Next to the lead interrogator, the same henchman. Slumped in his chair. Silent, staring at me. That day, instead of meeting at the Department of Foreign Nationals, they had "invited" me to a more incongruous place: a room in a big Tehran hotel. I went reluctantly. It was a few days after my press credentials had been revoked. On the phone, the boss had been brief. They wanted to see me as soon as possible. Without giving me a particular reason.

"Hello," I threw out casually, entering the room.

"Sit down!"

I jumped at the sound of the slamming door. It had closed behind me automatically. Obeying his orders, I took a seat in the empty armchair. A coffee table separated us. For a moment, I wondered if they had summoned me again because of Niloufar. She had taken the risk of reentering Iran. But as a precaution, we had chosen not to see each other since then. Oddly enough, she had nothing to do with this. That day, to my great surprise, they were interested in me.

"So, just like that, it seems they've revoked your press pass," he began.

An expression of mocking irony flitted through his gaze. He added:

"That's not very nice . . . And do you know why they did so?"

"Uh, no . . . ," I replied.

"There's surely a reason. Think hard."

A tense silence invaded the room. I didn't know if my pass had been taken away because of a particular article or interview. For the last few months, the censorship office at the Ministry of Culture had been going over my reports with a fine-tooth comb. Rumor had it that each journalist had been appointed a censor whose role was to scan his or her pieces, translate them, and underline in erratic red ink those passages deemed litigious. The amputee boss stared at me unremittingly, without saying a word. A heavy silence crashed over us.

"So?" he went on, sarcastic. "You really don't know why?"

"No," I replied.

In their eyes, they certainly weren't lacking for reasons. In my head, I started reviewing the potentially questionable subjects I had worked on. Was I being punished for visiting Montazeri's son? Or was it because of my escapade in the mountains? Or else my trip to the Basiji couple's home?

"You're even less talkative than the last time," he added coldly.

He sank into his chair, caressing its arms with his non-mutilated hand. Then he changed his tone:

"And yet, it seems that in the last four years, you've gained confidence. This country of your ancestors has become your own. Your vocabulary has improved. You travel a lot, you have new friends. You've even warmed up to your grandmother, it seems."

It was impossible to hide anything from him. He continued:
"Do you like Iran?"

"Yes," I replied, without hesitating.

"Would you like to stay here?"

"Yes," I repeated.

He paused, continuing to look me straight in the eye:

"Don't worry, we'll find a solution."

His voice had suddenly softened. It sounded almost friendly. As if he were trying to reassure me. Faced with my silence, he reiterated, in a compassionate tone, his desire to give me a hand. The reasons my press pass had been revoked were no longer important to him. He said that he found it all *regrettable*. A misunderstanding, certainly. A simple misunderstanding. He repeated again that I didn't have to worry. That there was probably a solution. That he knew how much I loved Iran. After all, I was a *hamvatan*, a fellow citizen, and he was prepared to help me.

"That's what friends are for, *Khanum* Minoui, right?"

Friends? I didn't know how to respond. He had changed so suddenly. I didn't see what he was getting at. He paused. A long pause. He straightened up, flashed me a fake smile. His gaze skimmed over the interrogation room door, double-locked. And that's when he offered me his "deal": the recuperation of my press credentials for a "favor."

"What favor?" I asked, breaking my silence.

I had replied quickly. Too quickly. In a rush to recover my press pass, I hadn't imagined what would come next.

"A small favor to do for us, nothing at all . . . Just a small favor . . . The next time you go to Paris, bring us back a list of successful Iranians who live in France."

So, that was it: a simple inventory of well-known Iranians—

dancers, photographers, doctors. I knew loads of them. Furthermore, their presence in France was common knowledge: Iranians of the diaspora stood out for their professional achievements. An hour spent surfing the Internet would be enough to draw up a list without much effort.

"Okay," I replied, naïvely, reassured by the simplicity of the request.

He smiled. He seemed satisfied.

"So, we'll see each other again upon your return!"

Then he led me to the door. He smiled at me. Again. The same fake, cold laugh. Then he put his hand on my wrist.

"I'm counting on you, Madam Minoui."

"Good-bye," I replied.

It wasn't until I arrived in Paris that I understood what he really wanted from me. A recruit! He saw me as a potential recruit . . . I had to be away from Iran to realize that his "deal" was nothing more or less than an offer to collaborate with the intelligence service. Immediately, everything became clearer. I better understood what Mr. Fingers wanted to happen. In that moment, Mr. Fingers had taken advantage of my weakness. He had grasped the fragility of my feelings. He knew I was enamored with the country that had been my home for the past four years. The names of successful men and women—theoretically, there was nothing confidential about that. But in agreeing to relay them to him, I would become one of them. A collaborator. And who knows what he would ask me to do next?

When I returned to Iran a week later, the telephone rang. Right away I guessed who it was. Mr. Fingers told me to meet him the next day in the cafeteria of the same hotel. I had no choice but to go, unenthusiastically. He was waiting for me, smiling.

"What about the list? Did you bring it for me?" he asked immediately.

Not at all. I had come back empty-handed. I told him no, just like that, without thinking about the consequences. "No," thinking of Emadeddin Baghi and all the brave freedom fighters who were paying the price for their commitment to democracy. "No," thinking of their courage, which I lacked. To give in to blackmail would be to betray their cause. In my head, I repeated several times the phrase I wanted to spit in this man's face: "A journalist cannot be bought. A journalist can only be endured." Faced with his somber gaze, his brow furrowed with anger, I didn't dare. I simply repeated, "No." Without offering any further explanation.

"What! You came back empty-handed!"

He was furious. "You came back empty-handed." When Mr. Fingers pronounced these words, referencing a well-known Persian expression, I had the confirmation of the blackmail I had almost given in to. Then he added, bluntly:

"No collaboration, no press pass!"

And he left.

SO THAT'S HOW it was. After so many years of my trying to reassemble the missing pieces of the Iranian puzzle, your country no longer wanted anything to do with me. I fell ill, worse than I had ever been. An aggressive sickness, a whirlwind that emptied my stomach.

The cramps started as I was heading home from the interrogation. At first, I tried to ignore them, telling myself it was just stress and fatigue. But the spasms intensified by the hour. Aggressive, vicious, relentless. I lay down on the sofa, thinking I would cure the illness with a long nap. Stars danced before my eyes, black holes, a chasm. I saw the floor lamp tremble, the walls teeter. I clung onto the cushions as if they were life preservers. The storm pelted down from every direction. My head was spinning, my fever rising. In my stomach, waves rolled in and rapidly rolled back . . . "Last name? First name? Age? Address?" Ouch . . . Always the same questions! "Madam Minoui, don't pretend to be stupid. You know very well what we expect from you." Chopped-off fingers pointed at me. They threatened me, clawed at me, flattened me . . . "No, no, I can't, Mr. Fingers! I can't take any more of your interrogations! What you're asking of me is impossible. Impossible! I feel sick. Sick to my stomach. Sick in my conscience. Leave me alone!" More rolling waves. My gut. Spasms, nausea, wanting to vomit, to cough everything up, to . . . "Let me out! Let me out!" I'm suffocating, my body . . . I'm hot . . . Let me out of my body! "No, Madam Minoui, you won't get out of here as long as . . ." What did I—but what did I do again? My head, my head . . . I'm drowning. "That's blackmail, Mr. Fingers! Blackmail . . . Leave me alone! I don't know anything! I can't do anything for you!" Pain, my body is only pain . . . I'm thirsty! I need water. Quickly! Cold water.

When I woke up the next morning, I was lying in the bathroom, one hand on my forehead, the other plastered to the tiles. Water was flowing from the tap in the sink. What time was it? How long had I been unconscious? What demon had inhabited me? I gathered my spirits and dragged my feverish body to the bedroom. Gripping the wall to lift myself up, I felt the spasms return. Even more intense. They tore through my abdomen. Between two convulsions, I managed to pull on my coat, tie my headscarf, and crawl to Dr. Rafat. He lived in my neighborhood, not far from Mohseni Square. Seeing me in that state, he immediately grabbed his large magnifying glass. Then he pored over his thick medical manual and announced his diagnosis: "Helicobacter. You have a helicobacter!" The scholarly word was written in black and white on page 102 of his big book, which looked like a medieval encyclopedia. He said I must have contracted it during a recent assignment in Afghanistan, when I took the road to Herat, after the fall of the Taliban. I had never heard of such a microbe, but the simple fact of being able to put a name to this strange pain reassured me a little. Once back home, I followed his "miracle diet" to the letter: grilled chicken to calm the gastrointestinal troubles, honey to kill the bacteria, and nothing else.

But the little pest was stubborn. In the following weeks, the pain got worse. Day and night, it scraped through my stomach. Getting up was a challenge. Leaving my home, a pointless endeavor. Outside, life had become foreign to me. A ballet of shadows along the walls, disappearing behind doors, a dancing procession of bodies without faces, hands without fingers . . . "Last name? First name? Age? Address?" The more the questions piled up in my head, the more my body abandoned me. I felt vanquished. Powerless. Paralyzed. "The Persian language bears the insanity of the inaccessible," the Iranologist Henry Corbin once said. For me, not only the language but the entire country was elusive.

I was disoriented. I thought I had finally mastered your country. I was too confident perhaps . . . Each reporting assignment was a dream opportunity to conquer a new city. The train had become my favorite mode of transportation. Sometimes, I took the bus in the middle of the night. I would stay with a local, in Qom or in Bandar Abbas. I was set on overturning the cliché of the woman reporter deprived of freedom. I had even convinced my editors in chief that there were so many other things than a nuclear Iran worth reporting on. I insisted that before worrying about the atomic bomb, we had to keep an eye on the social bomb. All those young people, women, intellectuals. My working conditions had also improved. Before my press pass was taken away, I had finally managed to live on my freelance salary. In my portfolio, I had just added *Le Figaro* to Radio France.

Meanwhile, the Iranian Spring had turned to autumn. After the arrest of Emadeddin Baghi, it was now Abbas Abdi, a former hostage taker who had helped plan the storming of the

American embassy, who wound up in Evin Prison. He was accused of having published a survey revealing that three-fourths of Iranians dreamed of closer Iranian-American relations. But I thought I had adapted even to that repressive atmosphere. Stories of intimidation and incarceration occupied my daily life. Fear became a companion like any other. I knew that the walls had ears, that I should never be too talkative on the telephone. That I had to refrain from mentioning dissidents' names. That the magic word for wine was *pomegranate juice*. That meetings were always arranged by email. I knew that living in Iran meant anonymous phone calls, pebbles thrown in the middle of the night at your window, taxi drivers who acted a little too curious . . . I was even starting to get used to Mr. Fingers. His repeated interrogations. His prying questions. His big eyes and his fits of rage. I told myself that it was all part of the reporter intimidation kit.

That last time, in the big, sterile hotel room, he had appeared under another guise. The executioner had become a "friend." But under one condition. A "small favor, nothing at all" . . . Just a "small favor" . . . With his proposition, he had offered me Iran by way of horse-trading. Since when is the love of a country negotiable? In refusing this pact with the devil, I had made myself vulnerable. I was unemployed. Undesirable in the land of my ancestors. Deprived of the password that had previously allowed me to exercise my profession. "No collaboration, no press pass," he had insisted. In my sickbed, his words mixed with pain. "You came back empty-handed" . . . "You came back empty-handed" . . . My stomach was still empty, too. In two weeks, I lost thirteen pounds. Instead of curing me, the diet prescribed by Dr. Rafat had hollowed out my stomach even more. On the phone, parents and friends begged me to leave Iran. I refused.

Leave? That would mean failure. Go back to see the doctor? What use would that be! To listen to him say that my helicobacter is a bacterium that resists even honey and grilled poultry? No way. After a month of suffering, I surrendered to the evidence: I had caught "Iran Fever," a tiny bit of your country had infected me like a bad virus. The illness ran through my veins, ate away at my insides. An incurable sickness that the best doctors would have been incapable of treating. I just had to learn to live with it. I had no choice.

WHO WOULD HAVE believed, dear Babai, that our paths would end up resembling each other?

Since I had caught Iran Fever, Papa called me frequently from Paris. Our conversations were always very brief. He didn't really know what to say to me. My determination to stay in your country perplexed him—he who had left many years ago. One night, he begged me for the umpteenth time to return to France, and my suffering inspired these words:

"Like grandfather, like granddaughter."

His comment caught my attention. Intrigued, I pushed to learn more. Papa took a deep breath. Then he confided in me that, before the revolution, the intelligence service had made a lot of trouble for you. Though he wasn't usually talkative, he started to tell the very detailed story of the blackmail you yourself had been subjected to . . . It was a summer morning in 1961. Before getting into your black Cadillac, you had taken care to put on the elegant navy-blue suit you reserved for special occasions. You had paired it with a new silk tie to celebrate the good news: you had just been offered the post of minister of national education. After all those years in the civil service, you had certainly earned the recognition. But the prestigious promotion carried a peculiar, pernicious condition: to collaborate with the SAVAK, the shah's secret police! This news was announced to you drily upon your arrival at the office. Obviously, you were shocked. The SAVAK! How dare they? You knew their repressive practices, you had heard about the torture in the prisons, their ways of getting people to inform on their fellow citizens, the disappearances . . . The notion was intolerable. Working with the SAVAK would mean renouncing your democratic convictions. Becoming a traitor to the cause. So you didn't hesitate for an instant. In short, you refused the offer. You said no, preferring isolation to betraying your people. Even though, that day, returning home, you understood that your career was over. With the shah, that's how it was. You were with him or against him. You knew that. But in your heart of hearts, you were proud of your decision.

I hadn't known about this part of your life. Among many others. While Papa was speaking, I stared at your photo sitting on my night table. You were wearing your signature black-rimmed glasses. In 2001, after Marie, your secret wife, had reappeared, I found them at the bottom of a dusty drawer while looking for a few more clues to solve the mysterious puzzle of your life. I put them on immediately, curious to know how you saw the world. Their lenses were so thick that a kind of blurriness obstructed my vision. I gave up understanding you then. I simply resigned myself to forgiving all your straying, seeing it as the weakness of a man with an oversize heart. I never would have imagined that they made you endure the same torments I was now enduring. That a half century later, your path would cross mine. Unbeknownst to us.

Papa took his time recalling the rest of your past. It was the first time he evoked your memory in this way. He told me how you were born in 1911 under the Qajar dynasty. Your father, Bagher Minoui, an ambitious landowner, was from Isfahan, also

known as Nesf-e Jahan, "Half the World" in Farsi. No place better illustrates the double identity, Persian and religious, of your
country's people than that city of roses and turquoise mosques.
Before you were born, your parents had decided to move to the
capital, attracted by a third facet of Iranian identity: modernity.
That race toward progress was instigated by Reza Shah, an ambitious monarch who, in 1925, put an end to the reign of the
Qajar dynasty by imposing his own: that of the Pahlavi. You were
only fourteen then. A teenager, you bore witness to the changes
that he inspired in your country, sometimes too rapidly and too
clumsily. Inspired by his Turkish neighbor, Mustafa Kemal
Atatürk, Reza Shah constructed new roads and tunnels all over
the place. And in a very controversial initiative, he imposed
"Western clothing" on the men, while forbidding women to wear
the veil. Your mother may have adapted to it, but your future
wife's mother, more pious and more traditional, was trauma-
tized. Like her, numerous Iranian women cloistered themselves
at home and stopped going to the public baths in order to avoid
going bareheaded through the streets. Irony of history: years
later, the Islamic Republic would set out, conversely, to hunt
down the "unveiled." But no one, at the time, could have predicted such a reversal.

In 1941, Reza Shah would be dethroned in his turn by his
own son, Mohammad Reza Pahlavi. Under his reign, you began
your career in civil service, after archeological studies that
brought you back, for a time, to Isfahan, where you had the rare
privilege of staying in the famous pavilion of forty columns,
Chehel Sotoun, a true jewel of Iranian architecture. An astute
observer of your country's evolution, you didn't hide your secular leanings, even if you were aligned with those who thought
it possible to reconcile Islam, democracy, and tolerance. Concerned with authoritarianism, you would consecrate a part of

your life to fighting in the name of human rights. Even if it meant paying the price.

The process of casting you out began in 1956. Three years earlier, the shah, under pressure from the CIA, had dismissed Prime Minister Mossadegh, a fervent nationalist who overshadowed him by overtly criticizing the Americanization of the country. Drunk with power, Mohammad Reza activated his security apparatus and started to hunt down potential enemies—that is, anyone who did not share his views. You had never been associated with a political party. And years later, you would keep your distance from the revolutionary movements. But your outspokenness was seen as a problem. The Iranian security classified you as a specimen to watch over closely. Or to keep out of the way. They would decide on the second option, offering you that cushy assignment in Paris: representing Iran in UNESCO. You jumped at the opportunity, seeing it as the bit of freedom you desperately needed.

On the phone, Papa stopped talking. I imagined him overwhelmed by his own memories. He was only ten years old then, and that move to Paris would mark the beginning of his new French life. For you, that UN job, at first very enticing, would quickly be at odds with your desire for independence.

Upon your arrival at UNESCO, Papa confided in me, only one order, in point of fact, was communicated from Tehran: "When a resolution is to be voted on in the General Assembly, do what the American representative does. If he raises his hand, you raise your hand!" Frustrated by this flagrant lack of autonomy, and feeling humiliated, you stopped attending the debates and putting on a show; you turned up only at the end, when they called for a vote. One day, when you hadn't even had the time to ask about the session's topic, you followed the example of the American. But on that occasion, a colleague signaled for you to abstain from raising your hand. "This time, the Americans asked that we vote *against* them," he informed you drily, giving no reason. They forced you to lower your hand, but you threw up your arm, irritated at the increasing American influence on the shah. Listening to Papa tell that anecdote, I thought again about Sardasht, of the nuclear arms race. In its own way, your experience explained your fellow citizens' heightened protectionism. Your personal history was merging with the larger history of your country.

Papa carried on with the story. He told me how you grew enraged, deprived of any responsibility and left to do nothing but run around in circles. You were beside yourself. Unable to stand the idleness, you enrolled at the Sorbonne. Literature became your refuge. An outlet for forgetting your troubles. You chose to write your dissertation on the life of Kashefi, a renowned Persian poet. The defense committee honored your work, and this meant so much to you, Papa explained.

I deduced that it was in this period that you developed a love for metaphor, which you shared with me so belatedly on your hospital bed, through Hafez. After your death, I remember poring over a bilingual collection of his poems at my neighborhood library. Opening the pages of his quatrains at random, I came upon one that said: "History repeats itself." Was I supposed to read a message between the lines? A warning to mull over? You used to echo your Iranian proverbs, saying I was "the light of your eyes." But without you, I felt more like "the dust beneath your feet." The space you left behind had never been so empty.

Lost in his memories, Papa added that, in 1961, soon after your return from France, the infamous SAVAK blackmail finalized your divorce from the state of Iran. Disgusted by their devious methods, you tossed your last hopes into the dustbin of history. You asked for an early retirement to distance yourself from everything to do with politics, directly or indirectly. But you remained in your country. Reading and writing became your comforts. Walks in the countryside, your only distractions. In 1979, from the distance of your couch, converted into an observation post, you followed the paroxysms of the revolution without participating in it.

Given how things turned out, I'm sure you didn't regret not getting involved. It seems that your apolitical stance and your distancing yourself from the SAVAK were in fact what saved you. For even though in the eyes of the new Islamist leaders you belonged to the *taghoutis*, the privileged, whose land was to be confiscated, you were not targeted as a man to be eliminated outright—even if Papa remains convinced that you were effectively killed by the cumulative effect of your property hassles with the Revolutionary Court.

Years later, in 1997, I was able to see to what extent Khatami's victory had restored your hope for your country. You thought he was different from the others. Perhaps because he, like you, expressed himself through poems? When you suddenly left us, a few months after his landslide victory, I regretted that you couldn't see with your own eyes this Iran that was learning to smile again, little by little. But, with hindsight, I tell myself it's probably better this way. Would you have been able to bear the sight, a few years later, of your country's dreams shattering once more against the shoals of reality?

AFTER YOUR TANGLES with the secret police, you chose to remain in your country, in internal exile. I chose to move to Iraq for a while. I thought that once I was on the other side of the border, I might manage to cure myself of this Iran Fever. No miracle remedy at hand, I had nothing to lose by trying. So, in February 2002, disheartened at not being able to get back my press pass, I headed first to the north and then made my way to Iraqi Kurdistan. The American invasion was imminent. Over there, the press was free. In a semiautonomous enclave, protected since 1991 from the claws of Saddam Hussein, many of the international media outlets had established their headquarters. Reporters for television stations, radio stations, newspapers—we were all standing by, waiting for the first signal that we could descend with all haste on Baghdad. When the regime fell in early April 2003, we all rushed to the Iraqi capital.

The city, only just liberated, was covered in a fine beige film of pulverized dust from the explosions. From east to west, American tanks controlled the main roads. As for the official buildings, the targets of missile strikes, there remained only mountains of rubble—with the exception of the very strategic Ministry of Oil. In the residential neighborhoods, the streets were as empty as my stomach. Deserted by their inhabitants. Eaten away by the fear of more bombings. Along the Tigris, only the windows held together with adhesive tape had withstood the blasts. Residents had used rolls of Scotch Tape, to limit the damage! I had only just arrived when I was immediately struck by one detail: that city of imposing concrete buildings, vestiges of Ba'ath architecture, bore no trace of its other war, the one Saddam had waged on the Islamic Republic of Iran more than twenty years earlier. Unlike in Tehran, the martyrs' faces were invisible. Nonexistent. Locked into a cult of personality, partial to outrageous murals of his image, the former Iraqi president must have felt that even the dead could overshadow him. But the rest of the city reminded me of Iran.

One day, as I finished up an interview in northern Baghdad, in the Shia neighborhood of Kadhimiya, my attention was caught by some music nearby—Persian! Thrilled by that familiar melody, I hurried to see where it could be coming from. Fifteen feet away, Iranian pilgrims were flowing into the street, cameras over their shoulders and bottles of water in their arms. There were a few hundred people, men in black, veiled women. The fall of Saddam Hussein, a member of the Sunni minority known for his fear of Shiites, had opened up the route leading to the mausoleums of their beloved imams, which for a long time had been kept under strict surveillance. So, Iranians were rushing from everywhere—from Tehran, Shiraz, and even Isfahan—to bow down before the tomb of Imam Kadhim, buried here in this district of Baghdad. The most zealous crossed the border at night, by foot, and risked stepping on one of the land mines left behind from the war in the '80s. They charged, heads lowered, as if rushing toward a rediscovered paradise. Their highly dangerous journey would lead them to Najaf, and then to Karbala, where Ali and Hussein, the most venerated of the Shiite saints, were buried.

And then there was an unexpected encounter with Hossein Khomeini, the grandson of Imam Ruhollah Khomeini, the Father of the Islamic Republic. He, too, had made the trip from Iran to pray before these holy sites. But another reason, a more unusual one, had precipitated his trip to Iraq: an insane, curious desire to savor the rediscovered freedom hovering over Iraq after twenty-four years of a tyrannical regime. I crossed his path randomly, while visiting a young Iraqi Shiite cleric who had just returned from a long exile in Dubai. Now in their forties, the two friends shared a villa overlooking the Tigris. In that spacious home echoing with canary song, they spent their nights playing the *tar* and welcoming a motley array of former opponents of the Ba'ath Party: politicians, intellectuals, and human rights advocates. They all shared the same hatred for Saddam, but also an astonishing admiration for the American GIs. Seated cross-legged on his sofa, Hossein Khomeini gave me a few explanations between puffs on his Miami cigarettes.

"As you know, Iranians are fond of freedom. An impossible dream, as long as religion and politics remain linked. If there is no way other than American intervention to obtain that freedom, I think that my people would be in favor of that solution. And I would be, too!"

His speech reminded me immediately of the words of Montazeri's son. The same outspokenness, the same dislike of the regime he had inherited. But Khomeini's grandson was taking it a step further: in the same Iraq where, during his exile in the '60s, his grandfather had proposed the famous *velayat-e faqih*, the "Guardianship of the Islamic Jurist," which enshrined the primacy of religion over politics, Hossein Khomeini not only challenged this principle, but claimed to be ready to welcome the enemy's tanks to Iran in order to put an end to it. Listening to him, I tried to imagine the scene: a succession of tanks over-running Enghelab, the famous revolutionary road. It sounded like something from a spy novel and sent shivers down my spine. How would Mahmoud, the death-obsessed Basiji, react to such a scheme? Or even Niloufar, who was such a patriot that she would align herself with the clerics to save her country? Even the most dissident of my Iranian friends had always been reluctant to accept foreign intervention in their country. They maintained that the change had to come from within, not outside, Iran. My astonishment didn't escape Hossein Khomeini.

"Today," he continued, "totalitarianism is eating away at Iran, as was the case in Iraq under Saddam . . . Since I came to Baghdad, I have noticed positive changes: the press is free, people are no longer afraid of speaking out, the Iraqis can breathe again. Their country is on the path to progress. It can't be denied: all of that wouldn't have been possible without the American-led intervention."

At these words, I felt a knot in my stomach. A burst of spasms, then another, shot through my guts. Was a Western offensive really the only recourse against a regime that oppressed its population? Could it really guarantee the establishment of a democratic system?

"A lot of countries, France included, were opposed to the war. Even the UN was against it. Some wonder whether there isn't a risk that American troops will turn into an occupying force," I replied.

"I disagree!" he shot back. "For me, they are forces of liberation, not occupation!"

I knew exactly what he was referring to. Before him, defenders of the American invasion had relentlessly tried to sell that war by comparing it to the American landing in German-occupied France during World War II. My maternal grandfather, then a prisoner in enemy territory, owed them his life. But, in this context, Hossein Khomeini's argument didn't convince me at all. I completely understood his frustration with the absurd political system installed by his ancestor that was mercilessly stifling its people; at the same time, I wanted to believe, like Niloufar and so many others, in the possibility of change from within. Was it the growing influence of my Iranian identity? In my view, a foreign intervention would compromise Iran. Worse, it would open the country to American GIs, which would be opening the doors to hell. The human cost of a military operation would be colossal. I believed it would radicalize the government and destroy the rising tide still resisting the regime. After so many years of suffering, did Iranians really deserve such a fate? Was there no other solution to end this tyranny? In my head, the questions jostled around to the rhythm of my cramps. By the end of the interview, it had become clear to me: the honey and grilled chicken might finally be starting to ease the pain, but I was far from being cured of Iran Fever. In Iraq, I was more Iranian than some Iranians.

I WASN'T TRAVELING across Mesopotamia on my own. At the beginning of February, I had reunited with my fiancé, Borzou, an American journalist of Iranian descent. We had met a year earlier, in Tehran, at the red carpet where Khatami was shaking hands with his guest of honor, Hamid Karzai. The first visit to Iran by an Afghan head of state since the fall of the Taliban regime.

Living in the United States since the age of four, Borzou had left the comforts of a major American magazine after witnessing, in person, the attack against the Twin Towers in Manhattan, from his neighborhood in Brooklyn. While the United States shut itself away in its extreme paranoia, he headed for the Middle East to feel out the other side. His new life as an independent reporter fit into a suitcase: a satellite telephone, a flashlight, and a few wads of bills. This minimalism had charmed me immediately. Like him, I had traveled light during my first visit to Iran. Like him, I considered luggage an unnecessary burden.

Together, we shared the same neurotic attraction to that region of the world, a predilection for complicated situations and a good dose of obstinacy. After Tehran, Kabul, and Baghdad, we rapidly became inseparable. It was also thanks to him that I had pulled myself out of my bed in Tehran and dragged my skeletal body to Iraq, in the hope of vanquishing the Iran

Fever. I had called Iran every name under the sun, convinced I would be forever chained to this country that was eating away at my stomach. But he succeeded in pulling me up from the abyss.

Like me, Borzou had a particular curiosity for Shiite mullahs. In his miniature suitcase, he had brought a reference book, *The Shi'is of Iraq*, which quickly became our guide to Baghdad's twists and turns. In it, Yitzhak Nakash writes in detail of the Iran-Iraq border, an unavoidable passage along the Shiite pilgrim route that for centuries has united the two countries, spiritually and geographically, from Tehran to Baghdad. Closed under Saddam, it had just been reopened and would become our path of choice during numerous trips to and from Iraq. We followed in the footsteps of countless Shiites.

Since the fall of Baghdad, Iraqi clerics exiled in neighboring Iran had returned to the country in droves. The Shiite awakening of Najaf, the Arab holy city, intrigued as much as it worried Qom, the Persian one. Unlike Khomeini's grandson, who was enamored of Americanism, the conservative mullahs, eager to preserve the supremacy of Qom over the Shiite community in the region, saw in this new chapter of Iraqi history a golden opportunity to regain their influence in the neighboring country. To such an extent that, years later, the United States would bitterly observe that they had given Iraq to the Iranians.

Back in Tehran, a few weeks after the fall of Baghdad, we set out for Qom, the capital of chadors, to meet with Ayatollah Haeri. The ultraconservative was said to be the mentor of Muqtada al-Sadr, a young anti-American Iraqi cleric who served the Iraqi city of Kufa, near Najaf. We were driven by a desire to better understand what was brewing between the two holy cities. Like me, Borzou had been stripped of his Iranian press credentials, but we thought the risk moderate, since we had not covered Iranian news in a long time.

We had just finished our interview with Ayatollah Haeri when our cell phone rang. Trying to save money, Borzou and I were sharing a phone.

"Hello," I answered.

"Put Borzou on," said the man on the other end.

"Who's asking for him?" I replied.

I knew that voice. I hadn't been able to erase it from my memory.

"Come on, *Khanum* Minoui, don't play dumb. You know perfectly well who this is."

Mr. Fingers! My Iraqi escape hadn't succeeded in making him forget about me. Except this time he wasn't calling for me. It was Borzou he was interested in. Hesitantly, I passed him the phone. I would have liked to save Borzou from Cerberus's claws, spare him the troubles I had suffered. Borzou took the phone. I saw him nod and heard him say yes a few times. Then he hung up, signaling to me that we had to get back to Tehran as soon as possible. The maimed man was in a hurry to see him. A routine visit, he had said. Words that rang familiar in my head.

When he came back from that meeting, Borzou, who usually had enough energy for the both of us, collapsed onto a chair in my living room. Mr. Fingers had greeted him in person, except that he was using a different name from the one I knew him by. In an icy tone, he had accused Borzou of traveling to Qom without a press pass, reproached him for breaking the country's laws, and then formally forbade him from writing anything. "Understand? Forbidden!" he had hammered home menacingly. Before ending his sermon, he had insisted that Borzou promise never to reveal to anyone what was said in that conversation. Of course, Borzou did the exact opposite. Knowing that we shared the same hell gave us the strength to resist; the waves of Iran Fever seemed easier to combat. We both agreed to publish our interview with Ayatollah Haeri at the same time—his in English, mine in French. A few days later, the phone rang again, "Unknown Caller" on the display. I knew right away what it was about. Mr. Fingers was furious. He wanted to see me immediately. And in a new location, "the stone building," in the north of Tehran.

The building, protected by a wall of white and gray stones, looked like a prison. I had to enter through a thick steel gate, which closed right behind me. Later, I learned that the sinister-looking structure, seized during the revolution from a Bahá'í businessman who owned the Coca-Cola factory, was one of the numerous buildings that housed the intelligence service. In the reception area, an assistant was standing behind the glass. He signaled for me to slide my passport and cell phone through the opening and immediately locked them in a small safe. I pretended this was normal. My heart was beating wildly.

They told me to sit in the waiting room. Staring down at me, portraits of Khomeini and Khamenei were my only company. Hung right in the middle of the main wall, they communicated something Orwellian that sent a shiver down my spine. An hour went by. Two hours . . . I was starting to wonder if I would ever get out of that hole when a door creaked open.

"Here you are!"

Mr. Fingers was standing in the doorway. Icy gaze, tight lips—still the same. He signaled for me to follow him into a small room with curtains turned yellow with age. I recognized my file on his wooden desk. It had grown much larger since my first summons. My interrogator didn't waste time on useless formalities. He got right to the point.

"How dare you write that Muqtada al-Sadr is Iranian!"

With his good hand, he brandished a page from the file. I recognized my most recent article, annotated in Persian.

"I never wrote that he was Iranian, just that he had an Iranian mentor."

"That's not what the translation says."

"I met him in Kufa. He didn't speak a word of Farsi. I can confirm for you that he *is* Iraqi."

"So why did you write the opposite?"

"I promise you, that's not what I wrote."

"And yet that's what I read, right here, in the margin."

"There must be a problem with the translation."

"You've become rather insolent since you started spending time with Mr. Borzou!"

What did my private life have to do with an erroneous interpretation of my article? What was he insinuating with that inappropriate remark? That he knew everything about our relationship, which was automatically illicit in his eyes because we weren't married?

"Your accusations are unfair!" I threw back.

He slammed his fist on the table.

"You write lies, and you do it without even having a press pass!"

He launched into a rapid monologue of accusations. In the torrent of words, I recognized *traitor, liar, illegal*—not much more. In fact, I understood only one out of every two or three words. I wanted to avoid giving in; I clung to my journalistic training. I took out my notebook, the only shield I had left. I wanted to copy down his sentences, to have them translated later in order to understand exactly what he was accusing me of. The more he spoke, the more I wrote.

"This isn't France!" he barked.

Like a robot, I continued to take notes.

"You really are obsessed with writing everything down! Didn't your friend Borzou inform you of my order? He is forbidden to write."

He said the name "Borzou" in a particularly disdainful tone. I was beside myself.

"He told me only that he had promised not to reveal any details of your conversation," I replied in an exasperated tone that came dangerously close to sarcasm.

Mr. Fingers did not appreciate this. He yelled:

"Do you know that I can charge you with lying and breaking the law?"

I swallowed. Getting ahold of myself, I repeated with resolve that I had never written that Muqtada was Iranian. I refused to cave. He was tearing into me, this man who had already destroyed my stomach. Pen in hand, I continued to fill the pages of my notebook.

He hit the table again:

"That's enough!"

I raised my head. His face was scarlet. I said nothing. I was stunned. His voice echoed off the walls. I didn't know what had compelled me to provoke him in this way.

"Next time, I'll see you in court!" he yelled.

And with his maimed hand, he showed me the door.

* * *

I met Borzou in a café right afterward. He was waiting for me, worried.

"What do we do now?" I asked, after telling him everything.

Neither of us had the answer. But could there be one, in a country with so many uncrossable, ever-changing lines? We went to knock on the door of Mohammad Seifzadeh, one of the few lawyers still walking free. In Iran, even the lawyers end up in prison. Seated around cups of tea accompanied by nougat from Isfahan, Seifzadeh repeated a paradox that we already knew: there is no law, despite the imposed restrictions, forbidding anyone from writing without a press pass.

"Write! Write!" he insisted. "It's the only way of saving what little remains of our besieged freedom of expression."

His audacity impressed us. He had defended Shirin Ebadi, the recipient of the Nobel Peace Prize, during her arrest; he had seen far worse cases than ours. It was clear that he was trying to reassure us. He told us we had no reason to panic. That, after all, we had alternate passports—an "escape route," he called it. That he would protect us in case of an emergency. But we felt vulnerable. The next day, we went to see Mashallah Shamsolvaezin, a pillar of the reformist press and the head of the Association of Iranian Journalists. A pipe in his mouth, he received us with open arms, laughing at our fears.

"What are you afraid of? You make me smile. If you stop writing, who will do it in your place? Who will tell people what's happening in Iran?"

He knew what he was talking about. Since the Tehran Spring, he'd lost count of the number of shuttered newspapers, jailed writer friends, exiled colleagues. He, too, had known the coldness of Iranian prisons, but without ever renouncing the struggle, despite having endured the worst humiliations. He told us how, during his last stint in jail, the judge had even fabricated charges of illicit relations between him and his secretary.

"When they can't manage to break you professionally, they break you personally."

Borzou and I looked at each other. There was no need to say

more. In a country of forbidden love, if we didn't want to stop writing, we had to keep our private life hidden.

"Freedom comes at a price. Each of us must find his own way of negotiating the lowest cost," Shamsolvaezin murmured by way of both advice and a good-bye.

Back at my place, we sank into the sofa, nestled against each other. By merely spending a night under the same roof, we were committing a "crime" that Mr. Fingers could use against us however he liked. And you, my absent grandfather, what would you have done in our place? Among the dusty cassette tapes salvaged from one of your old cardboard boxes that Mamani had kept, I picked out an album by Shahyar Ghanbari, one of the numerous exiled pop stars living in Los Angeles since the revolution. He sang, "The blue of the sea, forbidden! / The desire to see, forbidden! / Love between two fish, forbidden!"

Lulled by the melody, we were nodding off when the telephone rang. It was Borzou's mother. Where she was—Chicago—the sun had only just risen. With the time difference, she always called us around dinner. When she asked for news, at first we kept quiet about our troubles, but since the walls had ears anyway, we ended up telling her everything. She listened carefully, then exclaimed without the slightest hesitation: "Get a *sigheh*," she said. "A temporary marriage." I shrugged. But she was right. To protect oneself from the scorching strikes of the regime, it was better to stop playing with fire. I had denigrated the *sigheh* so much, but this "secret pact" would turn out to be the key to my survival.

The next day, I wore neither a crown of flowers nor a white scarf. Hastily, I called Laya, an Iranian friend. She came over right away while Borzou went to the pastry shop. She would serve as our witness, and the sweets as our festive decoration. We went to a matchmaker mullah discreetly recommended by an Iranian female colleague. He was located near Towhid Square, not far from the city center. "Don't worry, he knows his trade by heart," she had assured me. A few days earlier, he had married one of her Muslim acquaintances to a Zoroastrian from California for two weeks. The *sigheh*, a made-to-order marriage

"What can I do for you?" the mullah mumbled upon our arrival.

It hadn't been hard to find his address. "Marriages/Divorces," a sign written in Persian letters, announced his well-established business. Recently, an epidemic of divorces had struck Tehran. For a lot of rebellious Iranian women, who moved directly from the parental home to the conjugal home, it had become the final step in obtaining the freedom they dreamed of. And so this was what the cleric imagined had brought us to him.

"We're here for a temporary marriage," whispered Borzou, avoiding the taboo word *sigheh*.

The mullah sat up in his armchair, intrigued by our request.

"For how long?" he asked.

We remained quiet. We had thought of everything except the length of time.

"One week? Three months? A year? Four years?" he continued.

"Uh, let's say two years," Borzou replied.

His Persian, which he had spoken growing up, even in the United States, was much better than mine. But a strong American accent betrayed him.

The cleric turned toward Laya:

"Where are they from?" he asked.

"From here, and elsewhere," she replied.

"All right, sit down!"

Our case seemed to amuse as much as intrigue him.

He solemnly put on his glasses and then turned toward me.

"May God preserve you, are you a widow?" he asked me.

At my side, Laya translated his questions for me.

"No," I replied.

"Divorced?" he continued.

"Not that, either!"

In response to my astonishment at his questions, he added: "You mean to say that you've never been married?"

"No," I replied.

"Never?"

"No."

He leaned toward Laya, murmured a few incomprehensible words, started flipping through the pages of a book as if searching for a miracle solution, then crossed his arms, pensive. Embarrassed, Laya whispered in my ear:

"I think there's a problem."

"What?"

"A woman can't enter into a *sigheh* unless she's a widow or divorced. Normally, the condition is that she has already consummated a marriage, if you know what I mean."

I saw perfectly what she was trying to say. Since my discussion with Mehdi, the leather jacket–wearing mullah, the temporary marriage held no secrets for me. I also knew, thanks to the reappearance of your secret wife, Marie, that there were a thousand and one possible arrangements to seal this pseudo-religious pact.

"So tell him I was married before, if that will reassure him."

But it would take more than that to convince the matchmaker mullah: he wanted written proof of my "divorce" and the presence of my father, or at least his written authorization.

"No document, no *sigheh*," stated the mullah.

I turned toward Borzou. In this maze of rules, I felt I had exhausted every resource.

"Certainly there must be a solution," said Borzou.

The mullah was unmoved. He chewed on the frames of his glasses, watching us out of the corner of his eye. After a pause, he put his glasses back on and said, an eyebrow raised:

"What are you ready to give in exchange for a *sigheh*?"

Borzou and I glanced at each other again. I let him respond.

"Fifty dollars," he said.

Fifty dollars was a fifth of the average monthly salary.

The mullah's face suddenly relaxed.

"Okay, we'll find a way to marry your friends," he said to Laya.

We breathed a long sigh. So, it was a simple matter of money!

Looking very serious, he took out a sheet of paper from the bottom of a drawer. He stapled our two photos to it and meticulously copied a few phrases from the Quran, having us repeat them after him. Then he took out adhesive tape. After covering up the Quranic verses, he turned toward me:

"It's so as not to tarnish the words of God . . . during times of impurity."

I watched him append his final seal below our signatures. I didn't recognize his name in it. This man clearly marched to the beat of his own drum. My astonishment didn't escape him:

"I'm not the real mullah. I'm just an intermediary, working behind the scenes!"

We opened the box of sweets. Mullah or not, we had to celebrate our love visa before its expiration date. With the gleaming eyes of a glutton, the Quranic charlatan took a cream puff. Then he raised his head toward Laya. This time, she was the one being gobbled up by his eyes. When we got up to leave, he signaled for her to stay. He said that he had a secret to tell her. For her ears only. We waited for her at the entrance. A few minutes later, Laya joined us, looking pale.

"Everything okay?" I asked her.

"He offered me . . . a *sigheh*!"

ONE YEAR LATER, on the day of our "real" marriage, July 31, 2004, you were the only one missing. Faithful to our convictions, Borzou and I had opted for a civil marriage, in the middle of Normandy. At dinner, the guests' tables bore the names of the cities we had traveled through together: Tehran, Qom, Kabul, Herat, Baghdad, Fallujah, Kirkuk, Najaf, Samarra. The moon was our host, full and luminous. And Iran, our guest of honor. Before the meal, we kissed beneath two candy canes, according to the Persian custom, so that sweetness would guide our path. Laya surprised us by coming. In her red velvet dress, she enchanted us with a Sufi dance during the aperitif. For dinner, there were dishes from the East and the West, champagne, and bursts of laughter. A musician friend from Bandar Abbas crooned the melodies of Persian Gulf fishermen. Even Mamani had taken off her Medea mask. In the middle of the meal, she suddenly stood up. She put one foot in front of the other, snapping her fingers enthusiastically. Then, with her whole body, despite the burden of her years, she started to dance. Her face, normally so somber, glowed with the effect of half a glass of red wine. She laughed as she lit up the dance floor. My French friends couldn't believe it—I had poisoned them with stories of my killjoy grandmother. And I imagined you, somewhere up above, or else behind the waves, smiling at it all.

But a civil ceremony was worth nothing in the eyes of Iran. Before taking the plane back to Tehran, we still had to clear one last hurdle, this time at the Iranian embassy. Hassan Ferechtian, a doctor of theology accredited by the regime, greeted us at the first floor of the Centre Culturel Iranien, behind the Jardin du Luxembourg. I was wearing a white headscarf; Borzou, a cream-colored suit. According to the existing custom, Hassan Ferechtian recited a few verses of the Quran and issued us a marriage certificate in a burgundy folder. Once the formalities were over with, he handed us a gift: *400 Questions and Answers to Better Understand Islam*, a book of his that had recently been published in France. But he wanted to seal our union on a more romantic note. He turned toward Borzou and asked:

"Do you know Florent Pagny?"

"Floran who?" Borzou replied, staring at me inquisitively.

"Florent Pagny, the French singer?" I repeated.

I wasn't sure that I had heard correctly.

"Yes, Florent Pagny," Ferechtian insisted.

Hands on the table, he smiled at us:

"The marriage contract is a formality. Administrative paperwork. The important thing is to love each other. To love is to take and to give. To nurture the flame . . . In one of his songs, the French singer Florent Pagny says it much better than I can. So, here is a bit of advice: hurry and buy his CD."

Another Iranian paradox! He and the impostor mullah represented the clashing of two worlds. Touched by his ode to love, we took his advice. With Allah's blessing and Florent Pagny's album in our luggage, we had been immunized; we were ready to take on Iran once again.

IN TEHRAN, OUR Iranian honeymoon was abruptly cut short. At the Ministry of Culture and Islamic Guidance, our requests for press credentials were once again met with refusal. I was enraged to be subjected to such a sanction. I felt Iran Fever digging into my stomach again. Through much insistence, I managed to secure a meeting at the Foreign Media Department. "Other journalists before you agreed to do us a few favors. Take it or leave it," murmured the head officer, adding, "Sorry. There's nothing I can do for you." His response was clear, at least. Ours, too. To escape Iran's diktats, our only recourse was to go back to the other side of the border and settle in Iraq for good. It wasn't the best moment. Two weeks after our Normandy nuptials, our French colleagues Christian Chesnot and Georges Malbrunot had been kidnapped on their way to Najaf, in the middle of the "Sunni Triangle," a Sunni-Arab insurgency stronghold. Kidnappings for ransom were becoming common, and booby-trapped cars exploded without warning. At that time, Shiites and Sunnis were fighting for power against a backdrop of death squads and targeted assassinations. A post-Saddam conflict of unprecedented violence. In Iraq, there was no need for an alarm clock. The first bomb of the day always went off at around seven in the morning. In Iraq, you could die on any street corner, at any moment; it was like a game of Russian roulette.

But this war wasn't mine. I lived in it, but with a certain detachment. The fear that gnawed away at me didn't have the same texture as my Iranian anxieties. At night, I found something like comfort in letting myself be lulled by the purring of the generator providing our electricity. It was a change from the staccato that punctuated my Tehran nights, when passing strangers seeking to intimidate me sent stones ricocheting off my shutters.

In the winter of 2004, I was set on going back to Tehran for a few weeks. A personal visit, so I could give Mamani a hug and see my friends again. Love for a country can't be controlled. On the other hand, the Iranian intelligence service excelled at control. To perfection. I was waiting for my luggage in front of the baggage carousel in the large arrivals area when the loudspeakers spat out my name. A metallic voice ordered me to go to a vestibule. Behind a desk, a man in a black suit was there, waiting for me. Last name? First name? Age? Address? Again the same questions. Like a robot, I responded to the interrogation without batting an eye. Over time, I had gained confidence. My interlocutor then handed me an "invitation." The letter included a telephone number and instructed me to contact the "president's office" to arrange a meeting. I deduced that this was the intelligence service's latest tactic. Back home, I called my editor in chief. I wanted the secret police to hear that I was purposely informing Paris. That I was no longer as vulnerable as before. My composure caught them off guard. Later, when I contacted the number I'd been given, I was told that the interview had been canceled.

But the intelligence service didn't appreciate my little game. The day of my departure, three weeks later, they exacted their revenge. At passport control, a big bearded man approached me. Ear glued to his walkie-talkie, he demanded my papers; I

handed them over. He grabbed and rifled through them per-
functorily, then took off with them, weaving through a crowd
of passengers. After a half hour, I heard my name over the loudspeaker. This time, it was the airline: the last call before they
closed the gate. And then, I shuddered. I shuddered at having
played at defiance. I shuddered at being without my documents,
with no control over anything. I knew at that instant that the
worst could happen. The worst would be to disappear at the
airport and reappear, a few days later, in a prison cell. It was a
classic technique. Other travelers before me had experienced
it. On the loudspeaker, my name crackled again. I looked at
my watch. I had only fifteen minutes until takeoff. The minutes rapidly dissolved. Ten minutes. Five minutes . . . "Here
you go!" I jumped at the voice of the big bearded man. He had
reappeared, my passport in one hand, a photocopy of all its
pages in the other. "Here you go!" he repeated, handing me my
ID. "This time, we'll give you a chance to catch your flight." I
snatched my passport like a thief, saying nothing, neither "thank
you" nor "good-bye." I ran as fast as I could toward the plane. I
followed the long corridor, took the escalator as quickly as possible, leaped onto the Jetway, and then dove into the aircraft. I
was the last passenger aboard. My heart was beating furiously.
I cursed the bearded man. I cursed all of them. These people
had a talent for playing with one's nerves, fully aware of the unease they left in their wake.

My Iranian misadventures were not unique. They melted into
the white of that winter of 2004, one of the harshest Iran had
ever experienced. That winter, the snow enveloped Tehran in a

thick, cottony veil. On Valiasr Street, the wind had ripped the last leaves from the plane trees. During my three-week trip, I noticed that the promise of reforms had also flown away for good. Following the local elections of 2003, the conservatives had swept the legislative elections in 2004. It made you wonder whether the cold was influencing the political mood or the other way around. I remember shivering when I saw that antidepressants were flying off of the shelves of the pharmacy. Iranians were consuming them without moderation, like so many antidotes for seasonal affective disorder. Even Sepideh, my mischievous young friend, had given in to the pessimism. She had also achieved her dream of becoming a reporter with flying colors. Her valuable investigations of street children and of women in Ilam Province committing suicide by ingesting cement turned the best Iranian journalists green with envy. Still, under redoubled censorship, the daily newspapers were closing one after another. And Sepideh was sick of changing newsrooms as often as one changes a shirt. Her future looked unclear—violent, unpredictable, and dangerous. Like her colleagues, she never left home without slipping a toothbrush into her bag. "In case I get arrested," she told me one day when we met at our favorite coffee shop in Tehran, before I went back to Iraq.

During my nights in Baghdad, once the day's reports had been sent off, I often thought of her, my gaze fixed on the ceiling. I was passionate about reporting on Iraq, was by the side of the man I loved, and was finally making a living from my profession by freelancing more, but Iran constantly occupied my thoughts. Sometimes, for hours on end, I tortured myself with thoughts of not being able to work there anymore. I thought of the rebellious students. I dreamed of Qom, Bandar Abbas, Shahr-e Rey. I remembered the little beggar in Tehran, a canary on his shoulder, Hafez's verses in the palm of his hand. I also thought about you, my invisible grandfather. You would have been a precious comfort in those moments of uncertainty.

And then, one morning in the spring of 2005, almost at the same hour as the day's first bomb, the news I had stopped hoping for came in an email: "Your press credentials have just been renewed. Come by to pick up your pass when you like." The message was signed by the Ministry of Culture and Islamic Guidance. Without explanation, nothing asked in return. Dozens of times I reread it, thinking it must be a fake. But it was true: they were inviting me to return to Iran to cover the coming presidential election. A few days later, Borzou also received some good news: the *Los Angeles Times* had offered him a position as permanent correspondent in Baghdad. The offer was attractive, difficult to refuse. What to do? Stay in Iraq? Return to Iran? Heavy-hearted, we split the difference: for him, Baghdad; for me, Tehran. And for us, vacations in Jordan in between assignments.

HE NOTICED ME FIRST. He was going by on his motorcycle, at the end of my street. A Honda, what all the Basij militiamen ride when they roam the city from north to south. Mahmoud, the martyrophile, hadn't changed, with his chinstrap beard, dark pants, and nylon shirt.

"*Che khabar?* What's new?" he asked, giving me the uncomfortable impression that he may have been on the lookout for my return.

It was May 2005. There was something almost improbable about our reunion. Since our dinner in Darakeh, a little before I contracted my Iran Fever, we hadn't seen each other. Tehran is a vast labyrinth. One is easily incognito there, lost in a crowd of twelve million anonymous onlookers. Was our meeting a simple coincidence?

"We've moved. Now we live in the same neighborhood as you. See you soon, *inshallah!*" he hurried to say, as if he had read my thoughts.

And he disappeared into traffic.

The next day, he called me to politely invite me over for tea. I accepted, curious about the coincidence. Indeed, we were neighbors. Their new apartment was a few minutes' walk from mine, behind Pasdaran Avenue. When I arrived, I immediately noticed that two large sofas had replaced the traditional floor cushions. There was even a wooden table in the dining room. The decor was modern. More colorful. Nothing like the austere ambiance of their former home. In the bedroom, which could be seen from the hallway, the large tiles depicting the two Supreme Leaders had disappeared from the wall. My look of surprise didn't escape Mahmoud.

"It's the 'Fatemeh' touch," he said, with a grimace seeming to signify that this new layout wasn't in keeping with his taste.

"Do you like it?" a feminine voice followed.

I turned around. Head wrapped in a towel, Fatemeh had just emerged from the bathroom, trailing a sweet musky odor in her wake. Nonchalantly, she threw the towel on the sofa, revealing a new haircut, shorter and streaked with highlights. She was squeezed into a black T-shirt, and her silhouette was narrower. The loss of a few pounds suited her marvelously.

"What . . . What a transformation!" I replied, hesitating to compliment her on all these changes.

Mahmoud was quiet. His silence betrayed some discomfort. As if the emancipation of his wife damaged the image he wanted to project of their relationship.

"Praise God, she still wears the black chador when she goes out in the street," he interjected, to save face.

Then he quickly changed the subject:

"So, what's new with you?"

I didn't really know how to respond. I was still wondering why he had invited me over, what he really wanted from me. At moments like this my paranoia came back at a gallop. I decided to keep quiet about my problems with the press pass.

"Well, I'm married now, too!" I announced, to divert their attention.

"To a French guy?" Fatemeh asked eagerly.

"No, an Iranian."

"*Moborak!* Congratulations!" Mahmoud exclaimed with an approving look.

He, the nationalist, the living martyr, the fierce supporter of a homeland he worshipped to the extreme, was smiling again, probably proud deep down to see that Iran had rubbed off on the heart of such a Westerner. When I told him that Borzou was stationed in Baghdad, a new spark lit up his gaze.

"Ah, Iraq," he said in a dreamy tone.

Iraq, that country he had been too young to fight against, continued to haunt him. He confided in me that since the American intervention, he hadn't missed a single event. Like many Iranians, he had welcomed the fall of Saddam, a lifelong enemy, with relief. But the prolonged presence of the United States in a neighboring country worried him. For him, there was a hidden Manichean plan to occupy the entire region. Convinced that Iran was the next target in this "Western crusade," he said he was ready to take up arms if need be. That war would finally be his war, his generation's, the war he had been awaiting for so long. Furthermore, he confided in me that the Basijis had resumed their military training, which had been less frequent in the past few years. In a big suburb of Tehran, they were wielding Kalashnikovs again, readying themselves for a lopsided war. He found it necessary to prepare for the worst.

"And you?" he asked me, "you've lived in Iraq; what do you think of all this? What kinds of weapons are the GIs using? Is their firepower as invincible as they claim? In fact, would you be generous enough to share some photos you took there?"

His questions immediately took me back to Mr. Fingers. Was this a hunt for military information, at the behest of the intelligence service? Or legitimate questions from a half-*shahid* obsessed with everything to do with war?

His curiosity made me uneasy. I had to change the topic. To the coming presidential election, for example. Khatami was nearing the end of his second term. The names of the candidates to succeed him were starting to circulate: Mostafa Moin, the former education minister who had resigned after the repression of protests in 1999; Ali Akbar Hashemi Rafsanjani, the pragmatic conservative; Mohammad Bagher Ghalibaf, a former Revolutionary Guard now tempted by politics; Ali Larijani, the former director of the state television network.

"And you," I asked him, "who are you thinking of voting for?"

"Mahmoud Ahmadinejad!" he replied without hesitation.

Mahmoud Ahmadinejad. An unfamiliar name. Very little was known about the die-hard Islamist, except for the restrictions imposed on the Tehran City Hall, where he had presided since 2003: a ban on municipal employees wearing short-sleeved shirts; a ban on men using the same elevator as women; music concerts in cultural centers replaced by Quran-reading competitions . . . Mahmoud didn't seem to see any drawbacks to any of that; in fact, the opposite. For him, Ahmadinejad was a godsend. He idolized his religious fervor, his simplicity. He told anyone who would listen that his preferred candidate was the humble son of a blacksmith. Ahmadinejad had recently dressed in a garbageman's uniform to prove his closeness to the people. He had even promised to "put the oil money on the *sofreh*," the traditional mat used for eating on the floor. Furthermore, his home was not cluttered up with useless Western furniture. They ate on the floor, with the same simplicity as in Mahmoud's former home in Darakeh.

"And on top of that, he fought in the Iran-Iraq War!" insisted Mahmoud.

For him, it was the ultimate achievement, even if Ahmadinejad's role within the Basij was shrouded by a troubling mystery.

Rumor had it that he had a penchant for brutality against his adversaries. But to my host, these were all superfluous details. Mahmoud immediately identified with this Everyman, a model child of an "Islamic Revolution" that he supported 100 percent. For a week, he had been organizing meetings in his mosque in Darakeh to introduce the "real Ahmadinejad" to a wide audience.

"He's the kind of man we need to stand up to America!" he proclaimed.

I was curious to know how Fatemeh planned to vote. I wondered if she was leaning toward another candidate, as a large number of Iranians were. Or if she shared her husband's enthusiasm for Ahmadinejad. Silent, she had listened submissively without showing the least emotion. I turned toward her.

"And you," I asked. "Do you agree?"

She seemed taken aback that I would ask her such a question; she had grown up submitting to decisions made by men— father, brothers, husband. During Mahmoud's political diatribe, she had simply played with her wet hair. Now she took a deep breath and said:

"I'm not convinced he's the person we need."

Turning back toward her husband, she wore a mischievous smile, as if she had suddenly freed herself of a burden, as if, for the first time in her life, she had fully assumed her right to ask herself questions, to not endorse everything her husband said. Her right to be different.

"MY CONDOLENCES!" On the phone, I immediately recognized Sepideh's voice, drowning in sobs. It was Saturday, June 25, 2005. She was incapable of speaking, still in shock from the unexpected victory of Ahmadinejad. The unlikely president, the Islamist with a goatee and a shapeless jacket, the same man Fatemeh had reservations about, had just won the election. The news came at dawn. Stunned like so many others, Sepideh saw the news as the end of the Iranian Spring.

Yet she had chosen to believe in an impossible seasonal awakening. In the first round, on June 17, she voted for Moin, hoping the former minister of higher education would bring an honorable end to the political impasse solidified by the conservatives. But numerous Iranians took refuge in abstention. After the euphoria of the early Khatami years, they had shunned the ballot box, a protest vote against the political allies of "the Angel" in whom they had placed all their hopes. For them, the season of change had passed. Given the wide spectrum of candidates, no one thought the most radical, Ahmadinejad, had the slimmest chance. In the second round, he found himself in an unexpected face-to-face with the former president, Rafsanjani, who had led the country after the war with Iraq, and who was also said to have profited off the backs of the Iranian people. The matchup wasn't very encouraging, and the liberal press rushed to make a comparison with France, where, three years earlier, Jacques Chirac faced Jean-Marie Le Pen. With a jolt of panic, Sepideh and her colleagues had crisscrossed the city, going from place to place to encourage abstainers to vote for Rafsanjani. "A vote by default," she had conceded.

Fatemeh had also voted for Rafsanjani. The day of the second round, she had invited me to accompany her to the polling station. She had even insisted that I follow her into the voting booth, so she could fill out the ballot beneath my eyes. I felt in her the pride of a woman discreetly emancipating herself from her husband, the sign of a country pursuing, despite everything, a transformation in the shadow of the regime's crackdown. At night, back at home, I found hope again; I was convinced that all was not yet lost. With people like her or like Sepideh, Ahmadinejad had no chance of winning. Especially given that Rafsanjani had gone so far as to send his supporters parading down Valiasr Avenue on Rollerblades, handing out red roses—a symbolic gesture that would surely seduce a lot of young people. But that didn't take into account all the Mahmouds of that other Iran, to whom we Western reporters had less access but who came to the polls in droves. Far from the cameras, they had managed to activate their networks of Basijis, Pasdaran, mosques, and Islamic associations. In comparison with Khatami's lovely poetical flights of fancy, they used simple, concise language and promises of social services that appealed to the destitute and the traditional classes. Ahmadinejad was someone who stood up to the West, against America, someone who promised to turn nuclear power into an instrument of national pride.

When Sepideh called me that Saturday, June 25, to inform me of Ahmadinejad's victory, I understood everything all at once.

"I'm so sorry," I replied to her tears. "You never know; maybe he's not as terrible as they say."

My words rang false, sounded tactless. Between two sobs, she unleashed on me:

"You'll see. It's going to be hell. Hell!"

Sepideh had seen it coming. In the weeks, months, and years to follow, the new president would paint Iran in black. At lightning speed, he reactivated the nuclear program, declared a war of words on America, and set off an international frenzy with calls to wipe Israel off the map.

"WINE OR VODKA?"

Moses Baba, his head emerging from behind a mountain of trinkets, brandished two jerry cans, one filled with a red juice, the other with a beverage as translucent as spring water.

"So, wine or vodka?" he repeated in his mischievous voice, inviting me to sit.

Moses Baba had long performed his ritual of illicit *ta'arof*, his way of resisting. As soon as a visitor popped a head in the door of his small shop, he would immediately pour an aperitif before proceeding to his array of "treasures": old Torah manuscripts, Persian mosaics flanked by the Star of David, Quranic calligraphies, rugs from Isfahan, Qajar dynasty paintings. Often, he assigned them an age as unverifiable as his boast of being honored with a visit from the French actor Alain Delon during the time of the shah. It was over that anecdote that we had hit it off at the beginning of my time in Iran. In a French tinged with a Farsi that reminded me of yours, he told me of his nostalgia for the past, the "golden age" of his small business, when Western tourists still rushed to Iran, a time when his little community, which then included seventy thousand souls, lived in peace on that predominantly Muslim land. A serenity lost in 1979, the starting point of a massive exodus of Iranian Jews to Europe, the United States, and Israel. Moses Baba was the only one among his close relatives to have stayed, with the exception of one brother, Elyas, who refused to speak to him because of a silly financial dispute.

I had unwittingly taken advantage of this familial conflict without realizing it. Like Moses Baba, Elyas was an antiquarian, a niche profession popular among members of that religious minority, denied access to civil service jobs. Coincidentally, Elyas had a boutique on Pasdaran Avenue, opposite your street. I often stopped there, despite his grumpiness, because I knew that you used to go there to bargain hunt. I imagined your eyes riveted to the Persian miniatures that paid tribute to the feminine beauty ruined by the obligatory headscarf. With each visit to Elyas's, I surrendered to the temptation of a ceramic bowl, a kilim, or small bronze birds. My purchases made Mamani balk; she saw them as superfluous expenditures. *Au contraire*, I told myself, becoming Iranian also meant reappropriating a tiny part of your country's heritage.

As I amassed my collection, I noticed that the prices at Elyas's were almost double those at Moses Baba's. The day I mentioned this to him, Elyas jumped out of his seat and spared me the usual haggling, offering me the tray I'd had my eye on at half the price. A week later, I recounted the anecdote to Moses Baba, who burst out laughing: "That's my brother! He's refused to talk to me for years. I've tried everything to reconcile with him, but he hates me." Since then, we'd laughed about this brother who was so bitter that he was ready to sacrifice profits to compete with the only family he had left in the country. "When faced with someone who's trying to do you harm, laughter is an unbeatable weapon!" Moses Baba philosophized; he hoped that, with time, the brotherly tensions would diminish, a motto he preached among his small community, and which he further emphasized when he tirelessly brandished his jerry cans, thumbing his nose at the regime's extremists.

But the Iran of Ahmadinejad was not the Iran of Khatami. Seeing the two vessels dancing above his head, my heart skipped a beat.

"Moses Baba, is that really smart?" I whispered, discreetly signaling for him to conceal his illicit potion under the counter.

Once Ahmadinejad took power, not one day went by without the local press reporting the umpteenth outcry against the "Zionist entity." The new president had made Israel his obsession. Paying tribute to the late Ayatollah Khomeini's way of speaking, he strove to compare this small, controversial piece of land to a "cancer" that had to be "eradicated" at any cost. Once more, Iran's Jewish community felt vulnerable. And the worried eyes of the planet turned again toward Iran. That day, it was an article on this very topic that had brought me to Moses Baba's shop.

"One more threat won't change the face of the world!" sneered the old antiquarian, clinging to his jerry cans.

Then he signaled to Ahmad, his young Afghan refugee assistant, to give me a glass.

"We Jews, we're like fish swimming in a net. When everything is going well, the Iranians leave the net in the water. When things are going badly, they take it out."

I recognized his talent for metaphor, symbolizing the way in which the Islamic Republic used the country's Jews as scapegoats as soon as tensions with Israel mounted. Head in his memories, he continued:

"You remember the thirteen Jews who were arrested for 'spying for Israel.' Some of them were barely sixteen years old! Months of imprisonment, only to finally be freed in exchange for forced televised confessions . . . And that was in 1999, under Khatami, friend to all Iranians."

But Ahmadinejad was going even further. On top of his impassioned diatribes against Israel, he was a Holocaust denier, believing it was a "myth," one he contested in no uncertain terms. An Iranian journalist in exile had even spread the rumor that Jews in Iran would soon have to wear a star. When I brought up that rumor to Moses Baba, he finally resigned himself to putting down his jerry cans. But it wasn't a gesture of fear; it was, conversely, the expression of a man in a hurry to "reestablish" the truth, as he said.

"Let's be clear: all you have to do is watch Iranian TV to see that the Jews always play the role of the bad guy. Thieves, crooks, spies, to name a few. At school, when I was young, children would refuse to drink water from my glass. For them, I was *najes*, 'impure.' Even today, some customers avoid shaking my hand! Obviously, this social discrimination has strengthened since the revolution. But for them to want us to wear distinguishing symbols . . . The regime isn't that crazy! Those are myths spread by government opponents living abroad."

Though he was quick to ridicule the regime, he refused overly hasty categorizations. In Iran, the paradox was that the small Jewish community, though stigmatized, benefited from certain inalienable "rights": they had a representative in Parliament; they had schools, synagogues, a hospital. They could even produce wine, forbidden by Islam, for religious use, on the condition that they be discreet.

"I'll tell you a secret. If they catch me with my jugs of alcohol, the worst they'll do is call me a dirty Jew. But for Ahmad, it's guaranteed prison! Isn't that right, Ahmad?"

Seated on the stairs leading to the stockroom, the young Afghan nodded.

"Imagine: the Afghan refugees don't even have the right to buy a car, or send their kids to school! And we're not even talking about the Bahá'í, hounded by the regime; or the Sunnite minority, denied even mosques."

Eyes riveted to the portrait of Khamenei hanging on the wall, a "decoration" imposed on all shopkeepers, Moses Baba murmured:

"My wife begs me every year to join her in Israel. The truth is that even under surveillance, I feel at home here. Period!"

I was amazed that he didn't practice the "loose-leaf" technique, as those of his religion called it. It was a well-known strategy: a plane ride to the airport in Istanbul; a visa affixed to a piece of paper separate from the passport, to circumvent the ban on traveling to the "occupied territories"; and an incognito trip to Israel during summer vacation! He told me he had no interest, that he didn't see the point in all that secrecy. For nothing in the world would he give up, even for a few days, the taste of pomegranate juice or the scent of saffron. He celebrated Nowruz, the Persian New Year, with the same enthusiasm as Passover. Slowly, he took a jerry can and filled his glass with his bootleg drink. Then he raised it to the sky, saying he wanted to salute Shushtar, the site of the Tomb of Daniel; Hamadan, the site of the Tomb of Esther. And Cyrus the Great, who, according to the Torah, freed the Jews from captivity when he conquered Babylon in 539 B.C. He wanted to celebrate Iranian history and Jewish history. His was a bond that neither Ahmadinejad nor any other president would ever manage to break. And in a fit of hysterical laughter, he exclaimed:

"Going to Israel, to do what? I don't speak Hebrew. It's more expensive. For me, Iran is more tender even than a mother. It's my country!"

IN FACT, IN the Iran of Ahmadinejad, the stars didn't land on the Jews. They targeted students. On campuses, medieval sanctions rapidly put in place began stifling the slightest critical thought. A disruptive student, a star. A disagreeable slogan, two stars. A sign of dissent, three stars. Once you had four stars printed in black and white in your file, which was updated regularly by the disciplinary committee, it was automatic expulsion, for "violation of national security." Professors weren't spared in the hunting down of critical thought. If you were even a little too talkative, you could be fired on the spot, forced into early retirement. In the coming months, the scene grew even darker. Young people were arrested, their newspapers censored, and their friends threatened with the same fate if they, too, dared rebel against the new regulations. In the name of Islamicizing the curriculum, some courses were revised, others eliminated. In this attempt to castrate Iran, thought control was paired with a reconquest of the public sphere. One summer night, the new director of the Amirkabir University of Technology bulldozed the student association headquarters in order to replace it with a prayer room. With the disappearance of that symbol of intellectual ferment, an entire facet of student memory was erased.

At the same time, the Basijis were earning their stripes little by little, once again granting themselves the right to hunt down "poorly veiled" girls. And to mark their territory, they reburied the bodies of some of the martyrs of the Iran-Iraq War on university campuses. The full-scale reforms rapidly overflowed into other spaces. In Tehran, a Quran reading competition was added to rich music programming that dated back to Iran's most open period. In Qom, a Sufi lodge was razed to make way for a parking lot. For those who had witnessed the "cultural revolution" of 1979, this new era reawakened terrifying memories. A veritable machine to crush modern Iran had been set in motion. In the name of an outside threat, sometimes American, sometimes Israeli, Ahmadinejad knowingly declared war on his own people. Each day, he painted the country blacker, a permanent national mourning that stifled absolutely everything, even laughter. After throwing the last buds of the Iranian Spring into prison, he was stealing, from every single Iranian, the desire to breathe. To live.

AMID THIS NEW climate of terror, death came knocking at my door. Over the years, I had resigned myself to being in close contact with it. I no longer kept track of the number of dissident students I'd written about who had disappeared. But those stories were remote enough for me to maintain a certain separation from the daily tragedies. Until that gloomy night when I received a desperate call from an actor friend. On the line, he mumbled that he wanted to tell me a secret, the kind of secret you can't say over the phone. I told him to come over right away. I was at home. When he arrived, his face was so pale, I immediately understood the gravity of the situation.

In a trembling voice, he murmured:

"Do you remember Ardeshir?"

Ardeshir, the young actor who swore only by the theater of the absurd. The mischievous tightrope walker, hero of the *Book of Kings*. A name you don't forget! Right away, I imagined he'd been arrested. Ever since our crazy night at Niloufar's, interrupted by the morality police, I had followed his courageous progression through the twists and turns of Iranian censorship. After *The Blacks*, by Jean Genet, and then a few failed attempts to put on even more risqué plays, he had abandoned the stage for the film set. The seventh art was better paid. It also lent itself to greater flexibility. In theater, as a matter of course, you submitted the script to a screening committee, which then had to approve the final rehearsal before the first show. Once up and running, the play remained at the mercy of a raid by the Islamic morality police, who could cancel it without warning. In one minute, months of rehearsals and years of personal investment could go up in smoke. With cinema, it was different. All you had to do was present a phony screenplay, then shoot the "real" film, while saving a few politically correct sketches to shoot during impromptu visits from the censor. And that was it! Since the revolution, Iranian cinema had even benefited from this subterfuge, to the point of gaining real international renown.

"Cinema, that's just it," muttered our friend.

Cinema. A few months earlier, Ardeshir, at the age of twenty-eight, had finally finished his first feature-length drama. The end of filming coincided with Ashura, the annual period of national "mourning," commemorating the martyr Imam Hossein. Despite the restraint imposed during that Shiite celebration, Ardeshir's friends had convinced him to organize a small party at his apartment in the Tajrish neighborhood. The party was well under way. There were sandwiches, music, a few refreshments, and a password to enter. Very late in the night, plainclothesmen knocked on the door. They said they were the police and demanded that someone open the door. At first, Ardeshir and his partners in crime resisted. They simply turned off the music. But the knocks resumed with greater intensity. The night visitors started to break down the door. The guests panicked. The most acrobatic among them rushed to the balcony and straddled the railing, in order to jump onto a tree and run to the end of the garden. Ardeshir followed suit. He knew that gymnastic maneuver by heart, having practiced it during other parties.

But his apartment was on the fourth floor, and when he jumped, the branch gave way under his feet. The fall was fatal. "His friends immediately brought him to the hospital. The doctors did everything to try to stop the bleeding. Twelve hours later, he died of his injuries," added his actor friend. I was speechless. My tears had swallowed up my words. For days, the incident invaded my thoughts. Even today, I still think about it often. And I try to reconstruct in my head exactly what happened that night, that fatal instant when someone passes seamlessly from life into death. Music blasting, bursts of laughter, undulating dance moves, the scent of stolen freedom. Then the militia showing up, the knocks on the door, the police entering, the guests' pleas, the officers who won't hear any of it, who won't accept any concession, not even a few bills slid into a palm. Finally, the panic, the young people hiding under beds, others who lock themselves in the bathroom or take shelter on the balcony. And Ardeshir, who jumps onto a branch. How many other times had he managed that leap? Often enough that he thought he was invincible. Through practice, it had become a game, a game of heads or tails. And that last time, the branch hadn't held. Ardeshir the acrobat had fallen. Into the void. Death. The end of a dream. Murdered innocence.

DEATH, LIFE. Life versus death. As darkness gradually bled into our daily lives, punctuated by the new president's ominous warnings, a man of rare daring waged a relentless battle against the growing pile of funeral shrouds. That man was Emadeddin Baghi, the former Islamist revolutionary and a longtime journalist friend, an Iranian who never ceased to amaze me with his courage and clairvoyance. After three years in prison, he had regained his freedom in 2003. Banned from politics, he threw himself into social activism by launching a small association that defended the rights of prisoners. He was one of the few people to fight against capital punishment, another growing scourge plaguing Ahmadinejad's Iran.

I absolutely wanted to see him again. His daring was so precious in these particularly somber hours. His office on Haft-e Tir Square had closed a long time ago. He had been forced to put it up for bail and then ended up relocating to the top of a tower on Jordan Street, one of numerous high-rises obstructing Tehran's sky. The window of his new office looked out onto an improbable view: the courtyard of the "stone building," the stronghold of Mr. Fingers and other surveillance officials. I don't know by what coincidence, or coercion, he'd found himself in such close proximity to the intelligence service. Iran was a mountain of indecipherable paradoxes and surprises. I held myself back from asking him, focused as I was on understanding what force enabled him to keep fighting for those condemned to the gallows when he was condemned to his own troubles.

"Life is like the roots of a tree. Everything else is branches. If you take care to water the roots, only good will grow out of them. In other words, if we find a solution for capital punishment, there will be other opportunities for change."

Here was his usual wisdom. For him, there weren't only problems; there were also solutions. On his desk, the files accumulated, each more dreadful than the last: a dissident in solitary confinement, a man sentenced to life for ill-gotten wealth, an inmate cut off from his children. And all those condemned to death by hanging or public stoning for terrorism, homicide, even adultery. Several hundred every year in Iran, known for being among the five countries on the planet administering capital punishment most frequently, including to minors—with the numbers noticeably increasing since Ahmadinejad's arrival. As soon as he heard about a new case, Baghi would go to work finding the person a lawyer, helping the family, alerting the media when necessary. It was such meticulous work. Inch by inch. As a careful observer of his country, he acted from the belief that capital punishment was an act of violence against society as a whole. Abolishing it would ease tensions across the board.

I was curious why he had chosen advocacy as his means of combat, over politics or journalism.

"I don't have a choice. It's the only space left to me." Launched in autumn 2004, his new paper, *Jomhouriyat* (Republican), had been banned after only two weeks. The tightening of censorship had also kept him from publishing his latest work, *The Right to Life*, in which he, a sincere believer and theologian, strove to show that Sharia, Islamic law, was not incompatible with an equitable system of justice—one without capital punishment. For writing articles denouncing that barbaric practice, among other reasons, he had spent three years in prison. But far from breaking him, his prison experience had taught him lessons about his country, its idiosyncrasies and its faults.

"In jail, I spent a lot of time with common criminals. I lived with thieves, drug addicts, petty criminals. We intellectuals have the unfortunate tendency to believe that the rights of man are restored when one of us is freed. But we represent only a minuscule number of prisoners."

Spending three years in a completely different environment had, he said, opened his eyes to the breadth of the gap between the Iranian intelligentsia and the rest of society. In his view, it was this same gap that had brought about the recent victory of Ahmadinejad, with his populist slogans and promises to the poor.

"The reformers have been too focused on abstract notions like democracy, or even freedom. They should have been doing social work. That's what I'm trying to rectify today. In my own way."

His cell phone, atop a pile of documents, started to ring. Baghi picked up. The call was from an inmate at Karaj Prison, on the outskirts of Tehran. Accused of embezzling funds and condemned to ten years in prison, he had heard of Baghi's organization and was calling for help. Baghi scribbled a few lines in his notebook. In his soft, calm voice, he promised to find the man a lawyer. Hanging up, he fixed his gaze on the photo of a bird with folded wings nestled at the bottom of a series of rungs. The poster for his organization.

"There are a lot of prisoners who have no legal defense," he explained. "The majority of them don't even know that they have a right to one. The fact that they call us at all is already a victory. I am convinced that slogans are not what will help us achieve democracy. Sometimes, a simple action is worth much more than countless words chanted at the top of our lungs."

Baghi was a true freedom fighter. While doors were closing one after another, he had turned his organization into the ultimate escape from the censor. Accompanying me to the door, he told me he had a small favor to ask. He had heard about a book by Albert Camus, on capital punishment. He wanted me to help him get a copy, which he hoped to have translated into Persian. I didn't hesitate. I agreed on the spot. You don't refuse that kind of favor. Unwittingly, without thinking it through, I was shifting subtly from journalism to activism.

IN THIS DO-NOT-ENTER, access-denied Iran where everyone was withdrawing into his or her sanctuary, learning your language, Babai, became my ultimate refuge. So far, I had clumsily fumbled with the words, mangled them mercilessly, and I couldn't grasp the richness of their nuances. In fact, I had never made the time to wind between the *alef* and the *jim*, or to teach my pen to navigate from right to left. Ironically, the pervasive censorship gave me the opportunity to immerse myself in the language, for good. By chance, I met Sara, a young researcher in sociology. She was between projects, so she was teaching Persian to make ends meet. In our first class, Sara suggested I explore the language by reading blogs. She had one herself, dedicated to poetry. If you had still been among us, she would have moved you as much as she did me.

I was immediately won over by her methods, so different from the academic model. In those times of repression, blogs were booming. A parallel world, sealed away in the Internet, mocked the censors' archaic scissors. Combining spoken and written language, blogs also offered an ease of access that newspapers didn't: short texts, simple words, sentences with no verbs. An ideal introduction to that overly sophisticated Indo-European language. Farsi, which is written in Arabic script, is an eternal game of riddles. On paper, only the consonants appear. The vowels are contained within little accents, which disappear on computer screens. "Flower," *gol*, can thus be read as *gel*, the word for "mud." With Farsi, imagination is essential to sussing out the meanings of expressions. In your language, Babai, to say "my darling," you write "my heart." Friendship and love are declared through metaphors. A loved one proclaims that he is "the dust beneath your shoes." To express that you miss someone, you convey not solitude but a "restricted heart."

Persian, Sara explained to me, is in a permanent game of hide-and-seek with feelings. You constantly have to read between the lines to discover the real meaning. As if the language itself were designed to resist. In the seventh century, the Arab conquest imposed its alphabet on the Persian people. Under duress, they assimilated the letters of the invader, but were determined to preserve their own vocabulary. After the 1979 revolution, the ayatollahs tried once again to inject Arab words, the language of the Quran, into the spoken language—an offensive against which scholars like you were constantly shielding themselves by reciting rhymes as some recite Quranic verses. Sara, too, made it a point of honor to resist through words. I laughed to see her strive to speak a Persian as "pure" as Saadi's poetry. When I was with her, I didn't say *motshakeram*, derived from the Arabic *shukran*, to say "thank you." I said *sepasgozaram*. A subtle way of signifying opposition to the regime.

Sara was a waifish young girl brimming with energy, a woman-child full of contradictions that she hid behind an angelic smile. She came from a family whose enlightened faith had suffered greatly when the zealots ascended to power. Like Baghi, to whom they were close, her parents had lived through the hope and excitement of the revolution. Very quickly, they made the bitter observation that the Islamic Republic betrayed Islam more than

it served it. Her father, a man engaged in the opposition movement Melli-Mazhabi, religious nationalists, had paid a high price
and ended up behind bars. In her family, there were also *shahids* from the Iran-Iraq War and Mujahedin dissidents, a veritable cross-section of Iranian society, the perfect example of a
heterogeneous Iran. Sara was the real rebel of her family. She
had never joined any political organization. Her permanent penchant for defiance had instead turned her into a *roshanfekr*, a
"freethinker" in the true sense of the word. Married very young,
she confided in me that she had made her divorce a springboard
into freedom, moving alone into a minuscule apartment and
swapping the black chador worn by the women in her family for
a lighter headscarf. At university, the hallways buzzed with rumors when she passed by. She didn't care. At night, after prayer
hours, she escaped by writing poems. Often, inspiration came
to her in the middle of the night. By candlelight, once the city
was sleeping, she unleashed her words in a notebook. Unlike
in the Quran, the verses invoked freedom, love, drunkenness.
Sometimes she would sing while she wrote. Singing behind
closed doors, her precious stronghold. Just like her blog, where
her poetry had taken refuge since Ahmadinejad's arrival.

  With Sara, I gradually became immersed in another world—
that of words, the dance of words. Through our lessons, we
sealed a peculiar pact. She read me her poems as a sneak pre-
view, sometimes testing my progress in Persian based on my
level of comprehension. To prove my dedication, outside our lessons I would copy down the signs on my street that I was finally
able to decipher. She laughed when I told her that sometimes I
even dreamed in Persian. In return, I made fun of her insomnia
when, the day after a long night of writing, she would arrive an
hour late to our meeting. But we wouldn't have canceled our ses-

sions for anything. They constituted our escape bubble. In the *andaroon* of these Persian lessons, once the door was closed, we felt freer than we had ever been. Suddenly, everything vanished: our fears, our inhibitions, our uncertain emotions. We were so different, but with time, she would become my closest friend. That was the force of a common language: Sara was the first person with whom I spoke only in Persian. Thanks to her, I had reconnected with the other half of my identity.

One night, I decided to look again at the poem by Hafez, the one you left me. I felt afraid to confront again those verses and their Persian calligraphy. During my first years in Iran, I grasped only the tempo. But this time, like pieces of a puzzle, each word settled into its rightful place. The rhymes started to tickle the page. All at once, I was finally able to read that ode to the wave, to the voyage, that invitation to venture beyond the reassuring sands of the shore.

"A poem is never finished, only abandoned," said Paul Valéry. Without warning, you had bequeathed a few verses to me. After years of persistence, in the cycle of secret time, the poem about the wave made sense. And so did my life. That night, I realized more than ever that it wasn't just you, my enigmatic grandfather, I had come looking for in Iran; it was also a piece of myself.

WHILE I WAS learning Persian, Fatemeh the militiawoman was starting to learn English. During a dinner at her home, I discovered her new obsession with the language of Shakespeare. She and Mahmoud had just returned from Dubai, their first trip abroad. As mysterious as ever about his activities, he said he'd gone there for professional reasons. She had joined him, eager to window-shop and eat McDonald's in that shopping paradise that had arisen from the desert. The trip had completed her transformation. On the plane back, she devoured *Gone with the Wind*, bought in a bookstore in the Emirates, and shed all the tears in her body. A world unknown to her until then, a world of romance, suddenly opened its doors.

"The book never leaves my side. I reread it every night," she confided in me at this dinner, before making off to the kitchen.

She came back again right away, bearing a tray laden with dishes that were unusual for an Iranian meal: a green salad, some steamed vegetables, and Salisbury steaks.

"It's a 'light' recipe," she announced, eager to mention that she had discovered it on a German satellite channel.

I glanced furtively at the TV. Just above it, in place of the bouquet of plastic flowers, the only decorative element that had survived the move from Darakeh, a box blinked: it was one of those illegal receivers that allow you, with the help of a prohibited satellite dish, to connect to the outside world. In Tehran, all you had to do was count the satellite dishes all over the roofs to understand just how many Iranians violated the rules. In the end, this Basiji couple, too, had surrendered to the temptations of the outside world.

Fatemeh took me aside. She wanted to show me a photo of her slim figure in a bikini, taken with her cell phone in the shade of a hotel room balcony in Dubai.

"Don't tell your husband, okay?"

In fact, she was dying for me to tell Borzou, eager to project an image different from the one her conservative husband wanted to impose on her. During our last get-together, I had introduced them to Borzou. Every six weeks, the *Los Angeles Times* was giving him two weeks of vacation to escape the Iraqi quagmire. Along with the daily attacks on American forces, a religious war had sprung up between the Sunnis and Shiites. Obviously, Mahmoud, the failed *shahid*, had inundated Borzou with questions about the GIs. Fatemeh had dragged me into more intimate conversations about French lingerie.

She kept surprising me. The more time I spent with her, the more I saw her change. After that incongruous health-conscious meal, she started calling me regularly to go get coffee or ice cream. Under the pretext of practicing her English, she always managed to broach subjects that remained taboo with her husband: the contraceptive pill, abortion, love before marriage. She told me I was the only one in whom she could confide so openly. For Valentine's Day, which the hip young people of Tehran celebrated by exchanging little gifts, she offered me a scented candle inside a candy-pink champagne glass. "A token of friendship." She smiled at me. She adored all things kitsch. I had lost count of the number of red, yellow, and gold jewels she wore, concealed beneath the folds of her dark chador.

A few months later, she even abandoned her long, cumbersome veil, replacing it with a more practical headscarf-coat combination. Mahmoud had given in to her whims, on one condition: that she turn back into a black crow in the presence of his parents. Sometimes Fatemeh called me to go for a hike on Darakeh Mountain. At the summit, we met up with her husband to eat a kebab. The roles in their relationship were gradually reversing. He, who was normally so loquacious, always ready to defend Ahmadinejad and Khamenei, stayed in the background more and more. She was the one who, in her high-pitched voice, asked the questions and provided the answers. Astonishingly, Fatemeh was Westernizing at the rate that I was becoming more Iranian. As if we were rubbing off on each other.

I wasn't the only reason for her emancipation. One day, when she had dragged me to her favorite beauty salon, the one that drew the most beautiful eyebrows in Tehran, she gave free rein to her heart. "My sister just got divorced," she announced to me. The mother of two children, she had lost custody, an injustice suffered by a number of Iranian women—which Fatemeh had never realized, conditioned as she was by Basiji propaganda. Suddenly, the suffering of Iranian women exploded in her face. Revolted by the discrimination they were subjected to, she confided in me that she wanted to resume her studies, which she had abandoned after her marriage. It was law that interested her in particular: she wanted to investigate the roots of the marriage laws, to better understand the origin of gender inequality.

Although impressed by her growing empowerment, I was surprised when I saw her, fist raised to the sky, at the progovernment rallies commemorating the anniversary of the revolution or the American hostage crisis, continuing to proclaim her loyalty to the regime. Was there hypocrisy in her approach? Was it a pretext to keep her Basiji card and the social advantages that came with it? Or else another example of Iranian split personality? Fatemeh didn't weigh herself down with this kind of question. She fully inhabited her contradictions. Without reservation, she opened all the doors of her universe to me.

"That's enough political talk!" she said to me that day, in the middle of the small beauty parlor. "Tomorrow, I want you to come with me to a ladies' night!"

It was a "night" in the afternoon, starting at four o'clock. The small party was taking place at the home of one of her Basiji friends, not far from Darakeh. Entering the apartment, I noticed that Fatemeh's revolution had spread to her little world of militiawomen. At the entrance, black chadors hung from a coatrack like cadavers from the gallows. Their owners were already on the dance floor, in the middle of the living room, wriggling to the latest illicit tracks from "Tehrangeles," the "capital" for exiled Iranian singers. Their outfits rivaled one another in frivolity: form-fitting clothing, crimson bras under transparent blouses, fake-leather or leopard-print pants, studded belts. Of all her friends, Fatemeh was the "sexiest," with her exposed stomach and her lacy bustier. I felt like I was at a show. At the hour of the muezzin, I watched them turn the sound off and slip, one after another, into one of the bedrooms for the sunset prayer—only to reappear moments later on the dance floor, as if nothing had happened. Fatemeh was in her element. She shook her wild locks from right to left, like a lioness tossing her head as she escapes from her cage. Seated in a corner, like an anthropologist I took a mental snapshot of each of her gestures.

"What are you waiting for? Come dance with us," she beck-oned.

I hadn't budged from my armchair since the party started. Forcibly pulled up by Fatemeh, I ended up on the dance floor during a Spice Girls song. The women formed a circle around me and started ululating. I raised my hands to the sky, snapping my fingers in imitation of them. While I was dancing, the face of a deceased friend popped into my head: Ardeshir. I thought of our past conversations, of our exchanges on Iranian theater of the absurd. That acrobat had hit the nail on the head. And to think that those who had caused his death were in all likelihood from the same group as these militiawomen in full metamorphosis.

WOULD YOU EVER have imagined what happened next, Babai? Grandmother also joined the resistance.

One morning, she summoned me, triumphant, to her apartment below. Finger pressed insistently on the intercom button, she demanded that I come down to see her as quickly as possible.

"Look at my new outfit!"

She had resurrected her gray raincoat, the one that had survived all those storms. She had meticulously detached the old clasps, replacing them with buttons, perfectly vertically aligned. The golden buttons were hammered with an embossed face of . . . the former shah of Iran!

"I took them off one of your grandfather's old suits," she said.

"And you're going to go out in the street like that?"

"Why not?" she replied, hands on her hips in a gesture of defiance.

Looking at her in that moment, I understood the incredible deliverance a satellite dish could offer an oppressed society. The week before, I had become the latest victim of the magic saucer invasion, giving a dish to Mamani. Since the disappearance of Marie, your mutual "friend," she had retreated into her solitude. I figured that several hundred television channels would give her a bit of comfort, and company. At first, she had a hard time using the remote: she was baffled that sometimes the TV spoke English, sometimes Chinese, not always Persian. But the discomfort stopped abruptly on the day I wrote down the numbers for the Iranian channels, about thirty of them, broadcast from Los Angeles. There was something for every taste: musical, culinary, cinematographic, leftist, anarchist, monarchist. Run by Iranians in exile, they were the "voice" of dissidence abroad.

Mamani rapidly found her niche among the numerous televised debates, broadcast between video clips, in which a motley array of adversaries, experts, and know-it-alls unleashed hours-long, epic monologues on the future of their country. Their acerbic critiques of the regime started to radically reshape her way of thinking. She who had always stayed away from politics suddenly made elaborate speeches on death by stoning, attacks on freedom of expression, the mandated veil. She was unbeatable at naming all the furious ayatollahs, imprisoned students, exiled dissidents—nurturing a true affinity for the son of the shah, Reza Pahlavi, exiled in Virginia with his wife and children.

The episode with the buttons was only the first sign of an obsession exacerbated by the satellite dish. During this time, the heir to the throne, long ago forgotten, resurfaced in the media. He was making the rounds abroad, jumping from one capital to another doing interviews. Mamani could spend entire days cloistered in her bedroom, nose glued to her little screen, scrupulously keeping a lookout for appearances of the young shah. For fear of missing something, she even spurned the intercom. Her preferred mode of communication, the one she had long used to call me incessantly, was not compatible with her new pastime. I thought my ears were playing tricks on me.

One day, while I was sitting at my table, head buried in my Persian homework, the telephone rang. At the other end of the line, Mamani was overcome with excitement: "Quick, quick! Come look at the TV! His Imperial Highness Reza Pahlavi is speaking live!" I bounded from my chair. How could she be so reckless? Saying the shah's name on the phone, under Ahmadinejad's reign, was pretty risky. I hurtled down the stairs and charged into her bedroom. Index finger on my lips, I signaled for her to stop talking immediately.

Eyebrows raised, Mamani looked at me in bewilderment.

"But I didn't say anything bad! What's gotten into you? You're worrying over nothing!" she upbraided me.

I was speechless. There was such irony in the turn of events that had brought us to this moment. After all those years of ostracism and mistrust toward others, it was Mamani who was giving me lessons in courage.

IN AHMADINEJAD'S CORNER of the world, there was no room for critical voices. Nor for discontent. When the bus drivers started to complain, they, too, wound up behind bars—with their wives and children! Those same drivers, symbols of the common people whom the president had promised to support with the country's oil income, ended up paying a high price when they went on strike for better salaries, new vehicles, and access to social services. Upon their release a few weeks later, I received an email. It was summer 2006. One of their leaders, with whom I was in touch, invited me to meet them. They wanted to share their prison experiences, to talk about the threats and the end of a dream for a better future.

I knew the subject was risky, the kind of topic that sparks anger because it "sticks the pen in the wound," as the pioneering French investigative journalist Albert Londres would say.

Furthermore, my press pass had expired a few days earlier. I was waiting for it to be renewed. That same night, I was supposed to meet Borzou in Jordan. We hadn't seen each other in two months. Missing my plane was out of the question. So I hesitated. I was torn between the desire to practice my profession and the fear of exposing myself to risk. But I thought of Mamani's boldness. I also thought of Baghi, his resistance behind the scenes. I felt cowardly refusing the interview. If I declined the bus drivers' invitation, who would tell their story? I picked up a coin. Tails, I would do the interview. Heads, I wouldn't. I flipped the coin with my eyes closed. It flew, bounced back onto the table, and fell flat against the wood. When I opened my eyes, the choice had been made. Tails: I had to go.

I gathered my wits. I had to be especially prudent. As a precaution, I confirmed the meeting by email. At the bottom of my closet I found my longest black coat, and then grabbed the dark veil that went with it. I found an old shopping bag in the kitchen. On my way, I bought a big box of pastries to throw off curious bystanders. A few yards farther along, I hailed a taxi in the street. Under the pretext of a "family visit," I asked a driver to wait for me in front of the building. I climbed the stairs without looking around, as Iranian women do. On the second floor, a door opened. I slipped through the half-open space, mouth stitched closed. The apartment was somber and modest; it smelled like anger. Crouched on the floor, in a concert of whispers, the bus drivers spat everything out: the unpaid wages, stomachs hollowed out with hunger, the political disappointments, the desire to revolt . . .

Leaving the interview, I climbed back in the taxi, shopping bag over my shoulder. In the street, day was fading to night, that transitional moment at the end of the afternoon when the sky is covered in pink streaks. I had only a few hours to write my article and pack my bags before going to the airport. The driver took the first left, then the second right. There was no traffic. Only a few onlookers lost in the half shadows.

The car stopped suddenly. A screech, then the odor of burnt rubber. The taxi driver's grunt. I thought he had a flat tire. I raised my head. Two motorcycles were blocking our path, the same kind that Mahmoud rode.

"Where are you coming from?" barked one of the two
bearded men, brusquely opening my door.

Basijis!

I stuttered:

"A personal visit. A friend's birthday."

He didn't believe me. He repeated:

"Where were you?"

I didn't have time to respond. He was already seated to my
left, in the backseat. His companion had slid into the front passenger seat. Behind the wheel, the driver didn't say a word. He
was scared stiff. I grabbed my cell phone. I wanted to call the
first number on my contact list.

"No!" shouted my neighbor, forcing me to press Off.

Then he ordered the driver to lock the doors. How had I gotten into this mess? Was I under surveillance? Had there been
an informant among the bus drivers? Was Mahmoud, Fatemeh's
mysterious husband, in cahoots with my attackers? These two
bearded men were by no means nice guys. Colossal shoulders,
boxer physiques, walkie-talkies in their hands. It was hot in the
car. My head was starting to spin. I was angry with myself for
playing with fire. Through the window, the sun was waning.
That's when one of them yelled:

"Open your bag!"

I shook my head no. I was afraid of opening it. Afraid they
would find the interview recording. I wanted to protect the bus
drivers. Protect myself, too. The man growled. Got out of the
car. Behind the glass, I saw him tapping on his walkie-talkie.
I imagined he was contacting his superiors. Seated in front,
his associate couldn't see me. I had to take advantage of this
brief instant of madness and fright, when I was invisible to
them. I hastily slid my hand into my bag, searched by feel for

the back of the recorder. I grabbed the memory card and slipped it under my coat before concealing it in my bra. It all happened in a flash. I was covered in sweat. I straightened up in the seat. I couldn't save the notebook and the camera, at the bottom of my bag. I heard the door open again. The giant was already back in the car.

Sitting down again, he yelled:

"The bag! Or prison!"

Prison! I shuddered again, thinking of what I had just done. I lifted my eyes toward him. In the middle of his forehead, his prayer bump stared back at me, menacing. A third eye imprinted between his two eyebrows. Blood pounded through my head. I thought again of my meditation classes. Of those long nights spent preparing myself psychologically in case of an arrest. I had readied myself for this. Listening to the stories of former inmates, I felt as if I had already memorized Evin Prison's layout, its odor, its windowless cells, its interrogations. I knew the glare of the fluorescent lights, the sound of the iron doors, the cries that resounded through the corridors. But fear had left me gutless. In real life, you can never be prepared for an arrest.

"Come on, the bag!"

His voice crashed against the windows. It was an order. A real one. Like a slap, the face of Zahra Kazemi suddenly stung my memory. Zahra Kazemi, a journalist beaten to death in front of Evin Prison in 2003 for refusing to hand over her camera to the same sort of officials. I was paralyzed. I had never felt so vulnerable.

"The bag!" he repeated.

The bag. I gave in and opened it. Without protest, I watched my things disappear into his big hands: my recorder, my notebook, my camera.

Then the giant with the third eye ordered the driver to open the doors again. The poor man was rattled. He was shaking behind the wheel. Before getting out of the car, the officer tore a page from my notebook and scribbled a name and address, which he read aloud:

"Mr. Beheshti, Ministry of Foreign Affairs. He's the one who will give you back your equipment," he added.

He mounted his motorcycle, my things jammed beneath his arms. The other officer followed him, walkie-talkie in hand. Forehead against the glass, I watched them take off like bandits. I was exhausted. I was still shaking. The driver turned toward me:

"Those guys are criminals, Madam! You have to lodge a complaint. Let's go. I'll take you to the ministry right away."

I was touched by his kindness. A Good Samaritan in this hornet's nest.

At the ministry, there was no "Mr. Beheshti" in the roll of employees. And yet it was a rather common name! I showed the piece of paper to a variety of people, everyone from the security guard to the secretary. They all looked at me with pity, probably familiar with this kind of "procedure." I ended up calling the Ministry of Culture. They laughed into the phone: "You should have resisted! They were definitely thieves!" I was enraged. I was convinced that the entire country was conspiring against me. That they were trying to break me. When the taxi dropped me off at home, I rushed to my computer. I had just under an hour to write my article. In fact, I had nothing left to write. I no longer knew how to write. I was afraid of putting the cabdrivers in danger. I called Paris; I explained everything to my editor in chief. The response came like another slap: "I reserved you three columns in tomorrow's paper. You have forty-five minutes to churn something out!" I restrained my sobs. They were the only thing I barely managed to control. I sunk my fingers onto the keys of my keyboard and "churned out" my article. A basic piece, full of generalizations about the country's economy. Without a doubt, the worst thing I had ever written.

The telephone rang. It was Borzou.

"Are your bags packed?"

My bags. Good grief! I had only a few hours before my plane to Amman, via Dubai. I took a deep breath . . . and lied:

"Yes, yes. Ready!"

"How are you doing?"

"I'm fine." What a question!

Borzou wasn't convinced by my response, so I insisted in such a way that he would believe me. I wasn't in a condition to argue. In any event, we would be seeing each other in a few hours. We'd have plenty of time to talk.

Of course, I wasn't fine, not at all. Hanging up, I felt paranoia invade me, as if I were being watched from all sides. I said to myself: the Basij, the intelligence service, the ministry, they are all the same! I called a photographer friend. Without giving any details, I begged her to accompany me to the airport. I was worried about going there alone. I knew all too well that it was crawling with bearded men. Perhaps they had enough time to figure out that the memory card was missing from the recorder? Perhaps one of them was waiting for me at my gate? Perhaps they would escort me directly to prison?

None of that happened. I don't know by what divine grace I arrived in Amman in one piece. That's how it was in the Kafkaesque state of Iran: you could never predict when the troubles would start, nor when they would end. To this day, I still wonder if I was able to leave thanks to a cunningly calculated long-term strategy or a lack of coordination at the intelligence service.

Over dinner, I told Borzou everything. He was furious. He couldn't stand that I had lied to him on the phone.

"What if something had happened to you at the airport?"

"I didn't want to worry you," I replied.

Eyes half-closed, hands on the arms of the chair, he replied: "Worry me? Imagine how worried I would have been if you hadn't arrived in Amman! You think you're invincible!"

"No, I don't!" I said clumsily.

"In this profession," he continued, "there is only one motto: 'Stay alive today so you can keep reporting tomorrow'!"

He stood up. He looked out the window, as if searching for comfort in the calm of that Jordanian summer night. Outside, Amman seemed so peaceful compared to other Middle Eastern cities. Borzou turned back. He sat opposite me. He took a sip of wine. And he said:

"You have to divorce Iran!"

"Divorce Iran?"

"Yes, divorce Iran!"

His voice was serious. He sounded like someone begging an insane person to come to her senses.

"Impossible!" I replied.

How could I tear myself away from Iran? How could I detach myself from it? It seemed too late to amputate a part of myself. Iran, a country I had dreamed of, and reclaimed. I had lived all those moments of its recent history. I couldn't abandon it. Besides, there was no life for me after Iran. That country *was* my life.

Borzou looked me right in the eye.

"In Iran, they decide if you stay or leave. You have already stayed too long. You know too much. They don't like that.

They want to use their power to control you, but you elude them. They don't like that."

I withdrew into a long silence. I felt sobs invade my throat. To avoid crying, I changed the subject.

"And how was Iraq?"

"Oh, same as usual!"

I detected hesitation in his voice.

"Same as usual?"

He was pale; he had one of those looks that meant he was hiding something. After several minutes, he confessed.

"The other day, I went to Najaf. A routine report on the Shiites. At a checkpoint, men with guns made me get out of the car. They were Sunnis. They asked for my papers. I had made sure to leave my American passport at the hotel. I took out the Iranian one. In their eyes, it was hardly any better. They pointed a revolver at my temple. I thought I was going to die."

"And then?"

"And then they let me go. They told me they didn't want to see me again at that checkpoint. It was a really close call!"

I was livid, devastated by the turn our lives were taking. He had lied to me, too. Each of us had used lying as a shield to protect the other. Over time, we had learned to disguise our anxieties within pretense. Listening to Borzou's story, I became slowly aware of the point we had reached: having too long rubbed shoulders with fear, we no longer knew how to live without it. It was as if our bodies were programmed to endure it. We were ruled by fear; our movements made no sense except through fear: how to thwart an ambush; laugh off threats; hear a noise, deal with it; respond to a call; skirt danger. Each time, we promised ourselves it would be the last. And then we'd start all over again. Would we ever be able to live differently?

A few days later, I returned to Tehran. I could not help it. It was an urgent need. The stubbornness of someone lost. The more Iran mistreated me, the more I wanted it. Like a battered woman who refuses to acknowledge her scars. My days ranged between anxiety attacks and incomprehensible pleasure at being there, in the city that made me suffer and that I insisted on loving. And then came an unexpected call from the Ministry of Culture: "Come get your things. They were turned in." On a wooden desk in the Foreign Media Department, a plastic supermarket bag was waiting for me. The "thieves" had returned all my equipment. My press pass, though, would never be returned.

I didn't imagine that the "thieves" would travel all the way to France.

It was an afternoon in May 2007, nearly a year later. I was visiting Paris for a few days. Borzou and I had bought a studio apartment, as a refuge for whenever we needed to unload our stress. That morning, as I dropped off my bags, my Skype started ringing. It was Kourosh, my loyal fixer. He had just come back from a meeting with the intelligence service. The message from his interrogator had been as clear as it was incisive:

"Don't even think about working again with that *haramzadeh!*"

Haramzadeh, "haram child"—"bastard" in more familiar jargon. In Islam, it's a word saturated with hatred and contempt. I was speechless. Me, a *haramzadeh*? They despised me so much that they were trying to cut me off from those close to me. I slammed the door as I left the studio. I needed some fresh air. I ran along the quays, quickly crossed through the Louvre courtyard, then charged headfirst into the Jardin des Tuileries. I ran until I was out of breath. I was sweating all over.

Back at the studio, I felt wrecked. So was my apartment. Someone had forced the window wide open. My Iranian passport had been thrown on the floor. My French ID had been placed on the kitchen counter. I looked, panic-stricken, at the desk: my computer was gone. The hard drive, my portable memory, had also disappeared. All that was left of the camera was the bag. I turned toward the sofa. Laid out on the cushions were our wedding gifts, not a single piece of jewelry missing. Improbable survivors of a shipwreck. I was frozen to the spot. Incapable of even the slightest movement. In a few minutes, years of articles, interviews, photographs, and notes had evaporated. Immediately, I thought of the intelligence service. Were they sending me a final warning? Unless the paranoia gnawing away at me was setting off my imagination . . .

In a panic, I called my mother. My parents didn't live far. I needed advice, a reassuring presence. When she arrived, she convinced me to give a statement to the police. We went on foot. At the station, the officer told me to sit down. In a robotic tone, he explained to me that the neighborhood was "infested" with thieves from Eastern Europe. Undocumented Romanians, experts at quick burglaries. Then he added that it would be best to forget about my computer. That there was no chance of seeing it again. The same speech he must give all victims of theft. Then he asked me where I normally lived. When he heard "Iran," he leaped up from his chair. Within an hour, the judicial police were at the door of my studio. Three of them, two men and a woman, took fingerprints, studied the window opening, inspected every corner of the apartment. Like private investigators on the lookout for the tiniest clue. When they left, they assured me they would do everything they could to find the burglars. "If I were you, I'd say good-bye to Iran," one of them whispered politely before leaving.

When they were gone, I collapsed on the sofa. That sentence consumed me. I repeated it to myself on a loop. The rest was smothered in a hazy cloud. The disappearance of my computer felt like a violation—of my thoughts, of my past. Public life, private life—for the "thieves," there was no longer a border between the two. Our house was their house, if they so decided. In Tehran, in Paris. That day, in the confined space of my Parisian studio, I was faced with a reality I could no longer ignore: Iran wanted me out. Borzou was right: it was time for me to separate from your homeland.

THEY HAD STOLEN my memory; they wouldn't steal my notebooks.

Before giving up Iran, I had to go back one final time. To save the last fragments I had left of the country I had discovered, the scraps of all those years spent winding along the thread of your history. A few days after the burglary in Paris, I took a plane to Tehran. Arriving in front of your building, number 12 + 1, on a street that intersected Pasdaran Avenue, I took the stairs two at a time. At the door to the apartment, I hastily turned the key in the lock. I felt a sense of foreboding; this was the deciding moment. Had some undesirable visitors already been there? I walked through the living room diagonally. Heart in a knot, I opened the door to the office. Seeing my notebooks, I fell to my knees in relief. On a wooden bookshelf that took up an entire wall, there they were, lined up, numbered, arranged in chronological order, perfectly organized since my first trip to Iran, in 1997. My paper museum hadn't budged.

"*Salaaaam!*"

I jumped, raising my head. Mamani was there, next to the door, observing my little circus. I hadn't noticed her arrive. Despite her TV addiction and her tired legs, she had abandoned her TV screen to come up and greet me after hearing the creak of the front gate. She had no idea about all my troubles. I wanted to protect her, delay the moment when I would inform her of my departure.

She walked toward me.

"Look what I just found!"

In her hand was a pile of documents wrapped in cellophane. She said that she had unearthed them from the bottom of one of those old junk room cartons you left her. While I was packing my bags, she was reopening boxes. Her contradictory spirit had always contained something instinctive that never ceased to amaze me.

"Here. It's for you," she said.

I sneezed as I grabbed onto the plastic package. It gave off a strong odor of dust and mothballs. I opened it. It was full of letters: letters from when I was young, the ones I had sent to both of you. Me, in France. You, in Iran. I recognized them immediately. They were intact, meticulously stacked one on top of another. I opened them one by one. I analyzed everything: the paper, the words, the crayon markings. I laughed at my mania for reporting everything in detail: the facts, the dates, the ages. All those margins reserved for the doodles that innocently embellished my stories: the sandbox of the Parc Montsouris, our parents' office, my sister's new doll. All those little nothings that made up our daily life while you were stuck in Tehran during the Iran-Iraq War. In one of the letters, dated December 24, 1981, I had written, "Did Santa Claus bring something for you, too?" In these letters, I rediscovered my yearning to understand things. The pain of distance. The desire to know you. I said to myself: there are no coincidences in life. Just after your death, in 1997, I left for Iran as if in a dream, even if the dream ended up becoming a nightmare. After all, "Perhaps life is just that . . . a dream and a fear," Joseph Conrad once wrote.

Once Mamani had gone back downstairs, I immediately took out my black suitcase, the one I usually carried with me when I traveled, and filled it with my letters and notebooks. Now I needed to find a way to get that precious archive out of the country. I was more and more eroded by paranoia. I saw spies everywhere. On every street corner. Behind every door. Behind every wall with flaking paint. My friends didn't know what to tell me; they were also walled up in their own daily anxieties. "I don't even dare make love to my husband anymore," one of them whispered to me, confiding her fear that an official might be hidden behind the curtains. There remained only the French embassy, the final resort in this impasse. A kind friend at the embassy offices offered to send my bag via diplomatic pouch. I accepted without hesitation.

I waited for Grandmother to fall asleep in front of the TV before I snuck out. I didn't want her to see my suitcase. Then I rolled my bag along the *jub*, the little canal that ran the length of your street. When I crossed paths with three passersby on the way, I startled and sped up. Once on Pasdaran Avenue, I hopped in a taxi. Reaching the embassy had never seemed so perilous. The building was downtown, on Neauphle-le-Château Street, a name that was easy to remember, the same as Imam Khomeini's residence in exile. All the way there, I felt like a fugitive, constantly watched. I trembled at the sound of motorcycles. I lowered my eyes when I saw a beard. Fear is a lead weight when it pursues you. Greeting me, my diplomat friend smiled with compassion. We exchanged only a few words. I was in a rush to leave again as soon as possible.

The next day, first thing, I took a plane back to Paris. Before I left, Mamani hugged me on the doorstep, telling me she would be awaiting my return, and adding that she wanted me to bring her back some antiwrinkle cream. That's how she always made her good-byes. Once again, I took refuge in a lie. I agreed without batting an eye. I feared that she would be abandoned anew to the void to which you had condemned her. I lied to myself, too: the idea that I would never come back was unbearable. When one loves, one forbids oneself from letting love end. When one loves, there is no last time. So, I took off, leaving my apartment as it was: sheets on the bed, towel drying on the balcony, a few chicken skewers in the freezer. Still today, years later, Mamani chides me about those wasted skewers.

At the airport, I wasn't hassled. Not at passport control. Not at the gate. I figured that Mr. Fingers and his shadow men were relieved at my departure. Through intimidation, they had won the battle. A journalist outside the border causes less trouble. A journalist who resigns herself to suffering in silence makes less noise. On the plane, I slept the entire way. The trip had done me in.

A few days later, I received a call from the Quai d'Orsay. My precious suitcase had arrived in Paris. The receiving area for diplomatic pouches was in a building on the street adjacent to the main entrance. I went through a large iron door. An old reflex, I jumped at hearing it close behind me. Would I ever learn to live normally again? A little rattled, I gave a number to the attendant. He disappeared into a corridor before reappearing a minute later.

"It's a black suitcase?"

"Excuse me?"

"I said: a black wheeled suitcase. That's the one you're here for?"

"Uh, yes!"

The small conveyor belt started up automatically. It was cold, the same cold as at the Tehran airport. After a few seconds, my bag appeared. Stuffed like a fattened goose, pregnant with my notebooks. Ten years of reporting. Ten years of my life in a suitcase. It was all that was left for me of your country.

"Thank you!" I said clumsily.

"No problem," replied the official, accompanying me to the door.

And I left, pulling my luggage behind me.

Walking in the street, I felt drops of water on my cheeks. It was raining. The sky was filled with clouds. And I was crying as I looked up at them. I hadn't cried that much since your death.

BORZOU AND I ended up moving to Beirut. After Tehran and Baghdad, it was the city that suited us best. Beirut was a wounded place. Everywhere, traces of the Lebanese Civil War, scars from shrapnel, the imprint of missiles from the last conflict in 2006 against Israel. But it was a "free" sanctuary, perfect for fugitives, suited to all the region's pariahs, those forbidden to speak in their own countries. Beirut, a spillway for subversive ideas. Beirut, a city for escape.

Borzou had just been named Middle East correspondent for the *Los Angeles Times*. A reward for all his reporting in Iraq. In France, the media outlet I'd worked for hadn't offered me anything, apart from their "regret" at my leaving Tehran. And Lebanon was so saturated with independent reporters that I had no hope of freelancing. I was angry at my profession, I was enraged at the idea of coming up against rejections as soon as I pitched an article. But I resigned myself to following Borzou. After all, Beirut gave us the chance to start a new life together. It vibrated with all those little nothings that had vanished from our daily lives: the caress of wind in my hair, laughter on the phone, the pleasure of walking without turning to look behind me. Steeped in paradoxes, Beirut had a unique gift for distracting visitors from their torments. My black suitcase followed us on our move. We no longer had to hide it. To hide ourselves. In Beirut, we finally found a hint of normalcy.

After three years of marriage, it was our first time making a real home together. It was a sight to see us eagerly walking the streets of the Mediterranean city, from house to building, from stairwell to roof deck. Karine, one of the best real estate agents in the Beirut area, convinced us to live in Ashrafieh. It was a predominantly Christian neighborhood, to the east of the former demarcation separating the Christian and Muslim parts of the city. More stable, calmer. After a dozen visits, we found the apartment of our dreams. It occupied half the third floor of an Art Deco building. A Provence-yellow facade, a light-filled living room, a large office, balconies off every room. To the left, a mosque. To the right, a church. At the foot of the building, a sushi bar and a shop selling porcelain dishes. And opposite, the seller of electric batteries who rolled his r's and proudly sported a Mickey Mouse tie.

I felt at home immediately. During the day, we immersed ourselves in the twists and turns of local political conflicts. Come dusk, we flirted with the night, visiting the bars and discotheques of a capital that never sleeps. Good-bye long coats, passwords, the dread of an unexpected visit. We were living in the present. Like the Lebanese, immunized by years of war, we left our worries at the door. Amnesia was our party wear. Comfortable finery for anyone looking to flee her torment. Sometimes we would dance until early morning, before going to eat a *manousheh* while watching the sunrise over the Corniche. On New Year's Eve, we held our housewarming party. We invited about fifty people. Four times that number showed up. The next day, most of the shoppers greeted me at the supermarket. In French. In English. In Arabic. The city was a true polyglot village. My living room, the new neighborhood dance floor.

Lebanon was so much more than that. It was Sunni Tripoli and posters of Saddam Hussein. It was Shia Nabatieh and giant photos of Khomeini. Each city we visited gave us a feeling of déjà-vu. In a country where each community exists only in relation to its religion, Beirut was a multifaceted city. And I was a chameleon. My color changed depending on the neighborhood. In Ashrafieh, I was French. In Dahieh, a Shia Hezbollah stronghold, I was Iranian. Not by choice, but as a result of a simple mirroring effect. Indeed, I was the reflection of what each person wanted to project onto the screen of my face. Depending on their faith, the Lebanese had a surprising tendency to identify with a mother country. They were more French than the French, more Iranian than the Iranians, more Saudi than the Saudis. A survival instinct in that miniature country, so coveted, a permanent theater of proxy wars. I bore witness as I went from one neighborhood to another, scarf sometimes on my neck, sometimes on my head. No matter where I went, I wore Beirut like a custom-made dress. Never had my dual nationality found such a remarkable echo. Like opposites who attract and complement each other, my two halves found their balance.

It was during that time, I remember, that the desire to write came to me. Not an article, but a narrative—the story of the suitcase. Of the letters, the notebooks, the fear, of life unfurling like a wave, of my quest for self. I wanted to dedicate a postmortem homage to you. Without you, there would have been neither wave nor Odyssey. But how to shape this narrative? What to start with? My body was in Lebanon, my heart in Tehran. Words lurched on the page. An excess of contradictory sentiments kept me from gathering my thoughts. I was impatient to unwind that excess of emotions on paper. And yet, I was avoiding it. Each day, I would postpone beginning the manuscript. I felt that your story, my story, wasn't finished. Not yet.

SHIRAZ, TWO YEARS LATER

IT WAS IN SHIRAZ, March 2009, that inspiration finally came to me. For a long time, the city of your favorite poet had beckoned me to return. To explore the soul of Hafez, feed myself with his predictions. An indispensable step in this incomplete rite of passage. Two years had passed since my hasty departure from Tehran. Two years of traveling through other countries of the region, wherever my reporting took me: Syria, Yemen, Oman, Bahrain. Two years of trying to forget your country. Unsuccessfully.

Borzou and I had seriously hesitated before taking this trip. In 2009, the Islamic Republic was celebrating its thirtieth anniversary against a backdrop of reinforced repression. Roxana Saberi, an Iranian American colleague, had been arrested for "espionage." Eaten away by fear, several of my journalist friends had stopped working. Others had chosen exile. Even Mamani had left. After running around in circles in her "gilded cage," she had packed her bags for Paris, where she settled for good, near my parents. If Mr. Fingers decided to remind us of his existence once we were in Iran, we would have no family-related pretext to give him.

But after two years of absence and silence, this trip was far from the usual dizzying roads. It was a trip for *us*, a trip outside time, one that scoffed at politics and the dangers of reality. Upon landing in Tehran, we took the road south that leads to the tombs of the grand masters of Persian poetry. Together, we went to Hafez's tomb, north of Shiraz. A lovers' hideout, an oasis of serenity. Every month, visitors flocked there by the hundreds to place a hand on the mausoleum's cold marble while reciting a few *ghazals* by the great fourteenth-century poet: little good-luck charms that they pinned to their dreams, such as the one with the "wave" that you gave me as a gift. Eyes closed, we silently scrolled through the bygone years on the screen of our memories. There was too much restrained emotion to express it in words. Then we walked along the surrounding paths framed with elegant cypresses. In the garden, springtime scents of rose and jasmine floated through the air. At the gift shop, I bought Hafez's *The Divan* in its original version. My first Persian book without a translation.

Our pilgrimage complete, we went to visit Ali Jafarian, an old musician friend. He opened his door, one palm clutching the doorknob, the other searching for a cheek to kiss. Ali had been blind since fourteen, the result of a bad fall down a set of stairs. But in the kingdom of Islamic morality's paradoxes, his blindness worked in his favor: he was the only man authorized to direct an exclusively female ensemble.

"Good timing. The girls will be arriving soon," he said with a paternal smile.

Walking slowly, we followed him into the main living room. The couches were pushed up against the walls. Beneath a large window, the piano towered over an audience of folding chairs, thirty of them, arranged in rows. At the other end of the room, a woman in a pink top was busy adjusting the sound. I immediately recognized Pouran Dokht, the maestro's wife. That Friday, like every Friday, was a rehearsal day.

Pouran signaled for us to sit down before she disappeared into the kitchen. She came back right away, placing two glasses of cherry juice on a shelf in the living room, next to photos yellowed with time, singing hymns to the past. In one of the pictures, Ali Jafarian shone in his elegant Italian suit, posing next to divas in the days of the shah. As a child, he first dreamed of becoming a sculptor. After his accident, his mother decided to turn him into a musician. A cello prodigy who also had perfect mastery of the piano, he quickly established himself in the microcosm of Iranian artists, jumping from classical concerts to musical accompaniment for pop stars. After the revolution, numerous Persian musical stars fled, but he chose to stay, calmly enduring the police raids in search of "satanic" instruments: pianos, guitars, saxophones . . . Confined to darkness and silence, he discreetly used his talent for the benefit of the young girls of his town who were hungry for cultural escape, giving them music theory classes. Their dazzling progress coincided with a timid opening in the '90s. Under his direction, and behind the black screen of his glasses, one of the first postrevolution female orchestras came into being.

The doorbell rang. It was Bahareh, one of his oldest students. Once she had removed her headscarf, she undid her long braid, restoring life to her beautiful black hair, before tenderly embracing her music teacher.

"*Salam, Ostad!*" she called out to her teacher in a honeyed voice.

Thirty years old, the young woman was radiant in a silk dress cinched at the waist. An architecture student scrupulously attending to her studies in parallel with her music, she was the group's pianist. One after another, the musicians followed. I was amazed to see how gracefully they tried to outdo one another, flirtatious in revealing low-cut tops and heels once they had crossed the threshold. Seated in a corner, I feasted my eyes on this delicious spectacle. Leaning on his blind man's cane, Ali navigated from one to another, complimenting them on their perfume, teasing them about their absences, inquiring about their family lives. There were those who, driven by their possessive husbands, had renounced music, those who came here unbeknownst to their fathers, and those who had convinced their spouses to take classes with the maestro, too. In an Iran divided into bubbles, where everyone put on blinders to survive, Ali Jafarian's house was more than a refuge. It was a haven of peace, a place of resistance, where excellence defied religion and power. A modern metaphor for the garden of Hafez.

I was amazed that Ali's rehearsals had survived the tightening of the screws under Ahmadinejad. Since 2005, several of his concerts had been canceled, often without warning. After a deep breath, Ali leaned toward me:

"How many times have I thought of retiring!" He sighed.

Each time, his students had dissuaded him, threatening to sink into depression if they were deprived of their restorative Fridays. So Ali had given in, haphazardly throwing together rehearsals. After all, that was how he had functioned for years. Without any financial help, he had always paid for the orchestra out of his own pocket: instrument repairs, student meals, traveling to the capital for public or private shows.

"You have to be crazy to be in this line of work. Or else in love!" he said, shaking a tender hand in the air.

And then he burst into laughter.

His laughter was quickly lost in the cacophony of instruments. The girls had taken their seats, were tuning their sitars, adjusting their santurs. In the first row, the daf virtuosos were already making their fingers dance on the tight skin of their round instruments. Helped by Pouran, his wife, Ali took his place facing the musicians, standing behind his music stand. Head straight, chin pointed toward the congregation, he lifted his hands to announce the beginning of the first song.

First there were a few piano notes, then a storm of percussion, and then the voice of the soprano, Dorna, the orchestra's soloist.

My spring, my girl!
Wake up!

"It's a forbidden song," whispered Pouran.

I leaned toward her. I wanted her to tell me more.

"It was written by Fereydoon Moshiri. Then Marzieh sang it."

Those two names alone could have made Ali Jafarian a dissident worthy of being thrown into prison. Moshiri, the love poet. Marzieh, the Iranian diva in exile, a convert to the Mujahedin militant group after the 1979 revolution.

"This song," continued the maestro's wife, "evokes the true story of a certain Bahar, a first name that means 'spring' in Persian. At the time, the young Iranian, daughter of the composer Farhad Fakhreddini, died of an incurable disease, in the prime of her life. To console her father and dear friend, Moshiri dedicated this song to him."

I remember closing my eyes. Attentively pricking up my ears while letting myself be lulled by the lyrics.

Flower of my destiny
Oh sweet blossom
Spring arrives and you with it . . .
My spring, my girl!
Wake up!

That song of death and spring resonated with melancholy and hope. They say that Hafez's verses ease doubts and heal torments. In the heart of that city, within that closed session of the Shiraz orchestra, I wanted to see in that song a sign of possible rebirth.

BACK IN BEIRUT, *The Divan*, by Hafez, had become my wandering guide. A life companion, this little substitute for Iran that would never leave my side, there or elsewhere. It was lying on my bedside table, like a reflection of your memory, ready to supply a few keys to survival in moments of nostalgia. His verses cradled me. They cradled me in the same way as the song of spring, the sweet refrain of hope that inhabited my thoughts. Iranians have a unique tendency to abandon themselves to their destinies, to rely on oracles, imams, fortune-tellers, and poets to illuminate their foggy paths. I, too, had yielded to the charms of prophecy, in Shiraz. Borzou was confused by this. He was worried about my newfound optimism. He who had seen me collapse, six years earlier, under the effect of that Iran Fever, saw this as another recipe for disappointment. He found me too passionate. I accused him of excessive rationality.

Destiny ended up working in my favor. At first, at least. It was a morning in May 2009. In an email once again devoid of explanation, the Ministry of Culture announced its willingness to grant me a new press pass. Three years after the incident with the bus drivers, they were authorizing me to work in Iran again. This astonishing "miracle," a new example of the contradictions of Iranian power, coincided once again with an upcoming presidential election. In a surge of generosity, the regime had handed out more than six hundred press visas to international journalists. Borzou was also on the list of newly accredited reporters. Excited by the news, we packed our bags in a mad rush, leaving behind all our past worries. We were over the moon. The country we so loved and feared was inviting us to return.

On May 29, we landed in Tehran as if in a waking dream. At passport control, the customary pang of anxiety quickly dissipated in an ocean of good feeling. Despite its fluorescent lights, the airport had lost its usual austerity. At baggage claim, some passengers were talking about how they had made the trip explicitly to vote. Behind the glass of the entrance hall, hordes of cousins were waiting for them, arms full of flowers. Outside, the capital was plastered with new posters. Not the usual ones of regime leaders, but posters of three rivals to Ahmadinejad, who was up for reelection. On the sidewalks, streetlights illuminated their smiles. There were lipstick-colored garlands on the trees, carpets of leaflets at each intersection. On the way, the taxi driver confided to us his relief at the mere idea that the warmonger president might be ousted from power: "Because of him, the West takes us for a band of fanatics. His successor, whoever that may be, can only be better."

A strange wave was breaking over Tehran. An unexpected tremor, releasing a sense of revival, a festive air. In a few days, the wave turned green. The symbol of Islam. And of hope, too. Everywhere, green ribbons, green T-shirts, green headscarves, green nail polish . . . Green was the color of Mir-Hossein Mousavi. The primary adversary of the incumbent president had drawn the color by chance at the candidate lottery. Ahmadinejad had drawn red; Mehdi Karroubi, the former president of Parliament, white; Mohsen Rezaee, the former leader of the Revolutionary Guard, blue. Green, one more omen at the heart of what strangely resembled a new Iranian Spring?

June 3 brought a second "miracle." It was around 11:30 p.m. We had just turned on our television. Ahmadinejad took up half the screen, Mir-Hossein Mousavi the other half. It was the first in a series of televised debates the likes of which we hadn't seen in thirty years. To create a semblance of democracy, the Supreme Leader had made concessions to the media. A little hesitant, back hunched, Mousavi first struck me with his lack of charisma. Not much was known about the former prime minister from the '80s, with his gray hair and dark suit. After staying out of politics for nearly twenty years, he had replaced Khatami in this election on short notice, after Khatami had declined to put himself on the ballot. A mediocre orator, Mousavi seemed almost lost, faced with a very aggressive Ahmadinejad. Faithful to his reputation as a provocateur, the president took advantage of the occasion to brandish an illegible document for the camera: "proof," he said, that his adversary's wife had cheated to get into university. Mousavi immediately transformed. He leapt from his chair. His eyes gleamed with anger. In one breath, he retorted, "You are turning this country into a dictatorship!" And then, in an unexpected surge of audacity, he accused Ahmadinejad, haphazardly, of recklessness, instability, extremism, and superstition.

When the duel was over, we went for a walk down Valiasr Street, near the national television studio where the debate had been broadcast live. The streets were packed with clusters of young people draped in green shouting their hopes for restored freedom. Breaking with the self-censorship of the times, a young woman chanted, "Potato government, we don't want you anymore!" It was her way of denouncing the distribution of free potatoes by the pro-Ahmadinejad groups. Gathered around this brazen Iranian woman, the crowd took up the slogan in a chorus. Suddenly, four years of pent-up anger flooded the sidewalk.

In unison, the onlookers started up: "Mousavi! Mousavi!" That night, a new hero was born.

While I was writing my report back at the house, Mamani called me from Paris. She was hungry to know more about the electoral campaign. In her voice, I heard her regret at not being in Tehran. But her political opinions hadn't changed. "It's not an election. It's a selection," she muttered. She meant that the ballot was fixed in advance. That the candidates, whoever they were, had to pass first through the filter of the Guardian Council and then be approved by the Supreme Leader. Therefore, there was no reason to get excited about this temporary craze. I knew her refrain by heart.

However, day after day, the wave swelled even higher. At nightfall, joyous bands of people inundated the streets with their slogans and festive shouts. And then one night, the wave flowed all the way to our place, right under our windows. Drawn by the brouhaha, I went down to the street. At the end of our cul-de-sac, Pasdaran Avenue was swarming with people. A discotheque in the open air. "Ahmadi-bye-bye! Ahmadi-bye-bye!" they crooned. I raised my eyes toward a sign dancing above their heads. "I Will Rebuild You, My Homeland," read the slogan, inspired by a poem by the great Simin Behbahani. As I turned around, my gaze locked on the eyes of a person with a particularly familiar face. I rubbed my eyes to see better. Fatemeh, the Basiji's wife! She was there, in the middle of that excited crowd, wearing her midnight-blue headscarf paired with a coat audaciously cinched at the waist. Pinned to her lapel, an Iranian flag and a photo of Mousavi.

"*Khosh amadid!* Welcome!" she hooted at me, squeezing me in her arms. We hadn't seen each other since 2007. In truth, it wasn't that surprising to find her there, given her transformation over the years. I asked her where Mahmoud was. She shrugged her shoulders with a jaded expression, then pointed her chin in the direction of the opposite sidewalk. Over on the other side of the street, I recognized her husband. He was standing in the front row of a mob as dense as ours. But their signs displayed the bearded face of Ahmadinejad. And the girls on their side were wearing more austere veils. Faithful to his idol, Mahmoud was wearing the same baggy jacket as him. "Tchiz! Tchiz! Tchiz!" he chanted in unison with the crowd, ridiculing the slight lisp of Ahmadinejad's rival, Mousavi. From all around, people chanted the division of a country, one torn between a nationalist retreat and the desire for openness. Two opposite sides of the same coin. Two equal weights on the same scale. A few days from the election, Iran was cut in two (mirrored by this Basiji couple) and in all likelihood destined for a second round between the two main rivals.

And then, an unexpected turning point: all those Iranians—those disillusioned people, that silent mass so disappointed in the reforms, all those absent from the 2005 polls—renouncing their temptation to boycott the polls, started to speak up again. "It's best to choose the lesser of two evils" was their new adage. Among them were many women, many young people, carried by a common desire to take their destiny back into their own hands. Each day, there were more of them marching in the streets, jumping from a human chain to a pro-Mousavi concert. They marched as if surprised by their own courage, children on their shoulders, brimming with smiles. They marched while inventing slogans, as if composing melodies. Often, their slogans took the form of jokes. One of them: "Why does Ahmadinejad part his hair down the middle?" "To separate the male fleas from the female fleas." After four years of restraint, the public space had become an arena of so many possibilities.

On June 10, the last official day of the campaign, I briefly met Sepideh, my journalist friend, between two interviews. Since the start of the campaign, she had been racing between political meetings and street rallies. This new détente climate finally allowed her to write reports without having to self-censor. She exulted: "We've already won. It's the happiest day of my life!" In her fit of laughter, I immediately recognized the same enthusiasm she had shown at the end of the '90s, a hunger for life that had astonished me ever since we first met. Then she stopped and looked at her watch. "I have to go. I'm already running late with today's article. Let's see each other on the day of his victory! I'll bring cakes!" she yelled, before kissing me good-bye. I was captivated by her bubbly energy, such a contrast to the doom and gloom of these last four years. It was a spring without equal, a season of brio. I was starting to believe it as much as the Iranians. After all, maybe Mousavi did have a good chance of winning in the first round.

But in the crowd, I noticed more and more cameras filming the marchers, bearded men on motorcycles zigzagging from one cluster of people to another. That very morning, a leader of the Revolutionary Guard had dared compare Mousavi's campaign to a "velvet revolution." But the magnitude of the joy had chased away all fear, and no one paid him any mind.

On June 12, Election Day, the same enthusiasm poured out as citizens cast their votes. Several times, the authorities had to postpone the closing time for polling stations. When voting came to an end at 10:00 p.m., the polls already showed a record participation rate of 85 percent. It was as if a new Iran were being born. Driven by the ambient euphoria, I went back to the apartment on Pasdaran Avenue. My taxi drove past the skyscrapers, windows open to the wind.

In a concert of honking, a car overtook us. I raised my head.

Seated sidesaddle like an Amazon warrior across the rear door, a young woman mischievously waved her green headscarf into the night. Beneath the stars, her brown locks danced the farandole. Free, lighthearted, brazen. One last "click" capturing a city drunk with hope. One last vision to remember from that night, just before we crossed the threshold into the surreal.

"IT'S A COUP D'ÉTAT!"

On the phone, Sepideh was crying. It must have been around 10:30 p.m., that same June 12. Words garbled with tears, she added:

"Mousavi's headquarters were attacked by the Basijis. It happened a few minutes ago. I was there. They broke the computers, tore the posters from the walls . . . The leaders were taken away by the police. We don't know where they are now."

Her voice was lost in a thick silence. I tried to call her back. Without success. Her phone rang and rang. A few minutes later, my phone vibrated. I picked up quickly. It was one of Mousavi's representatives. An impromptu press conference was about to be held. He begged us to come as soon as possible. On the way, we made a flurry of calls. Well-informed friends confirmed Sepideh's fears: in tomorrow's paper, the conservative journal *Kayhan*, already going to press, was running a headline about Ahmadinejad's victory.

"I won the election. This is electoral fraud!" Mousavi yelled from his improvised podium.

He had just begun his speech when we arrived. In the confines of this little office in the middle of Tehran, a crowd of journalists huddled around the reformist candidate. Statistics in hand, his advisers said they had proof of his victory. The massive turnout of the youth and women had clearly worked in his favor. Circles under his eyes, face lifeless, Mousavi added that he refused to concede defeat; he would fight to the end. And then he disappeared through a small hidden door. Outside, a leaden silence crushed the stunned city. On the way home, I called Sepideh. She finally picked up.

"This time, the Basijis attacked the building of *Qalam-e Sabz* [The Green Pen], Mousavi's paper! I fear the worst," she said.

Something alarming was happening. But we were completely incapable of gauging its scope.

The next morning, the shockwave had made its way through Tehran. On the radio, a presenter played on a loop the announcement of the landslide "reelection" of Ahmadinejad, while rumors were already going around about Mousavi's house arrest, as well as those of other moderate candidates. In the street, shared taxis had transformed into places to let off steam. Borzou and I hailed one on the move. Once the door was closed, I turned on my recorder. The passengers were angry; they all wanted to talk. Beside himself, one of them started to tell us how campaign offices had been ransacked. A second affirmed that he had heard that activists were being arrested. He reported that he had also seen, the day before, with his own eyes, members of the reformist camp being held back from numerous polling stations. Another complained about no longer being able to send text messages, which were being completely blocked throughout the whole country. And then a collective lack of understanding: How can you claim a transparent election when the results are announced right after the polling stations close?

"They didn't even bother to count the votes!" the driver choked out with rage. "It was a fraud. I swear to you, a fraud! Write it in your papers! Ours are on the way to extinction," one of the passengers added. He was wearing a green T-shirt with blue jeans, on which the letter *mim*, Mousavi's initial, had been embroidered. He was enraged. He believed Khamenei was behind the fraud. That he had been overwhelmed by the extent of the pro-Mousavi excitement. That in the eyes of the Supreme Leader, the victory of the new "hero" put his own regime at risk. So he had blocked it. Just like that. No negotiation.

My telephone vibrated again. Another press conference was being held, this time at the headquarters of *Ettela'at*, the Persian-language daily. I asked the driver to take me there. Before I arrived, the police had already shut the place down. Along with Borzou and a few colleagues, I took refuge in a café on Valiasr Street. On the sidewalk, a young boy discreetly handed out leaflets. Calligraphy in black ink read, "Meet at Vanak Square to denounce the coup d'état." We weren't far from the rallying point. We rushed over.

"Where is my vote?" Fist held toward the sky, a young woman split the silence with a broken voice. Her words immediately ripped the tape from the closed lips of the first arrivals. "Where is my vote?" the crowd repeated in unison. Others took it a step further: "Death to the dictator!" "Death to the coup d'état!" There were hundreds of people gathered at Vanak Square. A swarm of disgruntled voters was growing rapidly. Men in overalls, disoriented students, old men in slippers. And then, suddenly, that metallic screech of chains lashed the cobblestones.

Riding on their Hondas, the Basijis charged at the protesters. Someone yelled for everyone to disperse. Fast. We ran with the crowd. A dislocated, nonsensical movement that zigzagged between cars. The roar of the motorcycles followed us. Along Valiasr Street, the stores lowered their iron shutters at the same speed as our frantic race. By some miracle, we ended up in a bookstore. The owner closed the door behind us, turned off the lights. In the dark, I could make out only shadows. Fugitives were jammed like sardines among the books. Next to me, a woman burst into tears. She was wearing a long chador, as black as the bruise blooming around her right eye. She had just been hit with a baton. She was sobbing, saying the regime had "betrayed" her: "I was part of the revolution. I believed in Khomeini. I gave martyrs to this country: my husband, my brother . . . And see how they thank me! By attacking me because I defended my right to vote! The regime is devouring its children. The trust is broken." I took a tissue out of my pocket. I handed it to her. Faced with her despair, it was the only gesture I could offer.

That night, I called Sepideh. I knew her fervor too well. I wanted to be sure that she was safe and sound. Her phone was off. Not even a ringtone. And Mahmoud and Fatemeh? Where were they during all this? Did they feel like victims of a "betrayal" like that ex-partisan of the regime, who yelled her disappointment into the face of a system she had supported her entire life? Or were they among those enraged militiamen chasing protesters at breakneck speed? I called both their numbers several times. They never picked up.

A rash of insomnia kept all of Tehran awake that night. Around the city, hotbeds of protest had broken out. Borzou and I went back out in the street. For hours on end, we walked along the raging streets, through clouds of tear gas, avoiding flaming dumpsters. On a bridge, protesters and Basijis were fighting, throwing stones at one another. Real urban guerrilla warfare like I had never seen before in Iran. Farther on, police vans were taking wounded protesters to who knows where. At Mohseni Square, riot police, resembling RoboCop, were making the rounds. We skirted them by taking side streets. As we turned down a back alley, danger caught up with us. Twenty Basijis on motorcycles stormed into an intersection. Borzou pulled me by the sleeve, just in time for us to hide behind a double door. In the dark, I heard them strike the air with their iron chains, like lions let out of their cages, before taking off in pursuit of protesters.

Breathless, we walked to Jordan Avenue. Behind their wheels, hundreds of drivers were protesting by honking their horns. When the militiamen reappeared on their motorcycles, we jumped in the first taxi to escape their attacks. We rode north. Passing in front of the stone building that was the illustrious landmark of the intelligence service, I shuddered. Was Mr. Fingers at the window, mocking this assassinated spring?

And then, a few yards from there, something happened that I will never forget. A protester fell, unconscious, beneath a torrent of blows. There were ten militiamen, maybe more, pummeling the poor man. A female protester in a black headscarf who had come out of nowhere hurried toward the window of our taxi. She didn't want our help; she just threw her bag on the backseat, begging us to look after it. And then she set out, head lowered, toward the group of Basijis, before collapsing in her turn beneath their blows. In the chaos, the taxi took off again. We could do nothing to save her.

Once back at the house, it was impossible to fall asleep. After walking in circles around the bag, we opened it. Without knowing us, this young stranger had entrusted her entire life to us: cell phone, wallet, keys to her apartment, ID card. A laminated document indicated that she was an architect. And where was she now? I couldn't stop myself from thinking the worst. I imagined she was gone forever. I thought of her parents, eaten up with worry. I opened her address book in search of a number to call. I wanted to give them what remained of their daughter. The book was empty. Around four in the morning, I nodded off, head on the blank pages. Suddenly, an unexpected melody, between an alarm clock and a cell phone ring, wrested me from my sleep. I opened my eyes. It was past noon on June 14. The stranger's cell phone was vibrating repeatedly. I picked up.

"*Salam*, it's Anousheh."

Anousheh! My heart leaped to the ceiling. I recognized the name printed on the ID card.

"*Salam!*" I replied enthusiastically, as if I had found an old friend.

"You . . . You have my bag?"

"Yes, of course!" I answered, giving her our address right away.

A few hours later, she rang the intercom. I pressed the button to open the door. In the stairwell, I saw a young woman come up the steps limping, eyes creased in pain. I took her arm, closing the door of the apartment behind us.

"Look what they did to me!" she moaned.

Then she took off her coat, pulled down her pants: her legs were lacerated with marks from the militiamen's blows.

"I wasn't even protesting . . . I only rushed over to help my brother. He had just been arrested. When I saw him collapse, I hurried to help him. The Basijis beat me up . . . Then they took both of us to the police station in a van. They kept us there all night before letting us go."

Her translucent face betrayed a profound lack of sleep. I still couldn't get over the fact that she had trusted us enough to give us her bag.

"Oh, a survival reflex!" she replied. "If something had happened to me, I at least wanted people to know where I had disappeared from. And also, I trust my people. Iran is a country of benevolent souls. By manipulating the election, the regime achieved only one victory: they brought us closer together. From now on, I will protest every day, in solidarity with my fellow citizens."

"Did you vote?"

"No. I've never believed in the system. Powerless to change it, I ended up resigning myself to it."

"So why take to the streets?"

"Now something different is happening: Iranians were tricked by a semblance of democracy. They came out to put their votes in the ballot boxes. And now they're being punished for voting. It's unacceptable! I'll protest for my compatriots' choice to be respected. And to be done with Ahmadinejad, Khamenei's pawn! You heard his speech today: he dared to call his opponents 'garbage.' It's scandalous! We're so sick of his arrogance. It's waking up even the most comatose among us."

I watched her speak, waving her hands. Sometimes a grimace betrayed her pain. Anousheh was one of those heroines from the shadows who defied suffering as she defied danger. Would Iranian women like her be the ones to rattle the regime?

"Pandora's box is open," she whispered. "The genie won't go back in the bottle so easily."

THE NEXT DAY, the unimaginable unfolded in front of my eyes. One of those magical moments when you would have been right at home, my epicurean grandfather, the aspiring poet, the passionate democrat. It was June 15, Khordad 25 in the Iranian calendar. I've kept the planner I had back then, the date circled in permanent ink. Beneath it, I scribbled a small note addressed to you. I told you how moved I was at having found all your ideas assembled in a single protest, the most dangerous and the most beautiful I had ever witnessed.

That morning, Mousavi the "hero" had canceled a heated protest for fear of a bloodbath. But the most audacious dissidents planned to meet at Enghelab Square at the end of the afternoon. Borzou and I headed downtown, our reporters' notebooks hidden in our pockets. The riot police were on the lookout. Spread around the University of Tehran, students formed mobile clusters. Their frozen faces revealed the uncertainty of the moment. They advanced slowly, brushing the windows of bookstores, exchanging a few furtive words, then walking a bit farther down the road. There were girls, lots of girls. With blue headscarves, red headscarves. And green, too. I lowered my eyes. They were all wearing sneakers. A sign: those girls were prepared to protest. And to run if needed. We followed them down Enghelab Street, toward Azadi Square and the unknown.

A stubborn silence accompanied our march. At the next inter-section, stray onlookers joined the movement. It was as if they had been waiting for this gathering to give meaning back to their miserable day. And then we passed other intersections, other streets, other buildings. And other protesters. I saw grandmoth-ers veiled from head to toe, businessmen with briefcases, work-ers in overalls, disabled war veterans in wheelchairs, children on their parents' shoulders. I observed them, their gazes to the sky, their moon-shaped mouths ready to shout their slogans at the signal.

In less than an hour, these little disjointed links had formed an immense human chain. Next to us, two old gentlemen, hand in hand, started belting out, "Give us back our vote!" One of them said that he hadn't left his home in a year. He added, "For how long have I dreamed of this day? Sometimes I closed my eyes, cried, and imagined this moment. And here it is before my eyes. Anything can happen to me now. I could die happy." He was trembling all over, stunned by his own feelings. And I listened to him as if it were you speaking. Farther on, a woman said that she had driven straight from Shahriar, about an hour from Tehran. She and her neighbors had rented a minibus to come protest. Her husband didn't know. "Down with the dictator!" she yelled. "Hey, Nuclear Ahmadi, give it a rest— you're tired!" added one of her companions. In Persian, the slogan rhymed. Even when they protest, Iranians express themselves in poetry.

Borzou and I went up on a bridge. The human wave un-furled as far as the eye could see. In the middle of the avenue, crammed on the sidewalks, on top of bus shelters, hundreds of thousands of Iranians were marching. Behind us, someone murmured that there were a million people, maybe two million.

Leaning over their balconies, onlookers cheered the absence of the police. Deterred by the size of the crowd, the security forces had vanished. Only a few helicopters skimmed the rooftops from time to time. Later, we learned that Mousavi had even risked a brief public appearance before disappearing again. I thought once more of the protests on Enghelab Street in 1999. Ten years later, the stifled cry of students had evolved into a cry of national anger that transcended generations. For the first time, all of Iran was in the street. An ocean of rebels.

The movement slowed as it approached a building guarded by Basijis. In this hive of activity, a few young people volunteered to form a protective barricade. A woman chanted at the top of her voice: "Don't be afraid, don't be afraid. We are all together!" Like a refrain, the crowd repeated her slogan. And then all that was left of fear and sadness was erased under the protesters' steps. The street was pulsating. The sun was splashing their faces. The light was warm and reassuring. I let myself be blinded, guided only by the sound of our steps on the cobblestones. I had lost Borzou in the crowd. I was alone in the middle of all those strangers. But unlike in 1999, I understood all the slogans, all the words, all the gestures. For the first time, I understood Iran in its entirety. I'd had to wait all those years to be able to penetrate its secrets. Beneath my eyes, in that defiant crowd, an entire country was revealing itself. Proud people, infatuated with democracy, were discovering that they existed; they were waking up in unison. Old men, zealots, disillusioned bearded men, the unemployed. The noose might tighten, bullets might whiz by, but, I told myself, never, never again would this pulsing wave of life be subdued.

At that moment, dear Babai, something inside me broke away. Anguish left me. I felt like a little link in that chain of rebels. I found something in their fight that resembled your convictions. My convictions, too. They were marching. We were marching. I was marching. Toward an unknown we no longer doubted. I had seen Enghelab Street red with roses, then with blood; now there was nothing left but the present, visible, the force of a desire for justice that grew with each second. The horizon was boundless. That march, although slow, resembled a frantic race, a dance that was brazen, uncertain, terrifying, and happy. It sucked me in; it filled me up. The world had grown larger around me, like an uncharted territory whose borders were constantly receding. In the middle of all these anonymous faces, I had forgotten my name, my profession, where I was, where I came from. My life melted into theirs. I was Iranian. We were all Iranian.

Back home that night, your memory continued to invade my thoughts. At the entrance to our street, normally so calm, a concert of *"Allahu Akbar"* rained from the sky. It wasn't the traditional call of the neighborhood mosque. It was a gentle, sinuous clamor, a chant that slid along the walls, caressed the leaves of the trees, and enveloped the melody of the *jub*. Intrigued, I opened the door to the building and climbed the steps that led to our roof, which hid our forbidden satellite dish. The chant amplified, grew closer, intensified. *"Allahu Akbar* . . . Death to the dictator!"* The voices answered one another from roof to roof, in perfectly orchestrated rounds. In a circular movement, I scanned the other roofs. Through the mesh of the black sheet of night, I recognized the faces of all those strangers I had walked past for so many years. The zealot neighbors from next door who got on our nerves with their litanies during the religious festivities of Ashura. The apathetic bourgeois who lived opposite our house and collected luxury cars. The old lady from the end of the street who never left her home. *"Allahu Akbar . . .* Death to the dictator!" Those people didn't know one another, perhaps detested one another. They probably had never spoken. But there they were suddenly chanting "God is great" in one voice. From one house to another, from one roof to another, they took up this rallying cry as their chorus, a strange echo of the 1979 revolution.

I thought again of that period, of your generation's revolt. Of that age when, at twilight, Tehran echoed with the same chant in the hope of overthrowing the shah. Through protesting, resisting, the dissenters had brought about the fall of the monarch. Would it be the same this time around? Would the Iranian people be heard? Would that astonishing national awakening bring down, if not the Supreme Leader, then at least Ahmadinejad? In 1979, passions had crystallized around a man, Khomeini, and an ideology, Islam. It was one of the reasons you stayed out of it, little inclined to sell your soul in the name of any dogma. This time the revolt was different. The movement had neither leader nor motivation other than respect for the people's choice. That was its weakness but also its strength. I asked myself what role you would have played. If, like all those rebels, you would have ascended to the roofs in protest. If you would have hummed *"Allahu Akbar,"* a chant of resistance henceforth stripped of its religious texture.

I wanted to call Mamani. I was curious to hear her opinion. In her apartment in Paris, she was stamping her feet at not being in Tehran. As when she was in Iran, she spent her days flipping between various satellite channels. In the course of the conversation, she was the one who told me that, at the end of the day, the protest on Enghelab Street had descended into violence after reaching Azadi Square. Several protesters had even fallen to Basijis' bullets.

"What do you mean, you didn't know? You're the journalist!"

In Tehran, text messages were blocked, and the Farsi BBC and Voice of America were jammed, complicating access to information. Internet filters made our task even more difficult. Apart from wildlife documentaries and video clips depicting the glory of the martyrs of the Iran-Iraq War, the state television didn't show much.

"Oh, and have you heard the latest? They're saying that some Iranian diplomats posted abroad are starting to quit," continued Mamani, triumphant.

At the other end of the line, her voice sounded young again. She told me she had heard this news about multiple resignations during a protest that day in front of the Parisian embassy of the Islamic Republic, on Avenue d'Iéna, in the sixteenth arrondissement. I thought I had heard incorrectly. I made her repeat it.

"You mean you went to a protest?" I asked.

"Well, yeah," she retorted, as if it went without saying.

I was astounded. Mamani, too, had joined the farandole of the unruly. Young Anousheh had been right: the entire population was waking up. Including your wife, the professional grinch, transformed late in life into an Iranian Joan of Arc. Before going to sleep, I replayed her words. If you had still been in this world, how would you have greeted her metamorphosis? I let myself imagine that you would have been seduced by her fervor. And that you might even have fallen in love with her again, this time for good.

THE NEXT DAY, I was finally able to see Sara, my Persian teacher. Since my return to Tehran, we'd had to keep postponing our reunion, repeatedly compromised by current events catching us off guard. Sara was particularly busy. During the day, she protested. At night, she went in search of her missing friends: she knocked on their parents' doors, made the rounds of the hospitals, visited the morgues, prowled around the prisons.

"Here. This is for you," she said, taking a surgical mask out of her bag.

This was the new shield for protesters. A modest armor to protect us from the tear gas. On the way over, she had taken time out of her busy schedule to stop at the pharmacy in her neighborhood before they ran out. In Tehran, these masks broke sales records. Sara wanted me to wear one, too.

"Can you imagine me wearing this?" I responded.

Actually, her gift couldn't have come at a better time. That morning, all press passes had been revoked. Several visiting reporters had received visits from the intelligence service in their hotel rooms. Others had been escorted to the airport. The order had been given from the Ministry of Islamic Culture and Guidance that we were no longer to set foot at the protests. I had to find a way to continue my reporting without being seen.

Facing the mirror, I pressed the square of fabric against my mouth. And as usual, I hid my hair under a black headscarf. With my sunglasses on top, I was unrecognizable.

"Perfect!" Sara said, proud of her find, inviting me to accompany her to that day's rally.

As a precaution, my notebook and camera were to stay at the house this time. Sara assured me that my cell phone would be more than enough. I took her advice. Before leaving, I turned to face her. Apart from the color of our headscarves, we were dressed like twins.

The procession began at Vanak Square, at around 5:00 p.m. Sara had received the details, scribbled in green felt-tip pen on a banknote. With no text messaging, this was the new way of passing on information. Sometimes, the banknotes could turn into antiregime pamphlets. Or even into poems. When we arrived, I saw the same mix of fear and audacity as the day before, the same brazen slogans. On a sign held overhead, someone quoted Mahatma Gandhi: "First They Ignore You, Then They Laugh at You, Then They Fight You, and Finally, You Win." Farther along, another protester was holding up the portrait of Ayatollah Montazeri. The day before, the turbaned wise man from Qom had emerged from his shell, calling for three days of national mourning in memory of the dead of Enghelab Street. Sara and I plunged into the wave. We marched side by side, accomplices on the same quest. A solemn calm accompanied our steps. The crowd was dense, faces on alert. An extraordinary scene I couldn't photograph. All those gleaming eyes I would have liked to immortalize. Then I saw Sara raise a hand in the air, the lens of her cell phone pointed at the crowd. A second cell phone followed. And a third. And a fourth. And then dozens of others. The hands were those of protesters. Holding tight to their cell phones, they filmed history in the making, the history that we, professional reporters, no longer had the right to document. True citizen journalists, at once participants in and witnesses to their own history. Without our having noticed, in the course of these events, a surprising switch had taken place. Sara, photographer by default. Me, impromptu protester.

In the following days, the little ritual happened again, even spreading to the sleepy provinces. At the end of each march, the next day's plan was announced by word of mouth. Or sometimes simply on pieces of cardboard exchanged between two subway cars during the protests. It was a moment of great conviviality. New friendships formed. Colleagues who had never spoken discovered one another. As soon as a protester learned that a reporter was among them, he or she would offer that person fruit juice and hugs. But each day, the regime's frayed nerves pushed us to redouble our caution. Borzou and I often went out separately, to dodge the intelligence service. In the crowd, he went by the name Behrouz. I was Élahé. It was the first time I had ever used my middle name, my Iranian name.

Our daily life had gradually taken the form of a play in which we were condemned to wear masks in order to keep on documenting what was happening. And to stay alive. It was a time of hope and apprehension. We didn't know what had happened to the majority of our friends. People said that Evin Prison was overflowing with prisoners. Never had we been so close to being behind bars. To this day, I still don't know what compelled us to take to the streets despite everything: passion for our work, love for country, addiction to risk, adrenaline. Or all of it combined.

On June 19, the Supreme Leader made his choice. After a week of silence, Ayatollah Khamenei stood with Ahmadinejad. Despite calls for a new election. Despite thousands of protesters in the streets. He made one speech, only one, delivered at the time of the Friday prayer. In his own words, he said that the party was over. That the rallies had to come to an end. Under threat of severe punishment. The speech issued a carte blanche to the Pasdaran and their paramilitary, the Basij, to repress all those who opposed the forced reelection of Khamenei's protégé.

By the next day, the face of Tehran had changed considerably. Like an open-air prison, the city was locked down by the police and riot squads. But the protesters persisted. All over the place, improvised gatherings defied the tear gas. There was indignation in people's wounded gazes. For two hours, I marched along the panic-stricken streets before turning back down Kargar Street, lined with flaming tires. It wasn't only Ahmadinejad who was targeted by the chants, but also the Supreme Leader. In one night, hope for a peaceful resolution to the crisis had been transformed into screams of rage against the Islamic Republic. In the middle of the road, a protester had transcribed his hatred in white chalk. DEATH TO KHAMENEI, his message read in Persian calligraphy. In the middle of the crowd that had come to applaud this subversive work, a man yelled, "Ahmadinejad commits crimes. The Supreme Leader backs him up." And he threw stones in the direction of the riot police. A roar of motorcycles muffled his words. Batons in their hands, the Basijis charged the crowd. The man fell backward, face bloody. The wave broke, crashing against the pavement of adjacent streets. Along with other protesters, I wound up pressed against the door of a building. It buckled under our weight. We dived into the stairwell. On the first floor, a grandmother in a chador offered us orange juice on a plastic tray. Another distributed bandages to wounded protesters. One of those surreal scenes that spoke volumes about the surge in mutual support emerging at every level of society. We climbed to the roof. It was packed. A makeshift refuge between two street battles. The tear gas seeped through the bars of the railing. It stung our eyes.

"I can't see, I can't see!" a woman was moaning when the first bullet whizzed by.

A leaden silence immediately stifled her cries. Our small group froze. It was the first time in Iran that I had heard such a close shot. A real bullet, no doubt. I shuddered, thinking of the stranger who had been hit in the middle of the street. And then came another barrage of bullets, this time farther away, followed by a confused commotion in the street. The sounds of chains and cries and tears mixed together. I peered through the railing. Below, the last protesters were dispersing in a surge of panic. "They're killing us! They're killing us!" one of them screamed. In the distance, the militiamen were only small black shadows. From the roof, we followed their trajectory before watching them disappear down a small side street. Someone whispered that it would be best to wait on the roof before going back out. So we stayed there, frozen in fright, caged up with the same macabre thought: a few minutes earlier, and that bullet could have killed one of us. In Tehran, no one was protected anymore from the violence unfolding over the city.

A half hour later, we recognized with relief the familiar

concert of horns. Outside, life was gradually resuming. A disturbing normalcy, as if nothing had happened. Single file, we left our shelter. In the street, we passed a woman, her face haggard. She confirmed that a young woman had been killed here by a sniper, the same shot we had heard. Along Kargar Street, I followed in the footsteps of other lost protesters. The sidewalks were dreary and severe. Everywhere, detritus. Under a half-burnt tree, a few scattered leaves blanketed the ground. Patches of assassinated greenery, lined up like cadavers on the scarred asphalt.

Back at home, I found Borzou again. He was leaning over his computer, head in his hands.

"Did you see what happened?" he asked, staring at his screen.

I grabbed a chair and sat down next to him. He had managed to get on the Internet. Though still bad, the connection worked better at night. Thanks to the magic of proxy servers that circumvented the censor, he had even managed to open Facebook and Twitter. The photo of a young woman filled his computer screen. He signaled for me to open another page. She reappeared, her porcelain face framed by a black headscarf.

"Here, look at this one, too," Borzou added.

I opened another site. I saw her again. The portrait of the unknown woman was everywhere, on every form of social media. I clicked on a video link. She was there again, the young girl with the face of an angel, on the ground this time, her big eyes turned to the sky. Blood ran from her mouth, flooded her cheeks. I squinted. Lying on the ground, she was dying in front of the lens of a protester who had filmed her death and posted it to the Internet. Below, a caption said that she was named

Neda. That she had gone to the demonstrations with her piano teacher. That she had been killed at the end of the afternoon from a bullet to the chest, not far from Kargar Street. So, she was the woman who had received that fatal shot. Who had died a few yards from our hiding place. The innocent victim of a Basiji bullet! Like thousands of other Iranian women, Neda had ignored her mother's orders. She had taken to the street to demand her right to be heard. She had joined the crowd with her music teacher. On the video, he was begging her to stay alive. In vain.

I was in shock. Neda was not the icon of bravery that destiny had made of her by broadcasting her photo all over the planet. Neither was she a militant or a combatant. Neda was a girl like any other, an everyday heroine. Simply a protester, nothing more. She was Sara, she was Sepideh, she was Anoushch. A young Iranian woman who dreamed of a happier future. She was only twenty-six years old.

In the morning, the telephone rang. It was Fatemeh.

"I hope I'm not interrupting anything?" she murmured.

I was rooted to the spot. After fruitless attempts, I had given up calling her. I had figured that, after Khamenei's speech, the Basiji's wife had rejoined the ranks.

"Poor Neda," she added.

Those two words said everything. They were enough to summarize her state of mind. So Fatemeh had chosen her clan. She was against brutality. She was opposed to repression through violence. Watching the death of a young woman, broadcast live, had devastated her as much as it had us. Perhaps even more.

"Let's get together, if you want?" I suggested.

I was dying to have a private conversation with her. She owed me an explanation. I wanted her to tell me what was going through the minds of the Basijis. Why this brutality, why this mess, why all these useless deaths? A few days earlier, we had learned that the militiamen had killed other young people, right in the middle of the Amir Abad dormitory. A raid like the one in 1999. Except that, this time, a video was already circulating on the Internet. These days, with social media, nothing could be hidden anymore.

"For now, we'd better not see each other . . . I'm sorry," replied Fatemeh.

I sensed that she was embarrassed. Her voice was hesitant. She told me that she didn't leave her house much. She had been warned not to go out. I thought of her father, a Basij leader in the suburbs. He must have given her orders. I didn't insist. She was already taking a big risk by calling me. I just asked about her health, according to the *ta'arof*, that customary Iranian pleasantry.

"Oh, I spend my days in front of the television. I like the satellite channels, when they're working. Because Iranian television is really a lot of nonsense!"

I recognized her veiled audacity. Her way of telling me that she wasn't being fooled. That she hadn't succumbed to the soup of propaganda the regime was ladling out every day. From morning to night, the Revolutionary Guards, known as the Pasdaran, multiplied their televised appearances, claiming that they had uncovered a plot "hatched by Iran's enemies," a "velvet revolution" orchestrated by the United States and Israel. The supporting "evidence," images of "crimes," was broadcast on Iranian TV all day long: satellite dishes, machetes and swords, laptops seized from protesters' homes. A few days later, we even heard that Neda had been killed by "a paid assassin hired by a BBC correspondent."

"And Mahmoud?" I asked.

I was itching to ask the question, even if I was afraid I already knew the answer.

"Mahmoud?" she repeated. "He's very busy. We don't see each other much at the moment."

There was a long silence. I figured she was hesitant to talk too much on the phone. Then she added:

"I think he's done with me . . . You know, I told him I didn't want to have children."

I sat down, ear glued to the phone. Tehran was crumbling, and Fatemeh, the reformed militiawoman, was opening her broken heart to me, turning to intimate secrets. Was she trying to divert the discussion, or was this her way of calling for help? I replied:

"Do you mean that you are thinking of divorce?"

"I don't know . . . At the same time, he's a good man. He doesn't beat me. Normally, he gives me my freedom. I can even go out with my girlfriends . . . The only problem is that he's married to the Basij . . . Really, he's cheating on me with the Basij!"

I could tell she was flustered, breaking down the usual boundary between public and private.

"Are you saying that Mahmoud followed the orders of the Leader?" I added, making an allusion to Khamenei's speech at Friday's prayer.

Fatemeh gave me the answer I feared:

"The other day, he came back home very late . . . His shirt was covered in blood."

I didn't know how to react. I already knew too much. The two of them, Fatemeh and Mahmoud, were symbols of an Iran that was destroying itself from the inside. In the ring, it was no longer "Islam versus Islam." It was turbans versus Pasdaran, a peaceful majority striving for an opening to the rest of the world, supported by distinguished clerics, versus a bellicose minority aligned against the West, preferring isolation and violence in the name of an obsolete ideology. Which of the two clans would win out? I needed to speak directly to Mahmoud. Had he, the aspiring soldier, transformed into an assassin? Hanging up, I called his number numerous times. It rang without response. At night, while I was writing my article about Neda, he called me back.

"What's up?" he asked in that indifferent tone I knew so well.

In the background, I recognized the irregular tumult of the street. He was still outside at that late hour.

"I have to ask you a question," I said right up front.

"Okay, I'm listening," he replied, surprised.

"You're not too rough with the protesters, right?"

He gave a fake laugh. He must have guessed that I had spoken to Fatemeh.

"Of course not. Don't worry! I simply bring the wounded to the hospital . . . Sometimes my shirt gets stained."

I stayed silent. I had nothing more to add. I was convinced he was lying to me, but it might have been my imagination. I didn't know if I should hate him, be mad at him, or share my suspicions with him. But was it wise to continue the conversation? He broke the silence:

"Don't worry! This chaos won't last. You'll see. In a few days, everything will go back to normal."

And with these words, he hung up.

IT WAS THE morning of June 22; I will never forget that day. In the living room, the television was set to the Iranian news. Exhausted from too many all-nighters, I was half listening to the bulletin. The presenter's voice accompanied my breakfast like background music. When I heard "journalist," I didn't notice right away. The sound was low. And then the word was said again multiple times. An unusual repetition. I raised my head. My photo took up half the screen. I jumped out of my chair. I think my mug of tea went flying. I gripped the remote. I wanted to turn up the sound. Listen to the commentary that accompanied the photo. The presenter was speaking too quickly. Other photos were displayed with the same speed. I didn't recognize the faces. I grasped only a few snippets: "Western conspiracy . . . manipulation by the foreign media . . . agents of Mossad and the Great Satan." Enough to understand that danger was closing in.

I called out to Borzou. He was in the shower. When he came into the living room, feet wet, the news had turned to something else. I didn't need to say much. Seeing my devastated expression, he knew there was something to worry about. The day before, Maziar Bahari, *Newsweek*'s Iran correspondent, had been arrested in his home. He was Iranian Canadian. Along with him and about ten other dual-nationality reporters, we were among the last representatives of Western media on Iranian territory. In the days before, all the press visas had expired and the last special correspondents had been kicked out. We had watched them leave, one after another, while choosing to stay. Had our hour come? Officially, we had the right to extend our stay. Our Iranian passports spared us such constraints. But they also exposed us to the risk of being arrested. Unbeknownst to us, we had become the potential hostages of a desperate regime. I shuddered, thinking again of what Mahmoud had said. Perhaps this was it, the return to order he had predicted.

The next day, a trusted friend came to see us, distraught. With a trembling hand, he unfolded a newspaper on the table. It was the latest issue of *Kayhan*, the mouthpiece of the regime. He flipped through it hastily and placed his index finger on the page he wanted to show us.

"Here. Read this," he said.

It was a short article. One of those tidbits you rarely pay attention to. A few words written from left to right, as brief as they were abrupt. "Western media outlets are dispatching their binational reporters to Iran to spy and glean information illegally," the text read. No need, for once, to tear my hair out trying to read between the lines. The message was clear.

"This is bad," said Borzou.

Our friend turned toward us, looking grave.

"Instead of accepting the demands of the people, our leaders have chosen to dream up a grand play entitled something like *The Velvet Revolution Incited by the West*. A piece of advice: leave. Leave before the casting office decides you're the best actors for the lead roles!" he said.

And then, flustered, he whispered that there were other reasons to worry about our situation.

"What?" I asked.

"I got a call from a guy in the intelligence service who knows you."

Mr. Fingers! My lead interrogator. I had almost forgotten about him. The passage of time had nearly managed to chase him from my memory. His reappearance didn't bode well.

"He wants to see us?" I interrupted him, already imagining a summons.

"No. It's worse."

We were hanging on his every word. He continued:

"He told me to warn you both. To tell you that he is no longer in charge. Neither he nor his cronies. Other 'services,' ones that are much more dangerous, have taken over. These people are no joke. If they catch you, there's nothing anyone will be able to do for you."

We understood immediately. It was the Revolutionary Guards who were steering the country. Mr. Fingers's call was a warning bell. The last one before prison. We had to leave right then. No more haggling for a few extra days. We had already stayed too long.

Within a few hours, we planned our departure. We would go in a group, with the last remaining dual-nationality reporters. We consulted one another via Skype, which seemed to be the most secure means of communication. We agreed to reserve the same red-eye flight for Dubai. It took off in the early morning. Then we packed our bags. We had never really unpacked them. Consumed with worry, Borzou and I sat one last time at our living room table to write an email to our close friends and family: a denial of the "confessions" they might extract from us by force if we were arrested. The document would serve, we hoped, to defend us.

In the late afternoon, Sara came to say good-bye. I wanted to give her one last hug before leaving. Wish her all the courage that I no longer had. I squeezed her very tightly. I could feel her bones beneath her blouse.

"You've gotten even skinnier," I said.

"Have you heard the latest joke? The Iranians started a super-trendy diet: lose weight by protesting. And the best part? It costs nothing!"

Her good humor impressed me. A shield against tyranny. Before taking her leave, she slid a piece of paper into my pocket. "My newest poem," she murmured. I told myself that I would have plenty of time to read it. In the plane or in prison.

Sepideh arrived immediately afterward. She was breathless. She had spent the day chasing after bad news. All around her, stories fell like flaming arrows. The leaders of the opposition had been put under house arrest. Their advisers, behind bars. And her writer friends were en route to the Turkish border. She knew they were looking for her, too. Each night, she slept somewhere new to avoid being caught.

"Leave. Leave before it's too late," she insisted.

"What about you?" I asked, my voice trembling.

My heart was on my sleeve.

"Don't worry. I've seen worse!" She laughed, cracking her shoulder, the one that had never fully set back into place after her first tangle with a militiaman, in the '90s.

I was frozen. I couldn't smile. Or even cry.

"But today they're much more violent," I said.

"Promise me just one thing," she added. "Don't forget us!"

I took her in my arms. She nestled her head against my shoulder, face buried in my hair. I felt her tears soaking through my T-shirt.

"I'm just tired. I'm just tired," she mumbled.

At that moment, I didn't imagine she would be arrested a few days after our departure.

By the time the taxi arrived, in the middle of the night, a lump of anxiety had lodged in my throat. The unthinkable had turned into the inevitable: we were leaving for good. My previous years had been an accumulation of false departures. This time, after such an endless game of hide-and-seek, I was shredding the map I had pieced together with my memories of Iran. Closing the gate to the building, I glanced one last time at the family home, where I had been the last resident. Who would come to water the plants in the garden? Who would feed the goldfish in the pond? Would I one day have the chance to see Tehran again, other than in a photo?

Borzou sat next to the driver. I sat in the back of the car. Outside, Tehran was colored with grief, wearing its veil of mourning. Forehead against the glass, I took a mental photograph of this city I had learned to love, that was slipping away from me yet again. The streets were deserted, the streetlights dimmed. The driver slowed while passing a makeshift Basiji checkpoint. In the twilight, just before turning onto the highway that led to the airport, he carefully slalomed between charred trash cans and burned cars. Last snapshots of a city on the brink of death. With a shudder, I told myself that soon there would be no more witnesses to tell the story. Beneath my headscarf, I was trembling. Everything in me rebelled against the turn taken by Iranian history, my history.

The taxi drives along gray lines. I'm scared. I know the road to the airport by heart. I've taken it many times. But I know that people who cause trouble disappear here. Glued to the glass,

I stare at those gray lines while torturing the ends of my head-scarf. Time seems so long when you are no longer capable of controlling your emotions.

A half hour later, perhaps a little less, a blinding light floods the taxi. We have arrived. The gigantic glass terminal is swarming with passengers; carts filled with luggage, cakes, and knick-knacks of every kind. We weave through the crowd. Mouths sewn shut, we check the departure time on the bright screen and then go through the body search checkpoint. At passport control, a light relief: our small group of reporter friends is here, too. Like sheep, we fall into the line together. On high alert, I keep an ear out for the loudspeaker. I wait for the bearded man to come looking for me. I try to imagine what will come next: Will he escort me to a small room to interrogate me? Or take me directly to Evin Prison? I haven't, however, committed any crime. No arrest warrant looms over me. My papers are in order. But I know that in this moment, anything could happen.

We end up passing through without any problem, one right after the other. Except for the last of us. Behind the glass, a security officer signals for our friend to follow him. We watch him disappear into a small room as we hold our collective breath. We hardly dare whisper. Five minutes later, our friend re-appears. False alarm. Marching robotically in single file, we reach the gate. It's terribly hot and stuffy beneath the lights. My heart bangs in my chest. A mixture of anxiety and exhaustion. Only a few minutes to go. Behind the counter, a flight attendant in a midnight-blue veil informs the passengers that the plane is finally ready for boarding. When the doors open, we rush onto the plane like fugitives.

When we finally take off, my headscarf slides furtively to my shoulders. I don't put it back on. A feeling of relief, of freedom, comes from shaking my hair loose. I lean against the window. Seen from above, Khomeini's gigantic mausoleum lights up the night. Like antennas pointed toward the sky, the minarets gleam as if nothing has happened and eventually disappear behind the clouds. In his tomb, the all-powerful imam is, no doubt, laughing at our distress.

I sink into my seat, a pillow behind my neck. I rifle in my pocket. I take out Sara's poem, the one she gave me before I left.

There's one upside to a tear-gas bomb
Like the starting gun to a race
You run
Your eyes burn
The first time, you're afraid
—Just like with the baton, just like with the cables used for
  torture—
The next times, you learn to take out
Your cigarette
You smoke
The neighbors scream at the window: "They're coming!"
You run again
It's so good to run
Along the plane trees of Valiasr Street
—no trace of self-righteous patrols—
From the bookstores on Enghelab Street
—So many banned books we found there!—
We run
If only you could run at our sides
You, our exiled friends
Our older brothers who lost your lives
For a simple manifesto

Or at the front
Or behind the walls of Evin
They tore us apart
We run
We miss you
The torch has now changed hands
May this race live on
We run
Eyes filled with tears
Toward freedom

I feel a pang in my heart. In 1997, I arrived in Iran with a poem. Twelve years later, a poem accompanies my voyage once again. It sings with a passion for life. The hope of a country that refuses darkness. A small firefly in the uncertain night.

POSTSCRIPT: PARIS, SEPTEMBER 2, 2014

MONTPARNASSE CEMETERY VIBRATES with birdsong.

This is the first time since your death, Babai, seventeen years ago, that I've come to your tomb alone. To think that it took all this time, all these miles, and a necessary distance from your country, to write this letter. And to place it on the cold marble that protects your last secrets.

I crouch down, hand on your headstone. I remembered it being smoother. Over the years, the rain has eroded the surface. I scan it with my eyes. An end-of-summer sun tickles the small mosaic of Ispahan, a subtle touch of color in the middle of a cemetery. Someone has placed flowers at the base. An old colleague from UNESCO? One of your former conquests? Another of your mysteries that will remain forever buried.

I close my eyes. In the disorder of my memories, I see your face again, your unforgettable smile. It floats among other faces of the deceased, imprinted forever in my mind. Ardeshir, the free-spirited acrobat who "died while escaping the police." Neda, the young Madonna with broken dreams. And all those others striving for democracy who left us too early during the 2009 crackdowns. How many had to pay the ultimate price for their dreams of freedom? How many were robbed of funerals, sometimes even of a grave, because those in power feared they might prove as dangerous, as provocative in death as they were in life? All those injustices would have outraged you as much as they have me.

Once more, I remember my hasty departure from Iran, at the end of that long journey you initiated. On June 25, 2009, I reluctantly closed the door to a country condemned to the blank page. It is the fear that all these memories might vanish that pushed me to take up my pen and dedicate this story to you. I recall, when I was little, writing to you from Paris, worried sick that you would disappear from my memory because you lived in Iran, so far away. In those letters, I recounted everything I could find—certain stories, anecdotes, details, sometimes trivial—to keep them alive on paper. I was convinced that this method would help keep you alive, too. Years later, when Iran pushed me once and for all toward the exit, the same obsession took over: write so as not to forget.

But I was affected by the censorship that had touched my friends. Sepideh was arrested at the end of August 2009. A few days before her arrest, she had written on her blog: "My pen is my totem." Isolated in her cell in Evin Prison, she was forbidden from having visitors, forbidden natural light, forbidden paper or even a pen. Freed after four months, she recounted her nightmare to me through a mutual friend: the cries for help that slam up against the iron door, the extended interrogations, standing blindfolded against a wall, the wandering hands of the guard . . . And then that ultimate affront by the judge on the day of the verdict: "Don't waste your time writing. You're starting to get old. You need to think about having children. Swear to me that you will make it your priority!"

Sara also had been consigned to the blank page. The poem she gave to me would never be published in Persian. At the Ministry of Islamic Culture and Guidance, the censorship committee settled for turning it into one more cadaver, buried at the bottom of a drawer. One night in 2010, she told me about it over Skype, her last window to the outside world. Taking refuge in her little apartment in Tehran, she repainted the walls of her living room a pistachio green. During sleepless nights, she made up quatrains that she wrote in green calligraphy on the white tiles of her bathroom. Rebellious and ephemeral words that were immediately erased with a stream of water. After a few months, even the most brazen protesters ended up going quiet under the weight of merciless repression, along with mass trials and forced confessions on television. A French researcher, Clotilde Reiss, even ended up on the defendants' bench. Arrested at the airport a few days after our departure, she became the hostage that I could have been.

How would you have reacted to that fierce repression? Would you have drawn sufficient comfort from Hafez's *The Divan*? Me, I was on the run. At the start of the "Arab Spring," in January 2011, I headed back out on the reporting trail, toward other revolts: Tunisia, Egypt, Libya, Syria . . . Afraid of reopening my Iranian suitcase and facing the dark memory of disappeared friends, I wrote about other martyrs whose deaths were just as violent, sometimes even more so. In reality, so many deaths made me forget the true meaning of life. It was time to pause in the middle of that insane race. At the beginning of summer 2011, I put down my reporter's bag in our apartment in Lebanon.

For the first time in my career, far from the clamor of the news and without my computer, I took a real vacation in the country of cedar. A month later, I discovered I was pregnant—the most beautiful gift.

If you had still been among us, you would have succumbed immediately to Samarra's charm. She was born in Beirut in March 2012, arms open to the world, just as one announces the arrival of a new spring. Her name means "Happy is the person who sees her" (*Soura Man Raa*) in Old Arabic. A nod to the ancient Mesopotamian city, where Borzou and I spent time during our stays in Iraq. And so, life goes on, interspersed with symbols that you taught me to appreciate through a poem you gave me just before your last breath.

In April, a month after Samarra's birth, we moved to Cairo, where we still live. After a few days, I finally unpacked my trunk of souvenirs and, taking advantage of my daughter's naps, started to fill in the first gray lines of the blank page. To my surprise, the words came together easily. The barriers were no longer so insurmountable. Samarra had given me back the strength to write. It was as if I needed to give birth to this small being before I could allow myself to bring my paper child into the world.

What came next, unpredictably, would have filled you with joy: in the spring of 2014, realizing a dream we had long ago renounced, we brought her to Tehran. A few days of vacation to celebrate Nowruz, the Persian New Year. Many things had changed since we left. In June 2013, after four gloomy years, Hassan Rouhani won the presidential election. In Iran, land of the unexpected, this moderate cleric advocated for openness and dialogue from that moment on. It was as if the fall of the region's dictators and the reinforcement of international sanctions on the country had prompted the Supreme Leader to endorse change.

Two years old, Samarra was amazed at everything: the goldfish, the dried pomegranates, the flaming twigs you step over to ward off the evil eye. The streets were in full flower, dotted with men dressed as Hajji Firuz, little minstrels in red hats singing of rebirth from their cars as they drove with their windows down. I felt such emotion at seeing the capital again through the eyes of a child. To see Sara again and read her poems, which she was finally going to publish. To hug Sepideh, who had regained her work permit and the pounds she'd lost in prison. Even the walls of the city were discreetly singing of the new spring. "It's the Spring of Freedom. Neda, You Are with Us," read graffiti on a wall.

On that trip, I also had a chance to see Fatemeh again. We met her in a "family" gathering in the gardens of the former palace of the shah, in the foothills of Niavaran. I saw her arrive hand in hand with a child, Mahsa, her four-year-old daughter, with Mahmoud at their side. Just like the country's political players, the Basiji couple had reconciled. At least in appearance.

I immediately recognized Fatemeh's spirit in Mahsa. The girl wasn't afraid of anything, climbing over off-limits lion cub statues, intruding into a teenagers' soccer match. Two years her junior, Samarra watched her with candid admiration. Would our daughters be friends one day? Would they be curious to rifle through their family history, as I had brought yours back to the surface of my memory?

On each trip to Paris, Mamani, along with my French grandmother, is one of the first people we visit. I like to listen to Samarra respond to her in Persian when Mamani sings Iranian nursery rhymes. They entertain themselves by gathering the jasmine flowers that Mamani grows on her balcony in remembrance of Tehran.

The echo of a bell tears me from my thoughts. I open my eyes. It's already 5:45 p.m., a quarter of an hour before the cemetery closes. Seated on your headstone, I gather my thoughts as I watch the summer drift away. Around me, the trees are already beginning to turn brown. The sun is low, drawing pink streaks across the sky. In its wake, a cloud has taken the form of a wave. I take a moment for a few final memories: Ali Jafarian, the marvelous conductor in Shiraz, who died suddenly due to a fragile heart; Moses Baba, the Jewish antiques dealer with the magic jerry cans, who also left this earth too soon. And then Ali Montazeri: his death, at the end of December 2009, came close to shaking up the powers that be. Never had Qom seen so many people pour out onto its streets as for the funeral of the enlightened ayatollah. A sign of a silent revolution that had not yet spoken its last word.

From time to time, acquaintances reappear through the magic of Facebook. Such as the mullah with the leather jacket, exiled in Europe, where he is currently working toward peace among religions. And Niloufar, the "godmother" of the youth. A few years ago, we met up on the terrace of a Parisian café. She made a comment that I have never forgotten: "Iran is like a broken glass whose pieces have been glued back together. For now, it's holding. But it could crack at any moment."

Mr. Fingers never reappeared. And it's much better that way. As for my computer, stolen in Paris, I never heard about it again, apart from a letter from the judicial police announcing that the case had been closed.

The bell rings again, even louder. In the distance, the Montparnasse groundskeeper signals that he's waiting for me to leave so he can close the gate. It's 6:00 p.m. Next time, I'll come earlier. I'll bring Samarra. Together, we'll read poems by Hafez and I'll tell her about you, the person who helped me reconnect with this invisible part of myself.

ACKNOWLEDGMENTS

This book almost never saw the light of day. "I don't think you'll write that book on Iran after all. Too much distance. Too much time. Too much delay," one of my former editors wrote to me, exasperated by my slowness, when I was still two years from finishing.

Nearly seven years passed between the earliest pages of this project, in 2007, and putting in the last period, in 2014. Seven years of intermittent writing, of introspection, of scribbling and rewriting, that resulted in a narrative thread much more personal than the simple journalistic account I had planned.

Obsessed with objectivity, reporter that I am, I had developed the reflex of boxing up my fears, preferring to hide behind facts rather than express my feelings. I was also anxious to write down everything, not to leave out a single detail, to relay all the voices inside, without exception. And then came a night when I was sharing my memories and a novelist friend, Hyam Yared, urged me to come out of my shell. "What if you focused your Iranian narrative on your personal history, and your grandfather?" Thanks to her, I found the courage to express this version of myself hidden behind a veil of reserve.

Other dear friends accompanied me on this long journey.

The filmmaker Katia Jarjoura was the only person with whom I shared this text from start to finish. More than a proofreader, she turned out to be an incredible adviser, from the selection of the people described in the book to the construction of the narrative framework—the arc to which we devoted so many nights. Rigorous, generous, she was of exceptional help to me.

I am also extremely thankful for my Colombian colleague Catalina Gómez, who is also passionate about Iran, for her moral support along the entire evolution of this project. Thanks are also due to my reporter "sister" Manon Loizeau for her enthusiasm and continuous cheering.

I would also like to express my gratitude to the incredible Hala Moughanie, who was kind enough to read and comment on the entire work in its final phase. Her suggestions proved to be infinitely valuable. Danielle Serpollet has also been of enormous help as we refined the English-language edition.

A special thank-you to my talented colleague from *Paris Match*, Alfred de Montesquiou, who, while my manuscript was at the halfway point, had the graciousness to speak to Éditions du Seuil about it.

I especially want to thank my Iranian friends, so many of whom opened their doors to me and shared their laughter, tears, and daily lives. Some of them appear in the book under their real names; others are protected under a pseudonym, as is the case for Fatemeh, Mahmoud, Niloufar, Sepideh, Leyla, and Kourosh. (They will recognize themselves, undoubtedly.) There are also those, whose shadows hover over these pages, who played a large role in my increasing passion for Iran over the years. I would need entire pages to name them. But I must express my faithful gratitude to my indispensable Iranian friends: the sociologist Masserat Amir-Ebrahimi, and the photographers Newsha Tavakolian and Zohreh Soleimani. Their energy and the beauty of their souls will forever remain a model of courage, a source of inspiration.

At Ershad, the Iranian Ministry of Culture and Islamic Guidance, I was fortunate to be able to count on the efficient and polite aid of many benevolent people, especially during my administrative troubles. I'm thinking in particular of Ali Reza Shiravi and Efat Eqbali.

I will never forget the great team at the French embassy in Tehran. Ambassadors François Nicoullaud and Bernard Poletti, with whom I share the desire for a better understanding of Iran, were always available and incredibly open-minded.

Since my early days in Iran, in 1997, I was fortunate to be able to count on the help of Marc Crépin and Gérald Roux, from Radio France, the first editors to encourage me to go to Iran and to assign me dispatches. A big thank-you to the team of L'Humanité for publishing my first pieces. I am obviously immensely indebted to Le Figaro, for whom I started to freelance in 2001, and for whom I ended up working as a full-time correspondent in 2009. I always counted on the professionalism and support of my respective editors in chief: Pierre Rousselin, Luc de Barochez, Philippe Gélie, and Arnaud de La Grange.

I am immensely indebted to Farhad Khosrokhavar, director

of studies at L'Ecole des Hautes Etudes en Science Sociales, and Fariba Adelkhah, research director at Sciences Po–Centre de Recherches Internationales, the first people to introduce me to the complexity of Iranian politics. Thank you also to Bernard Hourcade, research director at Centre National de la Recherche Scientifique, and Azadeh Kian, professor of sociology at Université Paris Diderot (Paris 7), whose keen knowledge of contemporary Iran was very useful in helping me better understand the country.

I also, of course, want to thank my family, and especially Mamani. Despite our difficult beginnings, she has been an exceptional grandmother, a woman whom I greatly admire and whose personal story was rich with lessons. I am also very grateful to my father, who, though belatedly, was a precious aid in awakening memories of Babai, my grandfather.

But it's for my husband, Borzou, that I reserve my most sincere gratitude. He has always been solid as a rock, handling all my qualms with exceptional composure. His patience and encouragement were an incredible aid to me.

Finally, I ask those who will feel flayed in the pages of this book to forgive me. For some, this history will perhaps seem apocryphal. It's a small piece of my story, steeped in a painful reality. But without pain, there is no story.

A NOTE ABOUT THE AUTHOR

Delphine Minoui, a recipient of the Albert Londres
Prize for her reporting on Iraq and Iran, is a Middle
East correspondent for *Le Figaro*. Born in Paris in 1974
to a French mother and an Iranian father, she now
lives in Istanbul.

A NOTE ABOUT THE TRANSLATOR

Emma Ramadan lives in Providence, Rhode Island,
where she is a co-owner of Riffraff, a bookstore and
bar. She is the recipient of a Fulbright scholarship, an
NEA fellowship, and a PEN/Heim Translation Fund
grant. Her previous translations include the gender-
less novel *Sphinx*, by Anne Garréta.